Deposition pg 165
Pg 170 demonstrative evidence
172 - palms up palms down
friends — NO

AF704589

# Techniques of Medical Litigation

# Techniques of Medical Litigation

*A Professional's Handbook for Plaintiffs, Defendants, and Medical Consultants*

RANDINE A. LEWIS

Q

QUORUM BOOKS
Westport, Connecticut • London

**Library of Congress Cataloging-in-Publication Data**

Lewis, Randine A., 1960–
Techniques of medical litigation : a professional's handbook for plaintiffs, defendants, and medical consultants / Randine A. Lewis.
p. cm.
Includes index.
ISBN 1–56720–088–5 (alk. paper)
1. Personal injuries—United States—Trial practice. 2. Medical jurisprudence—United States. 3. Medical records—Law and legislation—United States. 4. Medicine—Terminology. I. Title.
KF8925.P4L46 1997
346.7303'23
[347.306323]—DC20 96–32508

British Library Cataloguing in Publication Data is available.

Copyright © 1997 by Randine A. Lewis

All rights reserved. No portion of this book may be reproduced, by any process or technique, without the express written consent of the publisher.

Library of Congress Catalog Card Number: 96–32508
ISBN: 1–56720–088–5

First published in 1997

Quorum Books, 88 Post Road West, Westport, CT 06881
An imprint of Greenwood Publishing Group, Inc.

Printed in the United States of America

The paper used in this book complies with the Permanent Paper Standard issued by the National Information Standards Organization (Z39.48–1984).

10 9 8 7 6 5 4 3 2 1

# Contents

# Preface

With the tremendous surge of increased specialization in the field of medical litigation, lawyers are demanding more professional medical support. Attorneys need to work closely with medical professionals; doctors and nurses who also perform roles as consultants need to work closely with attorneys and their legal staff. Yet, the increasing complexity of each profession keeps them mutually exclusive.

This book bridges the gap between law and medicine, providing fundamental and practical information that will ensure that any medical case becomes less intimidating. It will familiarize you with the preliminary steps in preparing for a medical lawsuit: medical records acquisition, organization, interpretation, and summarization. You will be guided through clinical charts and given an introduction to drugs commonly found in the medical records. A complete guide to medical research, how to find a medical expert, and vast references are provided. Individual case scenarios are furnished; then you are guided through the steps involved in initiating a medical lawsuit, the discovery process, and trial organization and preparation. The last part of the book teaches you medicine by providing a commonsense approach to individual body systems, medical terminology, disease processes, diagnostic procedures, and drugs used in their treatment. The exhaustive appendix of medical abbreviations allows you to decipher the contents of the most complicated medical records.

Some portions of this manual seem to be plaintiff oriented; that is because certain steps in medical litigation pertain primarily to initiating the lawsuit and assessing the plaintiff's damages. This information is immensely important to counsel for the defense as well by taking the material presented and then reversing and countering the strategy.

I especially acknowledge Edward A. Lewis, M.D., whose support helped produce this manuscript.

Part I

# Preliminary Information

Chapter 1

# Introduction to Medical Litigation

Medical litigation arises when a claimant (*plaintiff*) sustains injuries allegedly caused by another's act, or failure to perform an act (omission), which caused harm to the plaintiff. The person, agency, corporation, or entity accused of committing or allowing the action that caused the injury, or of failing to do something within its control to prevent the injury, is known as the *defendant*. One claim can involve multiple plaintiffs and defendants. If the injury resulted in a death, the family will typically become plaintiffs on behalf of the decedent.

Medical claims can be broken down into: (1) medical malpractice, (2) personal injury, (3) wrongful death, (4) products liability, (5) chemical exposure, and (6) workers' compensation. The process for bringing a case into a court of law is similar for each and begins with the injured party's consulting an attorney to request assistance in filing a lawsuit. The attorney for the plaintiff evaluates the information provided by the client to determine if the incident warrants filing a lawsuit and to ensure that the *statute of limitations* (the time limit to bring a legal action to the courts) has not passed. Since an attorney may be penalized for filing a claim without basis, investigating the medical facts is crucial.

Get as much information from the client as you can on the initial meeting and document all pertinent medical facts. The client can fill out much of this information directly on an intake form. This information should be kept in the client's file for reference and should remain confidential. A sample intake sheet should include at least the following information:

**Client Information**

Name

Past Names Used

Date of Birth

Social Security Number

Address

Telephone Number

Work Address

Work Number

Spouse's Name

Children's Names and Dates of Birth

Facts Specific to This Case

Medical History (Surgeries, Illnesses, Diseases, Accidents)

Social History (Smoking, Drinking, Drug Use)

Psychiatric History (Any Counseling or Therapy)

Any Past Medical Condition That May Affect This Case

List All Doctors and Health Care Providers You Have Consulted in the Past for Any Reason

Date _____ Name _____ Address ________ Reason for Consult ________

Date _____ Name _____ Address ________ Reason for Consult ________

You may, of course, request any specific details your office may desire. The more information you can get initially saves much time and effort later. The client information material will allow you to obtain medical records and bills and begin researching the case.

The client must also fill out medical authorizations, copies of which must be submitted to the custodian of medical records of health care facilities, so that they may legally release the records and medical bills to you. Get ample copies of these documents signed; you will need them for ordering the medical records and bills.

## Chapter 2

# Obtaining Medical Records

Prior to any action taken in a medical lawsuit, it is necessary to obtain the client's medical records. The client may already possess his or her own medical records when seeking counsel; however, most often this is not the case.

Depending on the number of medical records necessary to suit, this process can become costly. If money is no object, you may order them all—but then you end up with volumes of records on each client. Determining which records are necessary can become an issue. Obviously, the records pertinent to the claim will need to be ordered.

### WHICH RECORDS SHOULD YOU ORDER?

You may have to rely on your client's recall of his or her past medical history to determine which records are crucial to your case. Relying solely on your client's recollection can place you at a disadvantage, however. You may not have the whole picture, since humans are selective by nature, and a client with a head injury may need assistance from the family in remembering past medical history. Plaintiffs' attorneys may need past medical history to contrast the healthy preaccident victim with the totally disabled client who must file suit.

Generally it is a good rule for plaintiffs' attorneys to obtain a complete set of medical records. By identifying providers through *interrogatories* (written questions presented to the opposing side for answers), defense counsel should subpoena those records. Plaintiffs' attorneys will receive copies of the subpoena, and if the records are determined to be irrelevant to the suit, they may file a motion to quash. As records are received and summarized, they may reveal additional health care providers of whom the client was unaware.

If you are working with counsel for the defense, a good portion of your argument may come from past medical history and preexisting conditions. Plaintiffs' counsel also must be aware of all conditions that could affect any allegations in their case. This is especially true with personal injury, workers' compensation claims, and some products liability suits. Prior medical conditions may lower awards for damages in certain injury cases.

Let us say that you are working for an insurance company, defending workers' compensation disability claims. You are assigned a case wherein a worker claims she injured her right shoulder while stocking shelves. She was lifting 15-pound bags of cat food and placing them on a shelf 6 feet high. She was 5 feet 4 inches tall. She claimed that her right shoulder "snapped," she suffered debilitating pain, and she still cannot lift her right arm at all. She is right-handed, and claims total disability. This was four and one-half months ago, and she claims no improvement after consulting numerous medical specialists.

Supposedly all records have been ordered pertinent to the claim. A legal assistant in the office ordered records from all doctors she has seen since the incident: a neurologist, an orthopedic surgeon, a chiropractor, and a chronic pain specialist. Medical bills are mounting, and she has been deemed as having achieved "maximum medical benefit." You look into the discovery folder and find that she listed all health care providers she has ever seen for any reason.

Three years ago, right after a divorce from her physically abusive husband, she made visits to an emergency room, a neurologist, an orthopedic surgeon, and psychiatric clinics, all within a few months' time. You decide to subpoena the records. You uncover the fact that just over three years ago, she visited an emergency room after being beaten by her husband. Her right shoulder had been dislocated, and she suffered a rotator cuff tear. After the repair had healed, she continued seeing her psychiatrist, who diagnosed her with a somatization disorder manifesting itself as unresolving shoulder pain. Strong defense!

As you can see, you cannot always count on records pertinent to the recent event being sufficient. If you are working for plaintiff's counsel, it should become apparent very early on which records will be necessary for working up your claim. If your client intake form or interview sheet is informative enough, you can start ordering medical records as soon as the client walks out of the office. You may need to wait until the answers to interrogatories are returned with the answers to past medical history filled out. Most medical malpractice claims rely on the hospitalization immediately adjacent to the injury.

Institutions from which you may need to order medical records include these:

- Hospitals—inpatient and outpatient facilities.
- Physicians' office records—consulting physicians often have their own copies of medical records, which they keep in their private offices. This includes additional billing. You may have to order records and bills individually from radiologists or anesthesiologists if the hospital record does not provide enough information or if there is additional billing.
- Psychiatric facilities—inpatient and outpatient services.

- Rehabilitation clinics—inpatient and outpatient. These may be for treating chronic pain, restoring function after injury, or treating substance abuse disorders.
- Skilled nursing facilities or other long-term care facilities.
- Home-based health care agencies (home nursing care, occupational or physical therapy, and so on).
- Dental records.
- Optometry records.
- Psychology records.
- Chiropractic records.
- Physical therapy records.
- Occupational therapy records.
- Pharmacy records.

## TRACKING MEDICAL RECORDS

When you have decided which records to order, it is critical to keep track of which records have been ordered and their current status at all times. (This process also pertains to medical bills.) A tickler system for following up on unfinished business is an excellent way to be reminded that you have not received the records you requested. Usually 10 days to two weeks is about time to issue reminders if your records have not been received as requested. If this process remains organized, you should know the status of any client's medical records within minutes.

A suggested means by which medical records and bills can be trailed is to keep a register to substantiate the present status. This may be accomplished via a computer or a binder with separate pages for each client. Then with the touch of a keyboard or the turn of a page you will have documentation of the current status at all times—for example,

| PROVIDER | CONTACT PERSON | COST | CHECK SENT | DATE ORDERED | STATUS | RECEIVED |
|---|---|---|---|---|---|---|
| Holy Cross Hospital | Edna Pfist 767-1335 | $335.87 | No - bill received 7/15 | 7/12/95 | | Yes 7/16/95 |
| Dr. Mertz | Ms. Lilly 766-4114 | $ 50.13 | Yes | 7/10/95 | Lost check, reorder 7/18 | |

Set up a table with the information that you find most helpful. This information may be set up on network computers as well.

Call the custodian of records and ask what the fee is to copy an entire file. In most cases, this person will be able to tell you before you make the request and you can enclose the check. Some providers bill after sending out records. Others send you a letter after receiving your request asking for prepayment before they will copy the records. Then you have to issue a check, reorder the records, and thereby delay the process unnecessarily.

## ACCESS TO MEDICAL RECORDS

Medical records are considered the property of the housing facility or the medical provider that generated the original document. Medical records are also considered confidential property based on the fiduciary relationship between a doctor and patient. Yet it is recognized in every state that patients have the right to access the information in their own medical records and copy them at their expense. (Third-party payers also have access to the same information.) The physician-patient privilege may be waived in two ways.

By an *express waiver*, the patient executes an authorization or consent for release of medical records. Most law offices have these authorization forms filled out and ready for clients to sign. These forms need to accompany a letter of request for medical records and a check, if applicable. (These consent forms are valid for a specified period of time only—check your local statutes.)

The other way is by *implied waiver*. By initiating a lawsuit, the patient is implying that he or she is effectively waiving the physician-patient privilege. Patients who commence litigation are inviting disclosure of the facts in question and, in effect, are placing their physical, mental, and emotional health and condition open for scrutiny. Thus, the way is paved for disclosing and procuring medical information via the subpoena. This process is not automatic, however. Counsel still may need to assert that physical or mental conditions about which you are requesting records affect or were affected by the incident at issue.

Psychiatric records require a special authorization or subpoena with distinct wording, making it abundantly clear that the patient is allowing disclosure of records pertaining to his or her mental and emotional well-being. This consent form or subpoena must specifically identify the nature of the records released.

## RECORDS SERVICES

Records services, available in almost every city, can do the work for you. You provide them with your client's authorization (or subpoena), and they will go to the health care provider and copy the records and bills, pick up x-rays, fill out an affidavit or whatever your particular needs are, and hand-deliver everything to you. These services are very time efficient but not very cost-effective. If you are in a time crunch and can afford the service, give them a try.

## SUBPOENAS

*Subpoenas* are issued by the clerk of the court where the action is filed or by the attorney as an officer of the court. The office you are working for should have access to court subpoenas and local rules that govern their deliverance.

The subpoena contains the name and seal of the court, the name and number of the case, the address of the person or agency being subpoenaed, a description of the items to be produced, and where and when they are to be produced.

If medical records or bills are to be produced, an affidavit is usually required by the custodian of medical records and bills to state that the following pages are a true and legible copy of the original and additional clauses that make the records or bills admissible as evidence. Once again, state statute prevails. Several examples follow.

**Letter to Health Care Provider**

TO: [Name and address of provider]

RE: [Name of patient]
[Name of patient's guardian, if a minor]
[Include maiden names and past married names]

DOB:
SSN:
Medical Records Number:
Inclusive Dates of Treatment:

Dear Provider:

Enclosed please find an authorization for release of medical [records/bills/photographs/x-rays] pertaining to and signed by the above-referenced patient. Also enclosed is a check in the sum of $_____ to cover the cost of copying the medical records [*or*, As is customary, please bill us for the cost of copying the medical records, and we will promptly reimburse you]. We have been authorized by our client to request a copy of all medical records pertaining to your care of the above-referenced patient.

Please have your custodian of records fill out the enclosed affidavit, sign and notarize it, and return it with the medical records. It is very important that this affidavit be returned, so as not to necessitate subpoenaing your custodian of medical records to testify in the event this claim results in a lawsuit. Please return to the attention of ________, at the law firm of ________, at your earliest possible convenience. Please call if there will be any delay. Thank you for your assistance.

Sincerely,

____________

[Once this letter goes out, start your tracking chart.]

**Authorization for Release of Medical Information**

TO:

RE:

DOB:

SSN:

This will authorize you to grant and allow the law firm of ________, P.C., and their representatives, orally, in writing, by photocopy, or as otherwise requested, free access to any and all medical, billing, physician, hospital, and/or other records and information regarding my condition while under your observation, care and/or treatment. This includes reports, charts, clinical abstracts, progress notes, orders, x-ray films, HIV testing records, your prognosis as to subsequent developments, and any and all facts and particulars which might be requested by ________ regarding my care.

Please grant and release to ________ all documents you have in your possession, custody and control concerning your examination, treatment, tests, findings, diagnoses and prognoses of me, my physical condition, injuries, and disabilities.

This medical authorization revokes any and all previous medical authorizations signed or otherwise authorized by me prior to the date of signing below.

[date] [signature of patient or legal representative]

It is agreed that a photostatic copy of this authorization will be accepted with the same authority as the original. Telephone inquiries about this authorization or the release of medical records should be directed to ________. Thank you for your prompt attention and consideration in this matter.

Notarization

Subscribed and sworn to before me, to certify which my hand and seal of this office on this ______ day of ______, 19___.

____________________________

Notary Public

In and for the State of ______

**Psychiatric Release**

**Special Consent for Release of Psychiatric Records [or Substance Abuse Records]**

I, ________, hereby authorize ________ Psychiatric Institute to release any and all confidential records concerning your psychiatric treatment of me [*or* your treatment of me for substance abuse] to the law firm of ________ or its representatives. The purpose for this disclosure authorized herein is to commence litigation and is limited [*or* is not limited] to: ________.

This authorization expires on ______.

[date] ________

[signature of patient]

**Affidavit**
**[accompanying medical records]**

BEFORE ME, the undersigned authority, personally appeared ________, who being duly sworn, deposed as follows:

My name is ________, I am over 21 years of age, of sound mind, and am capable of making this affidavit, and am personally acquainted with the facts herein stated:

I am the custodian of records of *[health care provider]*. Attached hereto are _____ pages of records, _____ photographs, and any hospital records, x-rays, medical reports, psychological therapy, or any other kind of medical record required to be maintained by *[health care provider]*. These _____ pages are all of the records made or maintained by *[health care provider]* for *[name of patient]* in the regular course of business, and it was in the regular course of business of *[health care provider]* for an employee, representative, or doctor of *[patient]* with personal knowledge of the act, event, condition, opinion, diagnosis, or necessary treatment recorded to make the memorandum or the record or to transmit information thereof to be included in such record; and the memorandum of record was made at or near the time of the act, event, or condition, or reasonably thereafter. These said records also include any and all records this institution has received from any other physician or institution pertaining to the above-named individual.

The records attached hereto are the original or exact duplicates of the original if it is a rule not to permit the original records to leave the premises.

__________

Affiant

SWORN TO AND SUBSCRIBED before me, on this the _____ day of _____, 19___.

__________

Notary Public

My commission expires:________.

**Affidavit**
**[accompanying medical bills]**

BEFORE ME, the undersigned authority, personally appeared ________, who being duly sworn, deposed as follows:

My name is ________. I am over 21 years of age, am of sound mind, capable of making this affidavit, and am personally acquainted with the facts herein stated:

I am the custodian of the medical bills of *[health care provider]*. Attached hereto are ________ pages of medical bills from *[health care provider]*. These said _____ pages are all of the medical bills kept by *[health care provider]* in the regular course of business, and it was in the regular course of business of *[health care provider]* for an employee, representative, or other person with knowledge of the act, event, condition for which these charges were incurred to make the memorandum or the medical bill or to transmit information thereof to be included in such memorandum or medical bill; and the memorandum or medical bill was made at or near the time of the act, event, or condition for which these charges were incurred or reasonably soon thereafter. Furthermore, I am familiar with the usual, customary and reasonable charges for such services in this community at the time they were rendered while *[patient]* was a patient of *[health care provider]*. These charges are the usual, customary and reasonable charges for like or similar services in the vicinity in which they were incurred, and of the time they were incurred, and were necessary for the proper treatment of the injuries sustained by this patient.

The medical bills attached hereto are the original or exact duplicates of the original if it is a rule not to permit the original medical bills to leave the premises.

__________

Affiant

SWORN TO AND SUBSCRIBED before me, on this the _____ day of _____, 19___.

__________

Notary Public

Now the medical records and bills are in presentable form for the courts and can become evidence in your case. (You may have to tailor your authorizations when requesting particular information such as x-rays, videotapes, photographs, or films.) Medical records must meet the following criteria before they may be used as evidence:

- The record pertains to the patient in question.
- It was compiled at the time the events occurred in the ordinary course of business.
- It was prepared by a person knowledgeable of the facts being recorded.
- It was prepared before litigation began.
- It is legible.

If you have any question as to the validity of the medical records obtained (e.g., times of entry in different sections do not match, signatures differ, items are crossed out, pages do not match copies that have been included with other doctors' referral notes), you may need to view the original documents at the hospital or clinic where they originated. You will need to contact the custodian of the medical records to find out the local procedure for viewing the original documents. Bring your copies to compare. If you see correction fluid used in a medical record, question it. Entries should be made in ink; if there is a correction, the original text should be crossed out and initialed by the writer. Some documents allow entries in pencil, but the document itself should state that pencil should be used and erasures are permitted. Errors should be obvious, and marked "ERROR." If it looks as if an error is trying to be hidden, it probably is.

## REPORTS

In some cases, you may need to request a report by the treating physician. This report will generally consist of a complete synopsis of the health care provider's examination, treatment, response to treatment, and prognosis. Be specific in your request. These reports can be expensive, so make sure you get what you want. An example of a report request follows:

### Report Request

TO: Health Care Provider

RE: Our client, your patient ________
DOB:
SSN:
Date of Accident:

We represent ________ for injuries sustained in an automobile accident on ______. It is our understanding that you have been treating him/her for these injuries. We have enclosed an authorization, signed by ________. Would you be so kind as to prepare a report outlining the following information regarding your care of ________ including the following:

Dates of treatment

History of the incident causing the injury

Any significant past medical history

Physical findings upon initial visit

Your treatment plan

Any limitations to activities, work, or daily living

Any referrals to other health care providers

Your prognosis for the patient

Has the patient's condition achieved maximum medical benefit, and if not,

What further treatment you deem necessary—including surgeries, devices, and additional medical care

Do you feel that the patient's condition is related in whole or in part to the accident, which occurred on ______?

Thank you for furnishing this information to us at your earliest possible convenience, and please bill us, of course, for the cost incurred.

Sincerely,

Attorney for the Plaintiff

By the processes outlined, you should have at your disposal the means by which you can obtain all medical documents you will need up to and including use at trial. The medical records, x-rays, reports, and so on will provide the evidence as to the client's physical condition. The bills document monies already expended in resolving the medical condition caused by the incident.

The *Physician's Current Procedural Terminology* (CPT), published by the American Medical Association, may assist greatly in deciphering procedural codes found in the medical records and bills. The following five-digit codes represent a systematic coding of procedures performed by physicians at hospitals and clinics:

| | |
|---|---|
| 00100–01999 | Anesthesiology |
| 10040–69979 | Surgery |
| 70010–79999 | Radiology (includes diagnostic ultrasound and nuclear medicine) |
| 80002–89399 | Pathology and Laboratory |
| 90701–99199 | Medicine |
| 99100–99140 | Anesthesiology |

These sections are further divided into subsections that describe almost every procedure found in medical billing records. Modifiers are also used to indicate specific circumstances, for example:

- A service has both a professional and technical component.
- A procedure was performed by more than one physician or in more than one location.
- A service has been increased or reduced.
- Only part of a service was performed.
- An adjunctive service was performed.
- A bilateral procedure was performed.
- A service or procedure was provided more than once.
- Unusual events occurred.

## WHAT TO DO WITH THE RECORDS

When you have collected all the medical records pertaining to a particular case, they must be organized. The most efficient manner to organize the records is chronologically. Depending on the type of case, you may want to have the most recent records in the front, followed by less pertinent records. If your intention is to create a story with the medical records, a more resourceful way would be to arrange them by date and time, from earliest to latest.

Voluminous medical records should be tabbed for easy reference. Many times throughout the case, you will need to find certain portions that come into question. Documents that must be referred to often should be tagged and highlighted for easy access. You may want to use adhesive labels, which are large enough to document pertinent items contained on the tabbed document.

Any medical case must be well supported. This substantiation is performed often by the records themselves. The medical reports will certify contentions made in the case and may become court evidence. This register must be *accurate* and *accessible, believable*, and *concise.*

If you can fulfill these three criteria, the time and money you will save in presenting your case will be immeasurable.

Once your records are organized, they must be chronologized or summarized with a description of what they contain. Obviously you will not need to include everything. You first need to review every document contained within the medical records to determine if it is pertinent. If it contains information that affects your case, tab it and make reference to it in the chronology. Otherwise pass it by. Never discard any medical documents; the record must remain a true and complete register of all documents contained in the office of the source of the records.

## MEDICAL BILLS

Arranging the medical bills is a more systematic task than organizing the medical records. Every medical bill the client has paid in association with the claim should be documented. This documentation ideally should consist of true copies of the medical bills accompanied by an affidavit by the custodian of medical bills. This will not always be the case, however. It may be necessary to obtain copies of other statements paid out in association with the claim. Insurance records may be a source. When adding up and recording amounts expended in the case, include only the amounts of the charges. Reimbursements need not necessarily be disclosed. A good practice note is to file the original document as is. Make copies of the original document, excluding items that are not pertinent, such as whether insurance has reimbursed the payee or intends to. These copies are filed behind the itemization of amounts expended. A sample medical bill itemization follows:

| ITEM NUMBER | DATE | DESCRIPTION | PURPOSE | AMOUNT |
|---|---|---|---|---|
| Exhibit #1 | 4/11/95 | Hospital A | Hospital stay | $ 3,672.45 |
| Exhibit #2 | 4/15/95 | Dr. B | Hand surgery | $ 1,314.07 |
| Exhibit #3 | 4/15/95 | Hospital A Anesthesia | Anesthesia | $ 857.43 |
| Exhibit #4 | 5/25/95 - 9/14/95 | Physical Therapy Assoc. | Ongoing therapy | $ 934.78 |
| **CURRENT** | **RUNNING** | **TOTAL** | - | **$ 6,778.73** |

Keeping track of the bills as they come in will help you assess the specials (costs specific to the case) you have obtained at any stage of the case. They should be attached behind the itemization list.

Other bills that you may want to include are any consultations that the patient required and any travel (including air fare, car rental, meals, and hotel stays). Psychiatric care may have been necessary. A parent of small children may have needed assistance with child care during the period of convalescence. These amounts are presented in the same manner.

Wages that were lost as a result of the incident will also be tabulated and included when you present your case. Calculations of lost earning capacity will become part of the case as well, if applicable.

## Chapter 3

# Contents of the Medical Records

Although hospital charts may vary in their organization, appearance, and format, they typically adhere to the documentation standards defined by the Department of Health and Human Services and the Joint Commission on Accreditation of Hospitals (JCAH). These organizations must deem the hospital as meeting certain criteria before they will accredit it and before Medicare and Medicaid reimbursement is allowed. Hospitals are often audited for their adherence to the JCAH requirements and their own local policies regarding the contents of medical documentation. Non-JCAH member facilities are not bound by JCAH requirements, but because of the wide acceptance, JCAH has established the standard. JCAH Standard I stipulates that "an adequate medical record shall be maintained for every individual who is evaluated or treated as an inpatient, ambulatory care patient, or emergency patient, or who receives patient services in a hospital-administered home care program." JCAH Standard II stipulates that "the medical record shall contain sufficient information to identify the patient, to support the diagnosis, to justify the treatment, and to document the results accurately." All medical records must contain at a minimum the following classes of information:

- Identification data; when not obtainable, the reason shall be entered in the record.
- The medical history of the patient.
- The report of a relevant physical examination.
- Diagnostic and therapeutic orders.
- Evidence of appropriate informed consent; when consent is not obtained, the reason shall be entered in the record.
- Clinical observations, including results of therapy.

- Reports of procedures, tests, and the results.
- Conclusions at termination of hospitalization or evaluation/treatment.

The format of the ICD.CM, the *International Classification of Diseases*, classifies diseases and injuries into 17 sections, using the following numeric codes:

| | |
|---|---|
| 001–139 | Infectious and Parasitic Diseases |
| 140–139 | Neoplasms |
| 240–279 | Endocrine, Nutritional and Metabolic Diseases, and Immunity Disorders |
| 280–289 | Diseases of the Blood and Blood-Forming Organs |
| 290–319 | Mental Disorders |
| 320–389 | Diseases of the Nervous System and Sense Organs |
| 390–459 | Diseases of the Circulatory System |
| 460–519 | Diseases of the Respiratory System |
| 520–579 | Diseases of the Digestive System |
| 580–629 | Diseases of the Genitourinary System |
| 630–676 | Complications of Pregnancy, Childbirth, and the Puerperium |
| 680–709 | Diseases of the Skin and Subcutaneous Tissue |
| 710–739 | Diseases of the Musculoskeletal System and Connective Tissue |
| 740–759 | Congenital Anomalies |
| 760–779 | Certain Conditions Originating in the Perinatal Period |
| 780–799 | Symptoms, Signs and Ill-defined Conditions |
| 800–999 | Injury and Poisoning |

Additionally, *V codes* are assigned when a person who is not sick encounters the health services (e.g., for vaccinations or to discuss problems), for treatment for certain diseases (e.g., kidney dialysis, chemotherapy), or when a problem affects a person's health status but in itself is not a disease condition.

*E codes* classify external causes of injury and poisoning. They ascribe codes based on the specific cause of injury or poisoning.

## FORMS: THE HISTORY AND PHYSICAL

An H&P (History and Physical) is a format by which a physician documents his or her evaluation of a patient. If you encounter an illegibly handwritten H&P, use the following sample as a guideline:

CC: CHIEF COMPLAINT: This is a _____ year old, race, male/female, admitted to the service of Dr. ________ , with a chief complaint of ________ .
*EXAMPLE: This is a 35 y/o LAF [Latin American female] who was involved in a MVA*

*[motor vehicle accident] this morning. She claims to have severe neck pain. There are multiple facial abrasions.*

HCC: HISTORY OF CHIEF COMPLAINT: Onset, duration, location, radiation, nature, frequency, and factors that relieve or exacerbate it.

*EXAMPLE: She enters the clinic wearing a neck brace; there is dried blood on her lip and chin. She stated she was a passenger in the vehicle driven by her 14-year-old son. Her head hit the windshield, shattering glass.*

PMH: PAST MEDICAL HISTORY: The patient admits to the usual childhood diseases without sequelae. The patient denies any history of rheumatic or scarlet fever, tuberculosis, diabetes mellitus, stroke, heart disease, cancer, ulcer, or venereal disease. There is not significant history of trauma, transfusions, or recent travel.

SURGERIES/HOSPITALIZATIONS:

*EXAMPLE: The patient had her gallbladder removed in 1978. Hospital stay was four days.*

IMMUNIZATIONS: The patient admits to the usual childhood immunizations. Last tetanus toxoid was ______.

ALLERGIES: Patient denies any food or drug allergies.

MEDICATIONS: Patient is currently taking ________.

SOCIAL HISTORY: The patient is of ________ (ethnic) origin, ________ (religion), and has a ________ level education, and is employed as a ________ at ________. The patient is married/single/divorced, and has ________ children. His/her hobbies are ________. The patient denies the use of tobacco, alcohol, caffeine, and recreational drugs. [Smoking history is usually defined in pack years.]

FAMILY HISTORY: Negative for asthma, alcoholism, cancer, convulsion, diabetes, heart disease, obesity, hypertension, jaundice, TB, gout, arthritis, ulcers, blood dyscrasias, kidney disease, emphysema, or psychiatric illness.

ROS: REVIEW OF SYSTEMS:

GENERAL: The patient denies any recent problem with weight gain or loss, fever, chills, night sweats or weakness.

SKIN: The patient denies any pruritis, rashes, unusual moles or warts, petechiae, or hair or nail changes.

HEENT: HEAD, EARS, EYES, NOSE, and THROAT: Patient denies any significant injuries or recurrent cephalgia (headache). Patient has required vision correction for hyperopia/myopia since age ______. Denies any recent changes in vision, glasses, blind spots, diplopia, redness, itching, burning, or dryness in the eyes. Denies glaucoma. Patient denies any loss of hearing, tinnitus (ringing in the ears), frequent infection, discharge, pain, vertigo (dizziness), or excess cerumen (ear wax.) Patient denies nasal fracture, sinusitis, epistaxis, or decreased smell. Septum deviates left/right. Denies any tongue or gum lesions or ulceration or decreased taste. Denies any tonsil or adenoid problems, recurrent sore throat or hoarseness. Denies thyroid or nodal enlargement.

RESPIRATORY: Patient denies history of asthma, pneumonia, bronchitis, emphysema, wheezing, cough, hemoptysis, shortness of breath, dyspnea on exertion, orthopnea, or TB exposure.

BREASTS: Patient denies any lumps, discharge, bleeding, pain, swelling, or tenderness. No history of breast implants. Last mammogram: ______.

CV: CARDIOVASCULAR: Patient denies any congenital defects, murmurs, palpitations, angina, syncope, edema, hypertension, claudication, cyanosis, venous varicosity, or phlebitis. There is no history of myocardial infarction, exertional dyspnea, or paroxysmal nocturnal dyspnea.

GI: GASTROINTESTINAL: The patient denies any nausea, vomiting, diarrhea, denies dyspepsia, abdominal pain, hematemesis, hematochezia, melena, tenesmus, clay-colored stools, pyrosis, excessive weight loss or gain, jaundice, constipation, dyschezia, or anorexia.

UG: UROGENITAL: Patient denies any polyuria, anuria, oliguria, dysuria, nocturia, pyuria, hematuria, urgency, frequency, hesitance, enuresis, dribbling, decreased force of stream, impotence, or veneral disease. Denies any history of cystitis, nephritis, prostatitis, or stones.

OB-GYN: Menarche occurred at the age of ______. Periods have been regular on a ___ day cycle and lasting ______ days. Flow is described as ______. Menopause occurred at age ______ and patient denies post menopausal bleeding. Last menstrual period was ___ and this was a normal period. Last PAP smear was ______/______/______. Patient denies dysmenorrhea, menorrhagia, metrorrhagia, and leukorrhea. Patient is gravida ______, para ______, ab ______, premature ______, living ______. Patient states all deliveries were vaginal/Cesarean, normal, and spontaneous/induced. Patient denies pelvic masses or pain, dyspareunia, sexual problems, or recurrent history of genital infections. Current method of birth control is ______.

MUSCULOSKELETAL: Patient denies injuries, swelling, stiffness, deformity, muscular weakness or atrophy, arthritis, or myalgia.

NEUROLOGICAL: Patient denies epilepsy, tics, twitches, convulsions, syncope, paralysis, paresthesia, dyssynergia, or dysphagia.

ENDOCRINE: Patient denies changes in voice, heat or cold intolerance, change in body hair distribution, change in skin, rapid growth, diabetes mellitus or thyroid disease.

HEMATOLOGIC: Patient denies fatigue, dizziness, easy bruising, history of anemia, transfusions, blood dyscrasia, and coagulation problems.

## PHYSICAL EXAM

A complete physical examination consists of an entire review of the patient's physical body. Rarely will you find an absolutely thorough physical exam; there is not ample time to check every physical possibility during most examinations. Anatomical landmarks are surface findings of internal structures. Common annotations are ASIS (anterior superior iliac spine), PSIS (posterior superior iliac spine), MAL (midaxillary line), MCL (midclavicular line), LCM (left costal margin), and RSB (right sternal border).

GENERAL DESCRIPTION: This is a ______ y/o ______ (race) ______ (sex) who appears to be in a good state of health and shows no signs of acute distress. [You might be likely to see this written as: WDWNBF, NAD—well-developed, well-nourished black female in no acute distress.]

VITALS: Vital signs are taken and listed as:

B/P: Blood Pressure, listed as systolic over diastolic.

TEMP: Temperature; may be listed as Celsius or Fahrenheit.

PULSE: Recorded as beats per minute.

RESP: Listed as breaths per minute.

SKIN: There are no rashes, ecchymoses, petechiae, nodules, stria, scars, or cyanosis noted. The skin is warm and dry and has good turgor and texture. Hair distribution, texture, fragility, and sheen are normal. There is no evidence of nail pitting, clubbing, splitting or malformation, and no splinter hemorrhages are present in the nail bed.
H/N: HEAD AND NECK: The head is normocephalic; no masses are noted. The scalp is intact without lesions or lacerations. The thyroid is in the midline and not enlarged to palpation. No bruits are auscultated. (Presence and strength of carotid pulse.) There is no lymphadenopathy noted. Neck is examined for suppleness, restrictions in ROM (range of motion).
EYES: Eyes move in a conjugate manner in six fields of primary gaze. Pupils are equally reactive to light and accommodation. Red reflex is present bilaterally, and there are no corneal or lenticular opacities. No scleral or conjunctival hemorrhage or exudates are observed. Sclera are nonicteric. Fundoscopic exam reveals intact retina without hemorrhages, exudates or papilledema. There is no nystagmus, ptosis, or exophthalmos noted.
EARS: The external auditory canals are patent bilaterally without erythema or discharge. Tympanic membranes are intact and have good cones of light, and are not bulging or retracted. Weber and Rinne tests are normal.
NOSE: The mucus is moist and pink. The septum is midline without perforation. There are no polyps or tender areas.
MOUTH AND THROAT: Teeth are present and in good repair. There is no bleeding ulceration or petechia noted. The tongue is moist and does not deviate. The pharynx is unremarkable and without postnasal drainage, discharge, injection, or exudate.
BREASTS: The breasts are bilaterally symmetrical and the nipples are everted. There are no masses palpated. No discharge, pain, swelling, or retraction is present.
C/L: CHEST AND LUNGS: The chest is symmetrical. Bilaterally CTA (clear to auscultation) and percussion. Respiration is regular and rate is rhythmical without the use of accessory muscles.
CV: CARDIOVASCULAR: Heart RRR (regular rate and rhythm) /s (without) murmurs. There are no palpable lifts or thrills. All peripheral pulses are normal and equal bilaterally. No peripheral edema, ulcerations, or varicosities are observed.
ABDOMEN: Abdomen flat, NT (nontender), +BS (bowel sounds are present), normal in all quadrants (RUQ—right upper quadrant; LUQ—left upper quadrant; RLQ—right lower quadrant; LLQ—left lower quadrant.) No evidence of organomegaly. There are no scars, masses or free fluid noted. Murphy's sign is absent.
GENITAL: *Male*: The penis is circumcised without lesions or discharge. Testes descended bilaterally without tenderness or masses. No hernias were palpated. *Female*: No lesions of the external genitalia are observed. The cervix is deep in the vagina, and no masses, polyps, or discharges are noted. The urethral orifice is unremarkable, as is the adnexa.
RECTAL: Sphincter tone is good. There are no fistulas, hemorrhoids, masses, or areas of tenderness noted. The prostate is firm and not enlarged. Hemoccult is ______.
NEUROLOGICAL: No sensory deficits are noted. Gait is normal. Cranial nerves II–XII are grossly intact and deep tendon reflexes are +2/4 and equal bilaterally. Babinski reflex is not elicited and ankle clonus is not observed. No atrophy, tremor, or fasciculation is observed. Rhomberg's test is negative. Mental status: A/O × 3 (Patient is alert and oriented to person, place and time). Judgment, memory, abstraction and calculation are intact.
MUSCULOSKELETAL. No areas of tenderness or spasm noted. Full range of motion

present in all extremities and spine. The extremities have normal, equal muscle strength. No scoliosis or osseous deformity is observed. No edema noted.

## PROGRESS NOTES

Physicians document the progress of a case, complications, consultations, change in diagnosis, condition on discharge, and instructions to the patient on the hospital chart progress record. Notations must be made at least daily. The note should be dated and signed, preferably with a time notation. Many progress notes will be made throughout the hospital stay, the frequency being proportional to the degree of morbidity or difficulty. Most progress notes commonly follow the format of SOAP notes:

*S*ubjective: How the patient feels, any complaints.

*O*bjective: Vital signs, physical exam, lab data, and so on, plus the physician's observations about the patient.

*A*ssessment: The physician's conclusions about the data received and impressions.

*P*lan: Any new labs or medications to order or start, changes or additions to orders, discharges or transfer plans, consultations requested and further testing planned.

If you note that a consultation has been requested by another service but has not been done, question it. Consultants issue reports focusing on their area of specialty. Numerous consultations may appear in one record (psychiatric consults, neurological consults, orothopedic surgery consults, etc.).

Electrolytes are documented by listing as:

| sodium | chloride |
|---|---|
| potassium | $CO_2$ |

SMA-6 (SMA-7) labs are shown as:

| sodium | chloride | BUN |
|---|---|---|
| potassium | $CO_2$ | GLUCOSE (CREATININE) |

## CONSULTATIONS

These forms are usually set forth in the same manner found in the history and physical, with emphasis on the particular medical specialty. Other disciplines, such as social services, nutritional services, and physical therapy, may be found throughout the hospital records. These records should also document problem areas, progress, and response to treatment.

## ADMIT NOTE

Hospital admission notes are usually a brief story about the patient. They consist of the following elements:

1. Chief complaint, sometimes written in the patient's own words.
2. Brief review of the chief complaint.
3. Previous medical history (should include only positives, e.g., "+ htn [hypertension] since 1986").
4. Previous surgical history (should list the operation and when it was performed).
5. Medications: prescription and over the counter.
6. Allergies. This is an important item, often overlooked in a hurry.
7. Review of systems, recording positive findings only:
   Eyes, ears, nose, throat (EENT)
   Cardiorespiratory
   Gastrointestinal
   Genitourinary
   Musculoskeletal
   Nervous system
8. Physical exam, recording positive findings:
   General: vital signs, etc.
   Eyes, ears, nose, throat (EENT)
   Cardiorespiratory
   Gastrointestinal
   Genitalia
   Musculoskeletal
   Neurological
   Mental status
9. Pertinent lab or x-ray data
10. Habits
11. Impressions
12. Plan, including expected therapy and consultations
13. Prognosis

## ORDERS

| DATE | TIME | ORDER | NOTED BY | DATE | TIME |
|---|---|---|---|---|---|
| | | | | | |

A physician's order sheet contains orders for medications, intravenous fluids, lab tests, and any special instructions for nurses (e.g., nasogastric suction, enema). This sheet usually has several separate entries on each page. Each time an order is written, it should consist of the date and time, and the exact order, including specific dosing information. Check the orders against other sections of the chart to ensure that all orders written were carried out. Make sure all actions carried out had orders for them. Telephone orders or verbal orders are also to be followed when given. These must be documented as such in the order section and be signed and dated by the physician within 24 hours.

Injection code sites are documented as:

RUOQ—right upper outer quadrant

LUOQ—left upper outer quadrant

RDM—right deltoid muscle

LDM—left deltoid muscle

RMLT—right mid-lateral thigh

LMLT—left mid-lateral thigh

RMAT—right mid-anterior thigh

LMAT—left mid-anterior thigh

AB—abdominal fat pad

## ANESTHESIA

Anesthesia is a branch of medicine that involves high risk. Anesthesiologists and anesthesia groups are often targeted for lawsuits. Certified registered nurse anesthetists can perform anesthesia for surgery or regional blocks, but they must be supervised by a physician—either an anesthesiologist or the surgeon of record. The administration of anesthesia for any procedure requires the patient's informed consent.

Anesthesia can be broken down as follows:

*Local anesthesia.* Involves injecting a numbing substance like lidocaine hydrochloride into the involved area. The drugs temporarily and reversibly block nerve conduction, reducing sensitivity to painful stimuli. They should be nonirritating and have low systemic toxicity.

*Regional anesthesia.* Involves injecting a drug to block the nerve that supplies a finger or toe, hand or foot, or even a whole extremity to be operated on.

*Conduction anesthesia.* Includes epidural and spinal anesthesia, where anesthesia is introduced into the spinal fluid through a needle injected into a certain level of the spine, between two vertebrae through the tough fibrous sheath enclosing the spinal column and brain. Epidural injections are made into the extradural space, and spinals inject local anesthetic into the subarachnoid space.

*General anesthesia.* The patient is made unconscious and insusceptible to pain by administering the anesthetic systemically. Desirable properties include a rapid and safe induction with limited effects on cardiovascular and respiratory functions. The actions produced are: hypnosis (loss of consciousness), analgesia (loss of pain), amnesia (loss of memory), and skeletal muscle relaxation.

The anesthesia record usually consists of information assessing the patient prior to surgery. A preoperative evaluation should contain variations of the standard questions prior to giving an anesthetic:

1. History of major medical problems (major organ systems: cardiovascular, pulmonary, renal, etc.).
2. Any medications the patient is taking.
3. History of allergies to medications and how the allergy manifested itself.
4. Any past problems with anesthesia.
5. Family history of anesthesia problems. (There are two inherited disorders that anesthesiologists are especially concerned with: *malignant hypothermia*, which is very rare and very severe, and *pseudocholinesterase deficiency*, when the body cannot break down succinylcholine, a commonly used paralyzing agent.)

The American Society of Anesthesiologists outlines risk categories to assign patients prior to surgery, from I to V, with V being most severe:

| | |
|---|---|
| I | Healthy with no systemic disease. |
| II | Healthy with one systemic problem that is well controlled (e.g., hypertension or diabetes under good control). |
| III | Two or more well-controlled disease processes or a past history of heart attacks, severe emphysema, and so forth. |
| IV | Uncontrolled disease process, which puts the patient at a high mortality risk (e.g., a recent heart attack, sepsis). |
| V | Expected to die despite surgical intervention (ruptured aneurysm, gunshot wound to the heart, etc.). |

Anesthesia care begins with the preoperative evaluation and ends with the patient's discharge from the postanesthesia care unit. Any critical problem during this time must be addressed by the anesthesiologist. The anesthesiologist responsible for pre- or postoperative care may not necessarily be the anesthesiologist who provided the surgical anesthesia.

Baseline vital signs should be taken in the holding area just prior to surgery and must be documented prior to giving an anesthetic. The anesthesiologist or anesthetist must monitor all vital signs closely during surgery. The general rule during surgery is that if blood pressure deviates more than 20 percent from baseline, the anesthesiologist should be alert to a possible problem needing immediate intervention.

Anesthesia complications may not be immediately evident. Critical problems that may be related to anesthesia may develop within the first 24 postoperative hours.

Surgical drugs are ordered and dosed based on body weight. The goal of general anesthesia is to induce a state of unconsciousness, analgesia, and skeletal muscle relaxation. Some of the most commonly used anesthesia drugs used today in surgery are:

*Induction/hypnotics*

Thiopental (Pentothal), a short-acting barbiturate for the induction of anesthesia.

Thiamylal (Surital), a short-acting barbiturate for the induction of anesthesia.

Methohexital (Brevital), a short-acting barbiturate for the induction of anesthesia.

Amidate (Etomidate)

Propofol (Diprivan). Not usually used in patients at risk for hypotension on induction or with severe coronary artery disease.

Droperidol (Inapsine)

Ketalar (Ketamine). Produces a dissociative state; used primarily for uncooperative children.

Lidocaine (Xylocaine)

Ketorolac (Toradol)

Innovar. A combination of droperidol (Inapsine), a butyrophenone, and fentanyl (Sublimaze), a potent short-acting narcotic, which together produce a state of indifference, decreased anxiety, analgesia, and bradykinesia, called *neuroleptanalgesia*, during which the patient can respond to command.

Diazepam (Valium). A benzodiazepine with a dose-related sedative and hypnotic action, usually lasting up to 6–8 hours.

Loazepam (Ativan)

Morphine, fentanyl, sufentanyl, and alfentanyl. Narcotics.

*Inhalation agents* are used to induce patients with compromised airways, children over 1 year of age who cannot cooperate with IV induction, or patients in whom anesthesia might be safer without fixed agents.

Nitrous oxide. Used only in combination with other drugs; should not be used in patients with compromised cardiac function.

Halothane (Fluothane). Easy, safe, and widely used but has been connected with liver damage.

Isofluorane (Forane)

Enflurane (Ethrane)

Desflurane (Suprane)

Methoxyflurane (Penthrane). Provides good muscle relaxation and analgesia but may produce high-output renal failure.

*Muscle relaxants*, or neuromuscular blockades that produce a state of paralysis during surgery.

Succinylcholine (Anectine). Depolarizing; most widely used.
Mivacurium (Mivacron)
Vecuronium (Norcuron)
Rocuronium (Zemuron)
Pancurium (Pavulon). Steroidal.
Atracurium (Tracrium)
d-tubocurarine (Tubocurare)

*Reversals* antagonize the action of certain drugs like narcotics or neuromuscular blockade agents.

Physostigmine (Antilirium)
Edrophonium (Enlon, Tensilon)
Flumazanil (Mazicon)
Naloxone (Narcan)
Neostigmine (Prostigmin)
Pyridostigmine (Regonol, Mestinon)
Glycopyrrolate (Robinul)

*Local anesthetics* produce a loss of nerve conduction in the order: (1) pain, (2) temperature, (3) touch, (4) proprioception, and (5) skeletal muscle tone.

Bupivicaine (Marcaine, Sensorcaine)
Cetacaine (Cetylite)
Lidocaine (Xylocaine)
Mepivacaine (Carbocaine, Polocaine)
Chlorprocaine (Nesacaine)
Prilocaine (Citanest)
Etidocaine (Duranest)

*Cardiovascular* drugs are often employed to ensure proper functioning of the surgical patient's cardiac status.

Hydralazine (Apresoline)
Trimethaphan (Arfonad)
Atropine
Brevibloc (Esmalol)
Calcium
Digoxin (Lanoxin)
Dopamine (Dobutrex)

Ephedrine

Epinephrine (Adrenaline)

Propranolol (Inderal)

Isoproteranol (Isuprel)

Labetalol (Normodyne, Trandate)

Lasix (a diuretic)

Phenylephrine (Neosynephrine)

Nitropruside (Nipride)

Nitroglycerin, sublingual (Nitrostat), transdermal (Nitro-Dur)

Halothane (Fluothane). Easy, safe, and widely used but has been connected with liver damage.

Verapamil (Procardia)

*Pulmonary* drugs are often employed during a surgical procedure to assist the patient's pulmonary status.

Aminophylline

Theophylline

Terbutaline (Brethine)

Albuterol (Proventil)

*IV Fluids* are given for perioperative fluid management. The anesthesiologist must monitor the patient's blood pressure and fluids lost during the procedure and ensure the replacement of water, electrolytes, and blood volume.

D5W

D10W

D5LR

Lactated Ringer's

Normal saline

Albumin

Dextran

Hespan

Mannitol

*Miscellaneous* drugs

Iodine, topical (Betadine)

Protamine. An anticoagulant protein.

Vitamin K (Aqua-Mephyton). Assists the clotting function.

Diphenhydramine (Benadryl). An antihistamine.

Prochlorperazine (Compazine). An antianxiety drug used to control nausea and vomiting.

Decamethonium. Produces a depolarizing block.

Phenytoin (Dilantin). An anticonvulsant medication.

Doxapram (Dopram). Stimulates respiration.

Ergonovine (Ergotrate). Controls postpartum hemorrhage.

Heparin. Keeps the blood from clotting.

Insulin. Keeps blood sugar levels from becoming too high during the stress of surgery.

Dextrose. Used in feeding solutions.

Papaverine. A smooth muscle relaxant.

Promethazine (Phenergan). A narcotic analgesic.

Oxytocin (Pitocin). Augments or induces labor.

Metoclopramide (Reglan). Used to prevent nausea and vomiting.

Hydrocortisone (Solu-Cortef). A steroid used to reduce inflammation or to prevent Addisonian crisis in patients receiving steroid therapy preoperatively.

Methylprednisolone (Solu-Medrol). A steroid.

Dexamethasone (Decadron). A steroid.

Chlorpromazine (Thorazine). Tranquilizer, antiemetic.

Ranitidine (Zantac). Inhibits gastric secretion.

Sodium bicarbonate ($NaOH$)

Potassium chloride ($KCl$)

Magnesium sulfate ($MgSO_4$)

Sodium chloride ($NaCL$)

Patients are often premedicated prior to surgery with a combination of narcotics for pain relief, diazepam to calm them, midazolam HCl to sedate and eliminate the memory of pain, and/or an anticholinergic agent, which decreases fluid secretions and counteracts the anesthetic effects on the heart.

During an operative procedure utilizing anesthesia, the anesthesiologist keeps a record that documents close monitoring of the patient's vital signs, the procedure being performed, whether the patient is intubated or catheterized, the type of anesthesia used, and many other variables.

The anesthesia record (Figure 3.1) is a complex and intricate form. The anesthesiologist or anesthetist performing the case will be identified here, as will patient identification factors including height, weight, blood pressure, pulse, allergies, if the patient is wearing dentures, hemoglobin and hematocrit, physical status, diagnosis, the operation performed, the surgeon, start and stop time, the type of anesthesia (general or regional), oxygen levels, any special procedures performed, and any special anesthesia care required.

Blood pressure readings are graphically represented by arrows (∨)(∧) through-

**Figure 3.1**
**Anesthesia Record**

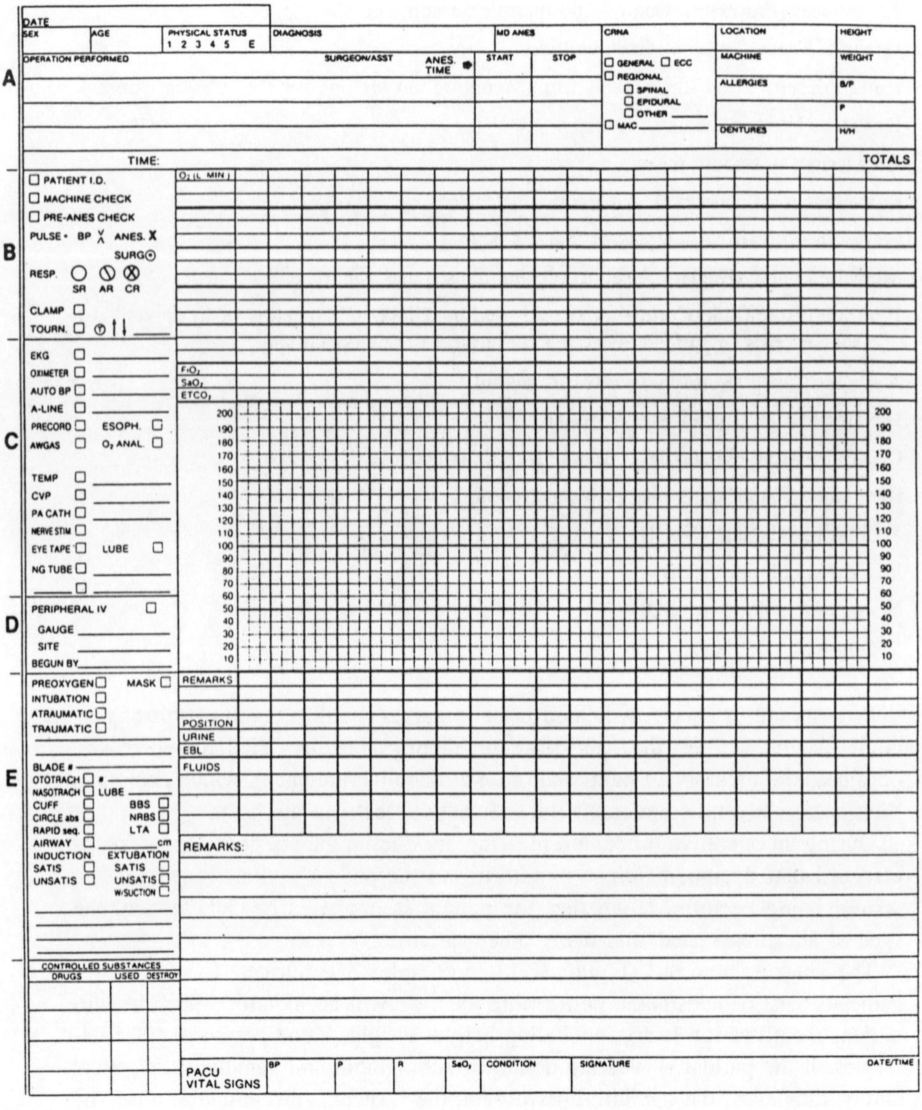

DATE
SEX | AGE | PHYSICAL STATUS 1 2 3 4 5 E | DIAGNOSIS | MD ANES | CRNA | LOCATION | HEIGHT

OPERATION PERFORMED | SURGEON/ASST | ANES. TIME ➡ | START | STOP | ☐ GENERAL ☐ ECC ☐ REGIONAL ☐ SPINAL ☐ EPIDURAL ☐ OTHER ____ ☐ MAC ____ | MACHINE | WEIGHT | ALLERGIES | B/P | P | DENTURES | H/H

A

TIME: | TOTALS

B

☐ PATIENT I.D.
☐ MACHINE CHECK
☐ PRE-ANES CHECK
PULSE • BP V Λ ANES. X
SURG⊙
RESP. ○ ⊘ ⊗
SR AR CR
CLAMP ☐
TOURN. ☐ Ⓣ ↑↓ ____

$O_2$ (L MIN)

C

EKG ☐ ____
OXIMETER ☐ ____
AUTO BP ☐ ____
A-LINE ☐ ____
PRECORD ☐ ESOPH. ☐
AWGAS ☐ $O_2$ ANAL. ☐
TEMP ☐ ____
CVP ☐ ____
PA CATH ☐ ____
NERVE STIM ☐
EYE TAPE ☐ LUBE ☐
NG TUBE ☐ ____
____ ☐ ____

$FiO_2$
$SaO_2$
$ETCO_2$

200 190 180 170 160 150 140 130 120 110 100 90 80 70 60 50 40 30 20 10

D

PERIPHERAL IV ☐
GAUGE ____
SITE ____
BEGUN BY ____

E

PREOXYGEN ☐ MASK ☐
INTUBATION ☐
ATRAUMATIC ☐
TRAUMATIC ☐
BLADE # ____
OTOTRACH ☐ # ____
NASOTRACH ☐ LUBE ____
CUFF ☐ BBS ☐
CIRCLE abs ☐ NRBS ☐
RAPID seq. ☐ LTA ☐
AIRWAY ☐ ____ cm
INDUCTION EXTUBATION
SATIS ☐ SATIS ☐
UNSATIS ☐ UNSATIS ☐
W/SUCTION ☐

REMARKS
POSITION
URINE
EBL
FLUIDS

REMARKS:

CONTROLLED SUBSTANCES
DRUGS | USED | DESTROY

PACU VITAL SIGNS | BP | P | R | $SaO_2$ | CONDITION | SIGNATURE | DATE/TIME out the case, showing systolic and diastolic readings. Blood pressures are monitored closely, as are heart rate, oxygen saturations, fluid status, and blood and urine loss.

## SURGERY

When a hospitalization includes surgery or other invasive procedure, there will be numerous forms to fill out, including a consent for surgery. This must identify the procedure and the physician and be signed by the patient, dated, and witnessed. A sample follows:

### Disclosure and Consent

*TO THE PATIENT: You have the right, as a patient, to be informed about your condition and the recommended surgical, medical, or diagnostic procedure to be used so that you may make the decision whether or not to undergo the procedure after knowing the risks and hazards involved. This disclosure is not meant to scare or alarm you; it is simply an effort to make you better informed so you may give or withhold your consent to the procedure.*

I voluntarily request Dr. ____________ as my physician, and such associates, technical assistants and other health care providers as they may deem necessary, to treat my condition which has been explained to me as: ______________________________

______________________________________________________________

I understand that the following surgical, medical, and/or diagnostic procedures are planned for me and I voluntarily consent and authorize these procedures: __________

______________________________________________________________

I understand that my physician may discover other or different conditions which require additional or different procedures from those planned. I authorize my physician, and such associates, technical assistants and other health care providers to perform such other procedures which are advisable in their professional judgment.

I (do)(do not) consent to the use of blood and blood products as deemed necessary.

I understand that no warranty or guarantee has been made to me as to result or cure.

Just as there may be risks and hazards in continuing my present condition without treatment, there are also risks and hazards related to the performance of the surgical, medical, and/or diagnostic procedures planned for me. I realize that common to surgical, medical, and/or diagnostic procedures is the potential for infection, blood clots in veins and lungs, hemorrhage, allergic reactions, and even death. I also realize that the following risks and hazards may occur in connection with this particular procedure: ______________

______________________________________________________________

I understand that anesthesia involves additional risks and hazards but I request the use of anesthetics for the relief and protection from pain during the planned and additional procedures. I realize the anesthesia may have to be changed possibly without explanation to me.

I understand that certain complications may result from the use of any anesthetic, including respiratory problems, drug reaction, paralysis, brain damage or even death. Other risks and hazards which may result from the use of general anesthetics range from minor discomfort to injury to vocal cords, teeth, or eyes. I understand that other risks and hazards resulting from spinal or epidural anesthetics include headache and chronic pain.

I have been given an opportunity to ask questions about my condition, alternative forms of anesthesia and treatment, risks of nontreatment, the procedures to be used, and the risks and hazards involved, and I believe that I have sufficient information to give this informed consent.

I certify that this form has been fully explained to me, that I have read it or have had it read to me, that the blank spaces have been filled in, and that I understand its contents.

DATE: __________ TIME: _____ SIGNATURE: ___________________________

PATIENT OR LEGALLY RESPONSIBLE PERSON

WITNESS: ___________________________________________________

ADDRESS: ___________________________________________________

Make sure you find this form in the records when an operation or surgical procedure took place.

Before any type of surgery, usually an assigned nurse will make sure that there is an operative permit; a history and physical have been taken; and valuables, dentures, glasses, contact lenses, prostheses, or hearing aids have been removed.

Preoperative lab values should be documented, including any specific labs ordered by the attending physician or surgeon. You will find these written on the physician's order sheet. Make sure they are documented in the chart. A common preoperative panel may include the following information:

Urinalysis

Complete blood count

Prothrombin time (PT) and partial thromboplastin time (PTT)

Bleeding time

Chemistry tests

- Electrolytes (Na+, K−, Cl−, $CO_2$ content)
- Glucose
- Blood urea nitrogen or creatinine
- Serum glutamic oxalacetic transaminase (SGOT)
- Lactate dehydrogenase (LDH)
- Bilirubin, total and direct

Chest x-ray

Electrocardiogram (ECG)

| **Blood type and screen** | **Abbreviation** | **Normal Values** |
|---|---|---|
| White Blood Count | WBC | $7.8 \times 10^3$ (+/−3) |
| Red Blood Cell Count | RBC | Male $5.4 \times 10^3$ (+/−0.7) |
| | | Female $4.8 \times 10^3$ (+/−0.6) |

| | | |
|---|---|---|
| Hemoglobin | Hgb | Male 16.0 (+/−2) g/dL<br>Female 14.0 (+/−2) g/dL |
| Hematocrit | Hct | Male 47 (+/−5) %<br>Female 42 (+/−5) % |
| Mean Corpuscular Volume | MCV | Male 87 (+/−7) fL<br>Female 90 (+/−9) fL |
| Mean Corpuscular Hemoglobin | MCH | 29 (+/−2) pg |
| Mean Corpuscular Hemoglobin Concentration | MCHC | 35 (+/−2) g/dL |
| Coefficient of Variation of the Red Blood Cell Volume Distribution Width | RDW | 13 (+/−1.5) % |
| Platelet Count | PLT | 130–400 × $10^3$ |
| Mean Platelet Value | MPV | 8.9 (+/−1.5) fL |
| Lymphocytes | Lymphs | 28 (+/−13) % |
| Lymphocytes | Lymphs | 2.0 × $10^3$ (+/−1) |

Elevations or depressions of these levels may alert the physician to abnormal processes within the body. For example, an elevated white blood count may mean an infectious process is occurring within the body. From the white blood cells, individual components may be analyzed as well. The term *left shift* pertains to elevations in immature white blood cells (neutrophils), indicating that the infectious process is an acute one.

Not all of the tests listed above are necessary in each case. Some abnormal findings will be found when there is no clinical abnormality. Therefore it is highly unlikely in minor cases for each of the above tests to be performed. A proposed preoperative testing schedule might be as follows:

| | CBC | Type & Screen | ECG | CXR | Blood Glucose | Electrolyte | PT/PTT |
|---|---|---|---|---|---|---|---|
| Minor surgery | | | | | | | |
| Major surgery | Yes | Yes | | | | | |
| Age <40 | | | | | | | |
| Age 40-70 | | | Yes | | | | |
| Age >70 | | | Yes | | | Yes | |
| Cardiac disorder | | | Yes | Yes | | | |
| Pulmonary disorder | | | Yes | Yes | | | |

| | | | | | | | |
|---|---|---|---|---|---|---|---|
| Malignant disorder | | | | | | | Yes |
| Hepatic disorder | | | | | | | Yes |
| Renal disorder | | | | | | Yes | |
| Bleeding disorder | | | | | | | Yes |
| Diabetes | | | | | Yes | Yes | |
| On Diuretics | | | | | | Yes | |
| On Digitalis | | | | | | Yes | |
| On Anti-coagulants | | | | | | | Yes |
| On Corticoids | | | | | Yes | Yes | |

This is subject to clinical judgment; it is not a finite rule. Other exams too may be necessary. Further diagnostic procedures may be ordered, in which case they should be documented in the order sheet, and there should be a report for each study performed included in the clinical records. The consultant who performed the diagnostic study will sometimes include his or her own progress notes in the chart in addition to the report of the study.

The operative note should provide at least the following information:

PATIENT:

SURGEON:

ASSISTANTS:

ANESTHESIA:

DATE AND TIME OF PROCEDURE:

PRE-OPERATIVE DIAGNOSIS:

POST-OPERATIVE DIAGNOSIS:

INDICATIONS FOR THE PROCEDURE:

FINDINGS:

PROCEDURE: Here you will find an in-depth, and most often quite technical description of the entire procedure including:

The positioning of the patient:

*Supine*: lying on back, facing up. These may be further broken down into:

gallbladder rest (midsection elevated)

lithotomy (knees up, feet in stirrups)

Scultetus (head down, feet up)

Trendelenburg (midsection and feet up, head down)

Thyroid (body slants down from shoulders, head back)

*Prone*: Lying face down.

hips flexed jack-knife (knees at feet parallel to body)

lift under pelvis (bent at an angle at the hips)

*Lateral*: placed on the side

flexed right or left

straight right or left

*Sitting*: bent at the waist and knees, head up, feet down.

How the anesthesia was administered.

Precisely how each cut was made and with what instrument.

How each organ was visualized and if it was altered in any way.

How many sponges were used.

How bleeding vessels were cauterized.

How much blood was lost.

How the incision was closed and with what suture material.

What dressing was applied.

Disposition of the patient at the end of the procedure.

COMPLICATIONS: If this section is included in the postoperative progress note, read it in depth, as something went wrong.

PLANS/PROGNOSIS: General information regarding the patient's follow-up plans

## POSTANESTHESIA CARE UNIT

Patients are monitored postoperatively in the recovery room, now called the postanesthesia care unit (PACU). This is where the patient recovers from the anesthetic to a stable condition not requiring monitoring, usually in minutes to hours. Recovery from the actual surgery itself may take hours to days in the same-day surgery unit or on the floor. Postoperative anesthesia care includes ensuring that the patient is positioned correctly, given oxygen or IV therapy if required, with instructions for further medications, and extubation criteria.

In the PACU, the patient will be assessed with a postanesthesia recovery (PAR) score, a system of evaluation based on objective, observable criteria. The parameters are circulation, respiration, activity, level of consciousness, and skin color. The criteria within each are scored from 0 to 2, and are taken upon admission, at 30 minutes, at 60 minutes, and on discharge. A total score less than 9 indicates that the patient requires continuous monitoring or further intervention and may not be discharged from the PACU until the supervising anesthesiologist approves the discharge.

Postoperative assessment includes the following evaluation standards:

*Respiratory*: Maintains patent airway. Respirations spontaneous, deep, effortless, without use of auxiliary muscles. Chest excursion symmetrical. Respiratory rate 10–20 for adults, 12–32 for pediatric. Breath sounds vesicular through both lung fields, bronchial over major airways, with no adventitious sounds. Sputum clear, if present. Nailbed and mucous membranes pink. $SaO_2 > 91$.

*Cardiovascular*: Heart rhythm unchanged from preoperative apical/radial pulse. Capillary refill returned in less than 3 seconds. Peripheral pulses palpable. No edema. No calf tenderness. Blood pressure stable and acceptable (determined by comparison with preoperative and interoperative blood pressures).

*Neurological*: Protective swallowing reflex present. Behavior appropriate to situation. Active range of motion of all extremities with equal strength. No paresthesia or numbness. Alert and oriented to person, place, and time, with verbalization clear and understandable before discharge. If pediatric patient, alert and verbalization appropriate for development age.

*Surgical Incision*: Dressing dry and intact. Wound edges well approximated. No drainage noted. Peripad to perineum—no drainage noted. Drains patent and activated by suction if appropriate.

*Neurovascular*: Affected extremity is pink, warm, and movable within patient's average range of motion. Capillary refill less than 3 seconds. Peripheral pulses palpable. No edema. Sensation intact without numbness or paresthesia.

*Gastrointestinal*: Abdomen soft, nondistended. Bowel sounds present. If nasogastric tube, drainage clear.

*Genitourinary*: Able to empty bladder without dysuria. Bladder not distended. Urine clear and yellow to amber. Continent of urine. Urinary drains patent with output greater than 30 cc per hour.

*Integumentary*: Skin color within patient's norm. Skin warm, dry, intact. Mucous membranes moist. No pressure sores developing.

*Musculoskeletal*: Absence of joint swelling and tenderness. Normal range of motion of all joints. No muscle weakness. Surrounding tissues show no evidence of inflammation, nodules, nail changes, ulceration, or rashes.

*Psychosocial*: Appearance, behavior, and speech should be appropriate to the situation. The patient's affect (external expression of emotion) should be appropriate, without mood swings. If pediatric patient, behavior appropriate for developmental age.

*IV Therapy*: Site should be healthy, without redness, swelling or drainage. IV should remain patent (unobstructed) with good blood return.

*Safety*: Side rails should be up constantly when staff is not at bedside. Bumper pads for protection of pediatric, restless, or combative patients. Stretcher wheels locked. ID bracelet on.

*Level of Comfort*: Clean, warm, and dry. Positioned to promote respiratory status. Positioned to reduce discomfort/swelling. No restrictive dressings. Minimal to no operative discomfort. Minimal to no nausea.

| **If the diagnosis is:** | **The goal for recovery will be**: |
|---|---|
| Alteration in respiratory function | Oxygen saturations over 91 percent on room air. |
| Alteration in circulation | Blood pressure and pulse within the patient's normal range. |
| Alteration in neurological status | Patient easily aroused and oriented to person, place, and time. |
| Potential for or presence of bleeding | No demonstrative signs or symptoms of hemorrhage. |
| Alteration in sensation/circulation | Patient's affected extremity pink and warm with palpable pulses, and with movement and sensation intact. |
| Alteration in gastrointestinal function | Patient will deny nausea. |
| Alteration in urinary elimination | Patient will have a nondistended bladder. If patient has a Foley, output will be over 30 cc. |
| Alteration in skin integrity | Patient will have no interruption of skin integrity other than the surgical site. |
| Alteration in mobility | Patient will move all extremities and sustain head lift. |
| Alteration in emotional status | Patient will have a calm, relaxed appearance. |
| Alteration in fluid volume | IV is patent, no redness or swelling at the site, infusing rate ordered by surgeon. |
| Potential for injury | Patient remains on stretcher with side rails up, wheels locked, and bumper pads used when indicated. |
| Alteration in comfort level | Patient will state that pain is alleviated or minimized. |
| Alteration in temperature | Patient's temperature will be equal to or over 95°F, and less than 99°F. |
| Received spinal or epidural | Patient should have 80 percent recovery in both sensory and motor areas before discharge. |

## PATHOLOGY REPORTS

If an organ or any body tissue has been removed or biopsied, the tissue should always be sent to the pathology lab, where the specimens are reviewed grossly and microscopically to identify the tissue or cells. The pathology report should include the clinical diagnosis; a description of the specimen received, including the site from which it was removed; the gross and microscopic examination results; and the pathological diagnosis. Following is a surgical pathology form:

*TO BE COMPLETED IN SURGERY*

ADMITTING PHYSICIAN DATE
OPERATING PHYSICIAN

PRE-OP DIAGNOSIS POST-OP DIAGNOSIS
BIOPSY SITE AND TISSUE REMOVED
[specify exact location and nature of tissue if indicated by surgeon.]

## NURSES' NOTES

Nurses' notes reflect instructions given by the physician and their implementation of the orders. They assess how the patient responds to treatment and general patient condition around the clock. Notes are usually made at shift change. Other notes must be recorded according to unit protocol.

## GRAPHIC SHEETS

This is a graphic representation of the patient's temperature, pulse, respiratory rate, and blood pressure.

## MEDICATION RECORD

This sheet records the following of instructions from the physician's order sheet. The medication record documents the time the drug is given, the name of the medication, the dose, and the route of administration. If the order and the medication record differ, question it. Any discrepancies should have reasons listed.

## POSTOPERATIVE NURSING ACTIONS

The nurse should make sure the patient is free from infection by:

- Maintaining aseptic techniques and utilizing principles of aseptic practice in varying situations.
- Initiating corrective action when breaks in technique occur.
- Classifying surgical wounds, making sure cultures are taken, and applying dressings.
- Monitoring drains and catheters.

The nurse also ensures the patient is free from injury related to surgical positioning by assessing the patient's mobility and range-of-motion limitations and using positioning devices and aids for proper body alignment. As well, the nurse:

- Ensures that the patient is free from injury related to electrical equipment.
- Ensures the patient's fluid and electrolyte balance is maintained.
- Makes sure the patient is free from injury related to the use of chemicals by assessing skin condition, allergies, and any pooling of prep solution.
- Ensures the patient is free from injury related to any retained foreign object.

## NURSING PHYSICAL ASSESSMENT

The patient should be evaluated and described using the following parameters:

GENERAL APPEARANCE—WNL (within normal limits); emaciated; obese; weak; acutely ill.

SKIN—WNL; pale; flushed; cyanotic; lacerations; abrasions; bruises; decubitus; jaundiced; clammy; swollen; petechiae; dry; rash.

CIRCULATION—WNL; edema; bleeding problems; peripheral cyanosis; calf pain; numbness; tingling.

EYES—bright; clear; dull; reddened; sunken; pupils dilated or contracted.

SPEECH—WNL; incoherent; slurring; aphasia; dysphasia.

TASTE—WNL; disturbed; lost; metallic.

APPETITE—good; poor; anorexic; fair; perverted craving for certain foods.

BREATH—WNL; sweet; fruity; sour; foul.

COUGH—absent; frequent; persistent; painful; spasmodic; hacking; productive; nonproductive.

RESPIRATION—WNL; quiet; rapid; shallow; labored; unlabored; apnea; Cheyne-Stokes; dyspnea.

VOMITUS—absent; small amount; large amount; blood-tinged; projectile.

DEFACATION—WNL; constipation; diarrhea; watery; blood-tinged; tarry; clay-colored; incontinent; enema.

GASTROINTESTINAL—WNL; nausea; vomiting; distention; abdominal pain/tenderness.

URINATION—WNL; involuntary; dysuria; hematuria; burning; urgency; nocturia; Foley.

NEUROLOGICAL—alert; disoriented; confused; seizures; lethargic; comatose; headache; dizziness.

POSTURE—standing; stooped; unsteady; semi-reclining; sitting upright.

PAIN—absent; severe; slight; dull; sharp; constant; localized; radiating; cramping.

PERSPIRATION—WNL; excessive; profuse.

BEHAVIOR—Appropriate; aggressive; combative; apprehensive; depressive; angry.

## DISCHARGE SUMMARY

This document should include a complete yet succinct synopsis of the patient's hospital stay by the attending physician. It should outline findings upon admission, laboratory values, physical findings, consultations made and their findings, results of any diagnostic tests, medications the patient was on, and so forth. Any procedures or operations performed and their results should be outlined. Complications during the hospital stay should be discussed, as well as how they were resolved. The patient's recovery should be followed, with any follow-up treatment and plans for discharge specified. The discharge summary should be completed even when the patient is transferred to another institution and will sometimes be called a transfer summary. If the patient died in the hospital, there will be a discharge summary, a death summary, or both. The discharge summary must be dictated within 30 days of the actual discharge.

## AUTOPSY REPORT

An autopsy is a pathological examination of the deceased with an attempt to determine the cause of death. If the cause of death is absolutely known, often an autopsy is not performed. Permission must be granted by the next of kin before an autopsy may be performed. (Coroners, however, must examine cases that are determined to be suspicious in nature.)

## EMERGENCY RECORD

This record may or may not be accompanied by an ambulance service activity report if an emergency medical team was required to transport the patient to the hospital.

The report should be very specific as to date, time, location, mode of treatment, time of dispatch, response codes, and other factors. Blood pressure readings, pulse, and respiration should be well documented, as well as status of consciousness, bleeding, and pain.

The emergency medical technicians will assess severity as nonurgent, urgent, critical, or dead. An injury will typically be described by its type, location, and probable cause. Illnesses will often be described by the symptoms exhibited and what type of body system is suspected to be affected.

Take note of the type of care that the ambulance crew provided: basic life support, advanced life support, and so forth. The ambulance record will also describe the training levels for all personnel involved on the run. This may become important in a lawsuit involving the transport company. Some types of runs require higher levels of training (e.g., registered nurse, paramedic). Training level determines the level of care that the crew is authorized to perform (e.g., basic or advanced CPR, IV fluid maintenance).

## CARDIOPULMONARY RESUSCITATION

Basic cardiopulmonary resuscitation (CPR) is used to resuscitate patients who present without a pulse or breath. The strategies use basic and advanced techniques.

### Basic Cardiopulmonary Resuscitation

This technique focuses on the ABCs in caring for an unresponsive patient:

*A*irway: Open the airway by tilting the head or removing any obstruction.

*B*reathing: Mouth-to-mouth respirations or artificial ventilation.

*C*irculation: Chest compressions/precordial thump.

### Advanced Cardiac Life Support

Advanced cardiac life support (ACLS) should begin as soon as the patient's underlying rhythm has been established. ACLS employs the use of advanced airway management, defibrillation, and drugs, along with effective performance of basic CPR. Since most cardiac arrests are unwitnessed events of ventricular fibrillation, we will address the following protocol for that situation:

1. Check for pulse. If absent, continue.
2. Perform basic CPR until a defibrillator is available.
3. Check the rhythm. If there is ventricular fibrillation, continue to step 4.
4. Defibrillate at 200 joules. If there is no conversion, continue to step 5.
5. Defibrillate at 200 to 300 joules. If there is no conversion, continue to step 6.
6. Defibrillate at full output: 360 joules.
7. Continue CPR.
8. Establish an IV line (suggested access in the antecubital fossa).
9. Give epinephrine 1:10,000 solution 0.5–1.0 mg IV push.
10. Intubate if possible.
11. Defibrillate with 360 joules. If there is no conversion, continue to step 12.
12. Give lidocaine 1 mg/kg IV push.
13. Defibrillate with 360 joules. If there is no conversion, continue to step 14.
14. Repeat lidocaine 0.5 mg/kg IV push. May give up to 3.0 mg/kg total lidocaine dose. Repeat boluses of 0.5 mg/kg are given at 8-minute intervals.

15. Defibrillate at 360 joules. If there is no conversion, continue to step 16.
16. Give bretylium 5 mg/kg IV push.
17. Consider bicarbonate (for acidosis; discouraged for routine CPR).
18. Defibrillate at 360 joules.
19. Repeat lidocaine or bretylium.
20. Defibrillate with 360 joules.

Other rhythm disturbances call for ACLS treatment as well. They are ventricular tachycardia, asystole, bradycardia, electromechanical disassociation, and supraventricular tachycardia. Pediatric CPR involves the same basic principles of CPR in the adult but with modifications in oxygen delivery and chest compressions. IV access is more readily obtained by femoral or external jugular vein cannulation. Drug dosages are decreased, and defibrillation should be initiated at 2 joules/kg.

## THE EMERGENCY DEPARTMENT RECORD

An emergency department, as defined by the American College of Surgeons, functions "to give adequate appraisal and initial treatment or advice to every person who considers himself acutely ill or injured and presents himself at the emergency department door." The JCAH has established the following criteria for accrediting hospital emergency medical services:

1. The emergency department shall be appropriately integrated with other units and departments of the hospital.
2. All emergency department personnel shall be prepared for their responsibilities through proper training and educational programs.
3. The emergency department shall be directed by a physician member of the active medical staff and shall be well organized, directed, and staffed according to the nature of health care needs anticipated.
4. Emergency patient care must be guided by written policies and procedures.
5. The emergency department shall be designed and equipped to facilitate safe and effective care of patients.
6. A medical record shall be maintained on every patient and be incorporated in the patient's permanent hospital record.
7. The emergency department shall establish appropriate quality control mechanisms.
8. As part of the hospital's quality assurance program, the quality and appropriateness of patient care provided by the emergency department should be monitored and evaluated and any identified problems should be resolved.

The emergency room record contains patient information, the attending physician and nurse, how the patient arrived at the emergency room and accompanied by whom, what the vital signs were upon admission, and how the patient presented. The condition on admission should be assessed; the record should contain a medical history and physical examination, the type of treatment given, whether the problem was diagnostic or medical, the disposition of the case, and the patient's condition on discharge from the emergency room. The emergency room physician will treat the patient for the emergency condition and then should refer the patient to an attending physician or the patient's private doctor. Often the patient is discharged to another service in the hospital or transferred for care at another institution. It is imperative to document consultations at this point. Transfer orders must be explicit. Many malpractice cases have originated because of defective orders at this stage. If the patient expires upon transport, the death is often blamed on the last service to document care given. The American College of Emergency Physicians has published the following patient transfer guidelines:

1. The health and well-being of the patient must be the overriding concern when any patient transfer is considered.
2. Emergency physicians and hospital personnel should comply with applicable state and federal regulations regarding patient transfer. A medical screening exam, mandated by federal law, should be performed by a physician. In the event a physician is not physically present in the emergency department 24 hours a day, the screening exam may be performed by properly trained ancillary personnel according to written policies and procedures.
3. The patient should be transferred to another facility only after medical evaluation and, when possible, stabilization. Stabilization includes evaluation and initiation of treatment to ensure, within reasonable medical probability, that transfer of a patient will not result in death or in loss or serious impairment of bodily functions, parts, or organs.
4. The physician should inform the patient or responsible party of the reasons for, and the risks and likely benefits of, transfer and document this information in the medical record. The competence of the patient to agree or refuse to be transferred should be assessed prior to obtaining consent. If the patient is incompetent to make this decision, a person legally responsible for the patient should accept or refuse the transfer on behalf of the patient.
5. The hospital and medical staff should identify individuals responsible for transfer decisions and clearly delineate their duties regarding the patient transfer process.
6. The patient should be transferred to a facility appropriate to the medical needs of the patient, with adequate space and personnel available.
7. A physician or other responsible person at the receiving hospital must agree to accept the patient prior to the transfer.
8. The patient transfer should not be refused by the receiving hospital when the transfer is medically indicated and the receiving hospital has the capability and/or responsibility to provide care for the patient. Economic reasons should not be the basis for transferring or refusing to accept a medically unstable patient.

9. Communication to exchange clinical information between responsible persons at the transferring and receiving hospitals must occur prior to transfer.
10. An appropriate medical summary and other pertinent records should accompany the patient to the receiving institution.
11. The patient should be transferred in a vehicle that is staffed by qualified personnel and contains appropriate equipment.
12. When transfer of patients is part of a regional plan to provide optimal care for patients at specialized medical facilities, written transfer protocols and interfacility agreements should be in place.

When a patient is discharged from the emergency room, the physician should supply the patient with instructions regarding follow-up care and medications. The patient should acknowledge understanding of the instructions. If the patient is not English speaking, an interpreter should be made available to promote understanding.

Figure 3.2 provides a complete emergency department medical screening examination and assessment record. This completed form is the ideal, yet rarely is this much information recorded in an emergency room record. Time is of the essence in order to assure proper care for the patients. The information is often recorded after the patient is stabilized, transferred, or discharged.

## THE INTENSIVE CARE UNIT RECORD

Patients in the intensive care unit (ICU) are those who require continuous monitoring and sometimes invasive care for a possibly life-threatening condition.

The (adult) intensive care record should consist of a patient care plan, order sheets, progress records, consultation reports, intake and output record, and a critical care flow sheet. It should also include a complete assessment of the patient, evaluating the patient's admission history, physical assessment, patient and family teaching needs, and discharge planning needs.

The following medications are commonly ordered in the ICU:

Adenocard—6 mg vials
Aminophyllin—500 mg vials
Aquamephyton—10 mg amps
Atropine—1 mg/10 mg syringe
Benadryl—50 mg tubex
Bretylium—500 mg tubex
Cardizem—50 mg vials
Cetacaine—spray can
Compazine—10 mg/2 ml amps
Decadron—4 mg/ml 1 ml vial

**Figure 3.2**

**Emergency Department Medical Screening Exam and Assessment Record**

DATE: TIME:

PATIENT NAME | DOB/AGE | PCP

TRANSPORT TO ED
☐ AMBULATORY ☐ W/C
☐ EMS ☐ ACLS ☐ BCLS

CHIEF COMPLAINT

**THERAPEUTICS**

| | |
|---|---|
| C-COLLAR | ICE |
| BACK BOARD | SPLINT |
| IV ____ | MEDS PTA |
| $O_2$ @ ____ | (List) |
| INTUBATED č ____ | |
| DRESSING | |

WOUND CLEANSED & DRESSED č ____

IMMUNIZATIONS UTD

PT STATES (DATE) ☐ YES ☐ NO ____

IMMUNIZATION INFO GIVEN/REQUESTED

TRIAGE VITAL SIGNS ☐ ORAL ☐ TYMPANIC
T ☐ RECTAL
P ☐ RADIAL ☐ CAROTID ☐ MONITOR
BP ☐ LEFT ☐ RIGHT ☐ TILTS
R
$O_2$ SAT

**PAST MEDICAL HISTORY**

DIABETES ☐ YES ☐ NONE
HYPERTENSION ☐ YES
SEIZURES ☐ YES
CARDIAC ☐ YES
ULCER ☐ YES
ASTHMA/COPD ☐ YES
SMOKER ☐ YES ____ PPD
OTHER:

**RESPIRATORY**

AIRWAY ☐ PATENT
RESPIRATIONS ☐ LABORED ☐ UNLABORED

WEIGHT (kg)

**CURRENT MEDS**

☐ YES ☐ NONE (LIST)

LMP ☐ Y
PREGNANT ☐ N

**MENTAL STATUS**

☐ CONSCIOUS ☐ UNCOOPERATIVE
☐ LETHARGIC ☐ COMBATIVE
☐ CONFUSED ☐ ALTERED
☐ UNCONSCIOUS ☐ BABY
☐ ORIENTED X ☐ HYSTERICAL

**SPEECH**

☐ COHERENT
☐ INCOHERENT
☐ SILENT
☐ BABY
☐ SLURRED
☐ CRYING

**PUPILS**

☐ N/A
☐ PEARL
☐ ☐ PINPOINT
☐ ☐ MIDPOINT
☐ ☐ DILATED
☐ ☐ FIXED
☐ ☐ RESPONDING

**MECHANISM OF INJURY** ☐ N/A

☐ AUTO ☐ DRIVER
☐ MOTORCYCLE ☐ PASSENGER
☐ ALL TERRAIN ☐ PEDESTRIAN
☐ BICYCLE ☐ EJECTED
☐ GUN SHOT WOUND SEAT BELT?
☐ STABBING ☐ YES ☐ NO
☐ FARM HELMET?
☐ BURN ☐ YES ☐ NO
☐ INDUSTRIAL ☐ UNKNOWN
☐ DIVING ☐ OTHER ____
☐ FALL
☐ SPORTS

**SKIN COLOR**

☐ PINK
☐ PALE
☐ MOTTLED
☐ CYANOTIC
☐ JAUNDICED
☐ OTHER

**SKIN MOISTURE**

☐ DRY
☐ MOIST
☐ DIAPHORETIC

**SKIN TEMP.**

☐ WARM
☐ HOT
☐ COOL
☐ COLD

ALLERGIES TO MEDS ☐ YES (LIST) ☐ NKDA

TRIAGE CATEGORY
I ☐ II ☐ III ☐ IV ☐

RN SIGNATURE

☐ PCP CALLED
☐ YES TIME ____ ☐ NO

PRIMARY NURSING ASSESSMENT TIME ____ ROOM ____

**RESPIRATORY**

AIRWAY
☐ NASAL ☐ AIRWAY PATENT
☐ ORAL ☐ NTT #
☐ $O_2$ ☐ ETT #
☐ CANNULA ☐ NON REBREATHER
☐ SIMPLE FACE
____ L/MIN.

RESPIRATION
☐ SPONTANEOUS ☐ STRIDOR
☐ ASSISTED ☐ RETRACTIONS
WHERE: ____
☐ ARTIFICIAL WITH BAG VALVE MASK

BREATH SOUNDS
☐ PRESENT ☐ R ☐ L
☐ CLEAR ☐ R ☐ L
☐ DIMINISHED ☐ R ☐ L
☐ WHEEZES/RHONCHI ☐ R ☐ L
☐ CRACKLES ☐ R ☐ L

CHEST EXPANSION
☐ SYMMETRICAL ☐ ASYMMETRICAL
☐ TENDERNESS-WHERE ____

COUGH
TYPE: ____
PRODUCTIVE ☐ NO ☐ YES - DESCRIBE: ____

**CARDIOVASCULAR** ☐ N/A

MONITOR ☐ YES ☐ NO
RHYTHM ____
PACEMAKER ☐ YES ☐ NO

CHEST PAIN
PT. DESCRIPTION: ____

☐ NON RADIATING
☐ RADIATING TO: ____
☐ SOB
☐ NAUSEA ☐ DIAPHORESIS
☐ NTG TAKEN
☐ EDEMA-WHERE ____
☐ HEART SOUNDS $S_1$ $S_2$
$S_3$ $S_4$ ☐ YES ☐ NO
☐ MURMUR

PULSE PRESENT
☐ CAROTID ☐ JVD
☐ RADIAL ☐ REG ☐ IRREG
☐ FEMORAL
☐ PEDAL

**NEURO** ☐ N/A

LOSS OF CONSCIOUSNESS ☐ NO
☐ YES HOW LONG: ____
PURPOSEFUL EXTREMITY MOVEMENT ☐ YES
DEFICIT ☐ WHERE: ____
PARALYSIS ☐ YES ☐ NO
WHERE: ____
HANDGRASP ☐ EQUAL ☐ UNEQUAL
WHICH: ____
DIZZY ☐ YES ☐ NO
DESCRIBE: ____
H/A ☐ YES ☐ NO
DESCRIBE: ____
GAIT ☐ STEADY ☐ UNSTEADY
OTHER: ____

**GLASGOW COMA SCALE**

| | | ARRIVE | D/C |
|---|---|---|---|
| **EYES** | | | |
| SPONTANEOUSLY | 4 | | |
| TO VERBAL COMMAND | 3 | | |
| TO PAIN | 2 | | |
| NO RESPONSE | 1 | | |
| **MOTOR** | | | |
| OBEYS | 6 | | |
| LOCALIZES PAIN | 5 | | |
| FLEXION/WITHDRAWAL | 4 | | |
| FLEXION ABNORMAL | 3 | | |
| EXTENSION | 2 | | |
| NO RESPONSE | 1 | | |
| **VERBAL** | | | |
| ORIENTED & CONVERSES | 5 | | |
| DISORIENTED & CONVERSES | 4 | | |
| INAPPROPRIATE WORDS | 3 | | |
| INCOMPREHENSIBLE SOUNDS | 2 | | |
| NO RESPONSE | 1 | | |
| SCORE | | | |

____
NURSE SIGNATURE

PELVIC SQUEEZE ☐ POS ☐ NEG

1. OPEN FRACTURE
2. AMPUTATION
3. GUNSHOT WOUND
4. DEFORMITY
5. STAB WOUND
6. BURN
7. PAIN
8. RASH

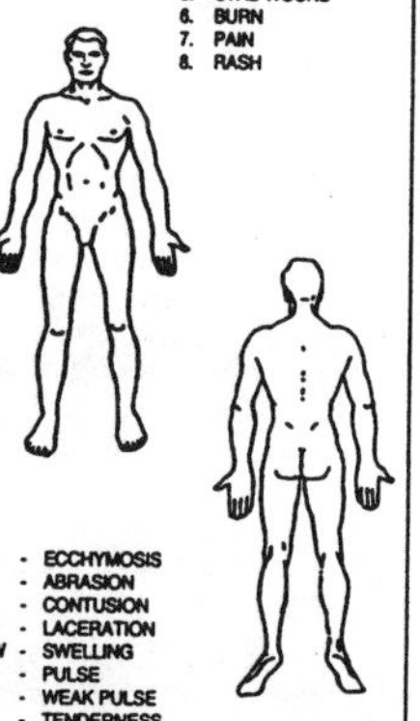

E - ECCHYMOSIS
A - ABRASION
C - CONTUSION
L - LACERATION
SW - SWELLING
P - PULSE
D - WEAK PULSE
T - TENDERNESS
S - SENSATION

**EENT** ☐ N/A

ORAL ☐ N/A
SORE THROAT ☐ YES ☐ NO
DYSPHAGIA ☐ YES ☐ NO
DROOLING ☐ YES ☐ NO
OTHER ____

EAR ☐ N/A
PAIN ☐ YES ☐ NO IF YES ☐ R ☐ L
DRAINAGE ☐ YES ☐ NO IF YES ☐ R ☐ L
OTHER ____

EYES ☐ N/A
EYE MOVEMENT ☐ INTACT ☐ IMPAIRED ☐ ABSENT
Acuity R ____ L ____
☐ CORRECTED ☐ UNCORRECTED
BLURRED VISION ☐ YES ☐ NO
DOUBLE VISION ☐ YES ☐ NO
OTHER ____

PUPIL SIZE
2 3 4 5 6 7 8
R - REACTIVE
S - SLUGGISH
N - NONREACTIVE
R ____ L ____

**GASTROINTESTINAL** ☐ N/A

NAUSEA ☐ NO ☐ YES
VOMITING ☐ NO ☐ YES X'S ____
COLOR ____
LAST BM ____
DIARRHEA ☐ NO ☐ YES X'S ____
COLOR ____
PAIN ☐ NO ☐ YES
WHERE ____
ABDOMEN
☐ SOFT ☐ DISTENDED ☐ NONTENDER
☐ FIRM ☐ TENDER

BOWEL SOUNDS
☐ PRESENT ☐ ABSENT

**GYNECOLOGICAL** ☐ N/A

PREGNANT ☐ YES ☐ NO
DUE DATE ____
FETAL TONES ____
FETAL MOVEMENT ☐ YES ☐ NO
GRAVIDA ____ PARA ____ AB ____
VAGINAL BLEEDING OR DISCHARGE ____
OTHER ____

**MUSCULOSKELETAL** ☐ N/A

NEURO STATUS INTACT ☐ YES ☐ NO
VASCULAR STATUS INTACT ☐ YES ☐ NO
CAPILLARY REFILL < 3 SEC. ☐ YES ☐ NO

**Figure 3.2 (Continued)**

NURSING DIAGNOSIS

- ☐ RESPIRATORY FUNCTION, ALTERATION IN, RELATED TO ______
- ☐ SKIN INTEGRITY, IMPAIRMENT OF, RELATED TO ______
- ☐ BODY TEMPERATURE, ALTERATION IN, RELATED TO ______
- ☐ OTHER ______
- ☐ COMFORT, ALTERATION IN, RELATED TO ______
- ☐ MOBILITY, IMPAIRED PHYSICAL, RELATED TO ______
- ☐ BOWEL ELIMINATION, ALTERATION IN, RELATED TO ______

GENITOURINARY ☐ N/A

| | | |
|---|---|---|
| FREQUENCY | ☐ YES | ☐ NO |
| BURNING | ☐ YES | ☐ NO |
| PAIN | ☐ YES | ☐ NO |
| BLEEDING | ☐ YES | ☐ NO |
| RETENTION | ☐ YES | ☐ NO |
| URGENCY | ☐ YES | ☐ NO |
| FOLEY # ______ | ☐ YES | ☐ NO |

OTHER: ______

DIAGNOSTICS

| | TIME |
|---|---|
| BLOOD DRAWN | |
| U/A | |
| STREP SCREEN (RAPID) | |
| ABG | |
| EKG | |
| RESPIRATORY Tx | |
| LUMBAR PUNCTURE | |
| OTHER | |

RESPIRATORY

| | TIME | PERFORMED BY |
|---|---|---|
| $O_2$ | | |
| INTUBATED | | |
| ETT # ______ NTT # ______ | | |
| OTHER | | |

GASTROINTESTINAL

| | TIME | PERFORMED BY |
|---|---|---|
| NGT # ______ | | |
| ☐ HEME + ☐ HEME - | | |
| CONTENTS | | |
| PERITONEAL LAVAGE | | |

RETURNS ☐ CLEAR ☐ PINK ☐ GROSS BLOOD

ENEMA

TYPE ______

RESULTS ______

| TIME | RESULT |
|---|---|
| | |

CARDIOTHORACIC

| | TIME | PERFORMED BY |
|---|---|---|
| CHEST TUBE | | |
| ☐ R# | | |
| ☐ L# | | |
| THORACOTOMY | | |

MAST TROUSERS ☐ LEGS ☐ ABD

TIME ON ______ TIME OFF ______

EXTERNAL PACER

PACER RATE ______ PACER MA ______

SENSITIVITY ______

OTHER

X-RAYS

| | TO | FROM | ESCORTED BY |
|---|---|---|---|
| | | | |

☐ PORTABLE ☐ ON MONITOR

| | | | |
|---|---|---|---|
| CT SCAN | | | |
| IVP | | | |
| ULTRASOUND | | | |
| NUCLEAR MED. | | | |

| CONSULTANT | TIME NOTIFIED | ARRIVED |
|---|---|---|
| | | |
| | | |

INVASIVE LINES

| | TIME | SOL. | GAUGE | SITE | INT. |
|---|---|---|---|---|---|
| 1. | | | | | |
| 2. | | | | | |
| 3. | | | | | |
| 4. | | | | | |
| 5. | | | | | |
| 6. | | | | | |

| | TIME | PERFORMED BY |
|---|---|---|
| CENTRAL LINE | | |

GENITOURINARY

| | TIME | PERFORMED BY |
|---|---|---|
| FOLEY ☐ # ______ | | |
| ST. CATH ☐ DAVOL ☐ | | |
| COLOR | | |
| ☐ HEME + ☐ HEME - | | |

INTAKE

| TIME | ORAL | CRYSTALLOIDS | COLLOIDS |
|---|---|---|---|
| | | | |
| | | | |
| TOTAL | | | |

OUTPUT

| TIME | URINE | N.G. | EMESIS |
|---|---|---|---|
| | | | |
| | | | |
| TOTAL | | | |

VITAL SIGNS

| TIME | TEMP | PULSE | RESP. | BP | $O_2$ SAT. | PUPILS | LOC | HAND GRASP |
|---|---|---|---|---|---|---|---|---|
| | | | | | | | | |

| TIME | MEDICATION | SITE | ROUTE | INIT. |
|---|---|---|---|---|
| | dT 0.5cc | | IM | |

| TIME | NURSES NOTES |
|---|---|
| | |

EVALUATION

| | TIME | PERFORMED BY |
|---|---|---|
| ☐ DISCHARGED | | |

☐ TRANSFER TO: ______ TIME ______

☐ INST. REVIEWED WITH: ☐ PT. ☐ PARENT ☐ OTHER

VIA ☐ LIFE FLIGHT ☐ AMB ______ IN ATTENDANCE

☐ ADMIT ______ ______ ROOM ______ REFERRING PHYSICIAN ______ ACCEPTING PHYSICIAN ______

NOTIFICATION OF FAMILY

PERSON NOTIFIED ______

RELATION ______

TIME ______ BY WHOM ______

CORONER

NAME ______

RELATION ______

BY WHOM ______

POLICE

NAME ______

DEPT. ______

TIME ______ BY WHOM ______

☐ COUNTY HEALTH ☐ POISON CONTROL

☐ MH/MR ☐ INFECTION CONTROL

☐ OTHER ______

TIME ______ BY WHOM ______

FOLLOW UP CALLS:

DATE TIME ☐ N/A ☐ WRONG NUMBER

SIGNATURES

AGE SPECIFIC CARE/CONCERNS

INFANTS
- ☐ PSYCHOSOCIAL
- ☐ DEVELOPMENTAL

TODDLER
- ☐ PSYCHOSOCIAL
- ☐ DEVELOPMENTAL

SCHOOL AGE
- ☐ PSYCHOSOCIAL
- ☐ DEVELOPMENTAL

ADOLESCENT
- ☐ PSYCHOSOCIAL
- ☐ DEVELOPMENTAL

YOUNG ADULT
- ☐ PSYCHOSOCIAL
- ☐ DEVELOPMENTAL

OLDER ADULT
- ☐ PSYCHOSOCIAL
- ☐ DEVELOPMENTAL

Dextrose—50% syringe
D10W—500 ml bags
D5–½NS—1000 ml bag
D5–⅓NS—1000 ml bag
D5–¼NS—1000 ml bag
D5LR—1000 ml bag
D5–Normosol-M—1000 ml bag
D5–Normosol-R—1000 ml bag
D5–NS—1000 ml bag
D5W—100, 500, or 1000 ml bags
Digoxin—0.5 mg/2 ml ampules
Dilantin—100 mg syringe
Dobutamine—250 mg/D5W—250 ml
Dobutrex—250 mg vials
Dopamine—400 mg/D5W 250 ml
Epinephrine—1 mg/10 ml syringe; 1 ml amps
Glucagon—1 mg vial
Hep-lock—100 units 1 ml
Heparin—1000 units/ml 10 ml vial; 10,000 units/1 ml; 5,000 units/0.5 ml
Heparin—1000 U/NS 500 ml bag or 25,000 U/D5W 500 ml
Hespan—500 ml bag
Humulin-N—U100 per dose
Humulin-R—U100 per dose
Inocor—200 mg amps
Isuprel—0.2 mg/ml 5 ml amps
Lactated Ringer's—100 ml bag
Lasix (Furosemide)—100, 40, or 20 mg vials
Levophed—4 ml ampules
Lidocaine—2g/D5W 500 ml
Magnesium sulfate-50%—2 ml vials
Mannitol—12.5 g, or 20% 500 ml bag
½NS—1000 ml bag
NS (normal saline)—100, 500, or 1000 ml bags
Narcan—1 mg/ml amps
Nitroglycerin—2% UNG 1 inch, or 50 mg/D5W 500 ml
Nitropress—50 mg vial
Nitrostat—0.4 mg tabs 25's

Pavulon—2 mg/ml 2 ml amps

Phenergan—25 mg amps

Potassium chloride—40 mEq Inj

Procardia—10 mg caps

Regitine—5 mg vials

Romazicon—5 ml vials

Sodium bicarbonate 8.4%—50 ml syringe

Sodium chloride—30 ml vial

Solu-Medrol—125 mg vials

Theophyllin—800 mg/D5 @ 500 ml

Thorazine—50 mg/2 ml amps

Tigan—200 mg supp

Tylenol—650 mg supp

Verapamil—5 mg/2 ml vials

Vistaril—50 mg/ml vial

Xylocaine—100 mg syringe, 1% 20 ml vial, or 2% 20 ml vial

The patient information should include name, age, marital status, accompanied by, origin, mode of arrival, chief complaint, and reason for hospitalization, in the patient's own words if applicable. Allergies should be listed and height, weight, and vital signs taken. Past medical history should include past illnesses, surgeries, and reactions to medications.

The health history of the patient and the patient's family should cover diabetes, stroke, rheumatic disease, genitourinary problems, hepatitis, heart disease, fainting or dizzy spells, liver disease, gynecological problems, psychiatric problems, hypertension, lung disease, gastrointestinal problems, cancer, or seizures.

Current medications should be documented along with the last dose taken. Social history should include smoking, caffeine, and alcohol consumption. Diet and activity level should be included, as well as living arrangements, religious preference, support systems, language spoken, and occupation.

The physical assessment should include the following parameters and are indicated if negative:

*Neurological assessment*: Alert and oriented to situation. Pupils equal and reactive to light. Active range of motion of all extremities with symmetry of strength. No parasthesia.

*Cardiovascular*: Regular apical/radial pulse. S1 and S2 audible. CRT less than 2 sec. Peripheral pulses palpable. No edema. No calf tenderness.

*Respiratory*: Respirations 10–20/min. at rest. Respirations quiet and regular. Breath sounds vesicular through both lung fields, bronchial over major airways, with no adventitious sounds. Sputum clear by history. Nailbeds and mucous membranes pink. CRT (capillary refill time) less than 3 sec.

*Gastrointestinal*: Abdomen soft. Bowel sounds active (5–34/min). No pain with palpation. By history, tolerates prescribed diet without nausea and vomiting/having BM within own normal pattern and consistency. Continent of stool. No appliances used.

*Genitourinary*: Able to empty bladder without dysuria. Bladder not distended after voiding. Urine clear and yellow to amber. Continent of urine. No appliances used.

*Integumentary*: Skin color within patient's norm. Skin warm, dry, and intact. No skin breakdown. Mucous membranes moist.

*Musculoskeletal*: Absence of joint swelling and tenderness. Normal range of motion of all joints. No muscle weakness. Surrounding tissues show no evidence of inflammation, nodules, nail changes, ulcerations, or rashes. No deformity.

*Neurovascular*: Affected extremity is pink, warm, and movable within average range of motion. CRT (capillary refill time) less than 3 sec. Peripheral pulses palpable. No edema. Sensation intact without numbness or parasthesia. No pain on passive stretch.

*Psychiatric/social*: Characteristics of appearance, behavior, and verbalizations appropriate to situation. Alert and oriented to person, place, and time. Memory intact. Affect appropriate. No mood swings noted.

*Perceptual pattern*: Without pain or experiencing pain that is managed effectively. (If pain, location, duration, description, precipitating/alleviating factors.) No sensory changes noted in taste, touch, smell, vision, hearing.

*Nutrition/metabolic patterns*: Eats regular foods, no change in eating or dietary patterns. No weight loss or gain in the past three months. Swallows without difficulty. No complaints of thirst.

*Activities/exercise, sleep patterns*: No assistance needed in feeding, bathing, toileting, grooming, dressing, home maintenance, or ambulation. No assistive devices used. No difficulty in falling sleep at night.

*Reproductive/sexuality*: If female, no vaginal bleeding/discharge/lesions. Normal menstrual periods. If male, no prostate problems/penile bleeding/lesions/discharge. No complaints of sexual dysfunction

*Safety assessment*: Under age 70, no history of confusion, falls, sensory deficit, impaired mobility, balance, and taking no medications such as sedatives, narcotics, tranquilizers, diuretics, and/or laxatives. (A patient who meets two or more criteria must be placed on the fall/alert program.)

The patient care plan includes monitoring of vital signs, respiratory status (including ventilator and suction when appropriate), infection control, hygiene, elimination, drainage irrigations, activity, dressing/treatment, diet, intake and output, traction, observations of behavior, special equipment, therapy (occupational, physical, speech) IVs, and catheters. Lab work is documented and monitored.

The critical care flow sheet monitors vital signs, arterial lines, oxygen pressure, pulmonary pressures, ECG readings, or any other monitoring devices the patient requires and documents them on a 24-hour sheet.

Figure 3.3 shows a sample critical care record.

## OBSTETRICAL RECORDS

Obstetricians are often the target of lawsuits, as much can go wrong during labor and delivery. Some states allow a child born with birth defects due to trauma of delivery up to 18 years in which to file suit in case the defects do not materialize in early childhood. OB-GYN charts should include the following information:

- age of patient
- normal height and weight
- past medical history, including smoking, drinking, and drug abuse
- family medical history
- allergies
- prescribed medications
- nonprescribed medications
- chronic illnesses
- menstrual history
- date of last menstrual period
- estimated date of confinement
- any history of sexually transmitted diseases
- history of past pregnancies (number, outcome, congenital disorders, multiple births)
- duration and frequency of prenatal care—any problems noted
- history of high blood pressure, swelling of extremities, proteinuria
- any bleeding or unusual discharge
- rupture of membranes
- appreciable change in fetal movement frequency

Pregnant women are described as: G #___, P #___ where G = gravida (pregnancies), and P = para (viable offspring). Ab = #___ will be listed if there is a history of abortion or miscarriages. *Primipara* means "first pregnancy," *secundipara* means "second pregnancy," and *multiparous* means the woman has been pregnant before (often referred to as a "multip").

A hospital admission should note contractions on admissions (frequency, duration, quality), membranes on admission (intact, ruptured), and whether there is vaginal bleeding (note type and amount).

Fetal assessment should monitor baseline, variability, accelerations, and decelerations. Uterine activity should be described by frequency, intensity, and du-

**Figure 3.3**
**Critical Care Record**

DATE: ______ TIME: 11-7 ______ NURSE: ______________

**NEUROLOGICAL** REFER TO NVS RECORD ☐

Pupils: mm BRISK SLUGGISH FIXED

R ________ ☐ ☐ ☐

L ________ ☐ ☐ ☐

L.O.C.: ALERT ☐ LETHARGIC ☐ OBTUNDED ☐ STUPOROUS ☐ COMATOSE ☐

BEHAVIOR: APPROP.☐ INAPPROP.☐ CONFUSED☐ AGITATED☐ COMBATIVE☐

ORIENTATION: X ________ PERSON ☐ PLACE ☐ TIME ☐

SPEECH: CLEAR ☐ SLURRED ☐ INCOMPRE. ☐ ET/TRACH ☐ APHASIC ☐

MOVEMENT: RA RL LA LL EXPRESSIVE ☐

VOL. ☐ ☐ ☐ ☐ RECEPTIVE ☐

COM. ☐ ☐ ☐ ☐

STR.(0-5) ____ ____ ____ ____

OTHER: ______________ GLASGOW: ______________

**CARDIOVASCULAR**

RHYTHM: ______________ LEAD ______

PM: N/A ☐ INT ☐ EXT ☐ SETTINGS

EXT # ______ TPW'S WRAPPED ☐ EKG ALARMS HI ____ LOW ____

HEART SOUNDS:

NORMAL ☐ GALLOP ☐ $S_3$ ☐ $S_4$ ☐ RUB ☐ DISTANT ☐ MURMUR ☐

OTHER: ______________

NAILBEDS: PINK ☐ PALE ☐ DUSKY ☐ CYANOTIC ☐

CAP REFILL: BRISK ☐ SLUGGISH ☐

TED HOSE: YES ☐ NO ☐ KNEE HI ☐ THIGH HI ☐

PULSES: TEMP RADIAL FEM POP DP PT

GRADE R ____ ____ ____ ____ ____ ____

1-4 L ____ ____ ____ ____ ____ ____

CHEST TUBES: N/A ☐ PLEURAL: R ☐ L ☐ MEDIASTINAL X ______

SXN ______ cm DRAINAGE SM ☐ MED ☐ LG ☐

SANG ☐ SEROSANG ☐ SERIOUS ☐

OTHER: ______________

**SKIN**

TEMP: WARM ☐ DRY ☐ COOL ☐ MOIST ☐ DIAPHORETIC ☐

COLOR: MEMBRANES PINK ☐ PALE ☐ DUSKY ☐ CYANOTIC ☐ JAUNDICED ☐

EDEMA: N/A ☐ AMT. ______ TYPE ______ LOCATION ______

HEMATOMAS: N/A ☐ LOCATION ______________

INTEGRITY: INTACT ☐ SEE SKIN CARE DOCUMENTATION RECORD ☐

OTHER: ______________

**RESPIRATORY** ROOM AIR ☐ ASSISTED ☐

RATE: EVEN ☐ UNEVEN ☐ SLOW ☐ RAPID ☐ UNLABORED ☐ LABORED ☐

DEPTH: SHALLOW ☐ DEEP ☐

BREATH SOUNDS:

| | CLEAR | DIMINISHED | FINE CRACKLES | COURSE CRACKLES | WHEEZES |
|---|---|---|---|---|---|
| RUL | ☐ | ☐ | ☐ | ☐ | ☐ |
| RLL | ☐ | ☐ | ☐ | ☐ | ☐ |
| LUL | ☐ | ☐ | ☐ | ☐ | ☐ |
| LLL | ☐ | ☐ | ☐ | ☐ | ☐ |

CHEST EXPANSION: EQUAL ☐ OTHER: ______________

AIRWAY/$O_2$ NC ☐ ____ VM ☐ ____% NRB ☐ ETT ☐ ____ (SIZE) TRACH ☐ ______ (SIZE/TYPE)

VENT SETTINGS: VT ____ RATE ____ $F_1O_2$ ____ PS ____ PEEP ____

AC ☐ SIMV ☐ T-Tube ☐ CPAP ☐ OTHER: ______________ ALARMS ON ☐

OTHER ______________

**GASTROINTESTINAL**

ABDOMEN:

SOFT ☐ FIRM ☐ FLAT ☐ DISTENDED ☐ NONTENDER ☐ TENDER ☐ ____ (QUADS)

BOWEL SOUNDS: PRESENT ☐ X ____ (QUADS) ABSENT ☐ X ____ (QUADS) HYPO ☐ HYPER ☐

NG TUBE: N/A ☐ NARE R ☐ L ☐ ________ cm PLACEMENT ✓ ☐

DRAINAGE: SM ☐ MOD ☐ LG ☐ COLOR: ______________

FEEDING TUBE: N/A ☐ NARE R ☐ L ☐ PLACEMENT ✓ ☐ TYPE: ______

DIET: NPO ☐ PO ☐ ______ (DIET) ENTERAL FEEDING ☐ ______ (TYPE/RATE) TPN ☐

RESIDUAL ______________ STOOLS ______________

**RENAL** VOID ☐ FOLEY ☐ ANURIC ☐

COLOR: COLORLESS ☐ YELLOW ☐ STRAW ☐ AMBER ☐ PINK ☐ BLOODY ☐

CLARITY: CLEAR ☐ CLOUDY ☐ SEDIMENT ☐ CLOTS ☐

AMT: MINIMAL ☐ ADEQUATE ☐ COPIUS ☐

DIALYSIS ☐ HEMO ☐ PERIT. ☐ CAVHD ☐

GRAFT ☐ RA ☐ LA ☐ THRILL ☐ BRUIT ☐ AV ACCESS ☐

OTHER: ______________

**DRESSINGS** N/A ☐ ______________

______________

______________

BED WHEELS LOCKED: Y ☐ N ☐ HEARING AID Y ☐ N ☐ ______ (LOCATION)

BEDRAILS UP: Y ☐ X N ☐ DENTURES Y ☐ N ☐ ______ (LOCATION)

ID BAND ☐ GLASSES Y ☐ N ☐ ______ (LOCATION)

FALL RISK ASSESSMENT DONE: Y ☐ N ☐ OTHER: ______________

SAFETY DEVICE/RESTRAINTS: Y ☐ N ☐ TYPE ☐ ______________

PURPOSE: ______________

ORDER ______________

## ICU - CCU FLOW SHEET

DIAGNOSIS:

| ALLERGIES: | DOCTORS VISITED |
|---|---|
| | |
| | |
| | |
| | |

| DAILY | 7-3 | 3-11 | 11-7 |
|---|---|---|---|
| BATH | | | |
| BACK CARE | | | |
| ORAL HYGIENE | | | |
| LINEN CHANGED | | | |
| | | | |
| ROUTINE | | | |
| FOLEY CARE | | | |
| TRACH CARE | | | |
| IV TUBING CHANGE | | | |
| ARTERIAL LINE CARE | | | |
| ARTERIAL LINE ZERO | | | |
| SWAN GANZ CARE | | | |
| SWAN GANZ ZERO | | | |
| CVP LINE CARE | | | |
| CVP LINE ZERO | | | |
| PACER SITE CARE | | | |
| E-T TUBE Reposition | | | |
| RESTRAINT CIRC. | 8A 10A | 16P 18P | 24A 02A |
| CHECKS & RELEASE | 12P 14P | 20P 22P | 04A 06A |

| DIET: | | | FAMILY VISITED |
|---|---|---|---|
| % TAKEN: | LIQUID | SOLID | |
| BREAKFAST | | | |
| LUNCH | | | |
| DINNER | | | |
| H.S. SNACK | | | |

**Figure 3.3 (Continued)**

## DIAGNOSTIC TESTS

| TEST | EKG | XRAY | LAB | ABG | |
|---|---|---|---|---|---|
| TIME | | | | | |
| LAB TEST RESULTS | | | | | |
| TIME | | | | | |
| NA | | | | | |
| K | | | | | |
| CL | | | | | |
| $CO_2$ | | | | | |
| TIME | | | | | |
| HGB | | | | | |
| HCT | | | | | |
| BUN | | | | | |
| CREAT | | | | | |
| TIME | | | | | |
| CPK | | | | | |
| LDH | | | | | |
| SGOT | | | | | |
| SGPT | | | | | |
| TIME | | | | | |
| BS | | | | | |
| C&A | | | | | |
| INS. | | | | | |
| TIME | | | | | |
| PT | | | | | |
| PTT | | | | | |
| TIME | | | | | |
| pH | | | | | |
| $PCO_2$ | | | | | |
| $PO_2$ | | | | | |
| $HCO_3$ | | | | | |
| $O_2SAT$ | | | | | |
| WBC | | | | | |
| PLT | | | | | |
| | | | | | |

## INTAKE

| | PO | NG | IV | IV | WB | PC | AL | | |
|---|---|---|---|---|---|---|---|---|---|
| 7:00 | | | | | | | | | |
| 8:00 | | | | | | | | | |
| 9:00 | | | | | | | | | |
| 10:00 | | | | | | | | | |
| 11:00 | | | | | | | | | |
| 12:00 | | | | | | | | | |
| 1:00 | | | | | | | | | |
| 2:00 | | | | | | | | | |
| 8HR | | | | | | | | | |
| CREDITS | | | | | | | | | |
| | PO | NG | IV | IV | WB | PC | AL | | |
| 3:00 | | | | | | | | | |
| 4:00 | | | | | | | | | |
| 5:00 | | | | | | | | | |
| 6:00 | | | | | | | | | |
| 7:00 | | | | | | | | | |
| 8:00 | | | | | | | | | |
| 9:00 | | | | | | | | | |
| 10:00 | | | | | | | | | |
| 8HR | | | | | | | | | |
| CREDITS | | | | | | | | | |
| | PO | NG | IV | IV | WB | PC | AL | | |
| 11:00 | | | | | | | | | |
| 12:00 | | | | | | | | | |
| 1:00 | | | | | | | | | |
| 2:00 | | | | | | | | | |
| 3:00 | | | | | | | | | |
| 4:00 | | | | | | | | | |
| 5:00 | | | | | | | | | |
| 6:00 | | | | | | | | | |
| 8HR | | | | | | | | | |
| | 24 HOUR ITAKE | | | | | | | | |
| CREDITS | | | | | | | | | |

## OUTPUT

| | UA | GI | CT | EM | HV | BM | |
|---|---|---|---|---|---|---|---|
| 7:00 | | | | | | | |
| 8:00 | | | | | | | |
| 9:00 | | | | | | | |
| 10:00 | | | | | | | |
| 11:00 | | | | | | | |
| 12:00 | | | | | | | |
| 1:00 | | | | | | | |
| 2:00 | | | | | | | |
| 8HR | | | | | | | |
| CREDITS | | | | | | | |
| | UA | GI | CT | EM | HV | BM | |
| 3:00 | | | | | | | |
| 4:00 | | | | | | | |
| 5:00 | | | | | | | |
| 6:00 | | | | | | | |
| 7:00 | | | | | | | |
| 8:00 | | | | | | | |
| 9:00 | | | | | | | |
| 10:00 | | | | | | | |
| 8HR | | | | | | | |
| CREDITS | | | | | | | |
| | UA | GI | CT | EM | HV | BM | |
| 11:00 | | | | | | | |
| 12:00 | | | | | | | |
| 1:00 | | | | | | | |
| 2:00 | | | | | | | |
| 3:00 | | | | | | | |
| 4:00 | | | | | | | |
| 5:00 | | | | | | | |
| 6:00 | | | | | | | |
| 8HR | | | | | | | |
| | 24 HOUR OUTPUT | | | | | | |
| CREDITS | | | | | | | |

DATE: __________ WEIGHT ( ________ kgs.) ________ kgs. ± ________ kgs.
PREVIOUS CURRENT DIFFERENCE

| SHIFT | INITIAL | SIGNATURE |
|---|---|---|
| SHIFT | INITIAL | SIGNATURE |
| SHIFT | INITIAL | SIGNATURE |
| SHIFT | INITIAL | SIGNATURE |
| SHIFT | INITIAL | SIGNATURE |
| SHIFT | INITIAL | SIGNATURE |

PATIENT TEACHING

| Time | NURSING OBSERVATIONS |
|---|---|
| | |
| | |
| | |
| | |
| | |
| | |
| | |
| | |
| | |
| | |
| | |
| | |
| | |
| | |
| | |
| | |

Neuro Vital Signs Legend

GLASGOW COMA SCALE

| | | | |
|---|---|---|---|
| Eyes Open | | Spontaneously | 4 |
| | | To verbal command | 3 |
| | | To pain | 2 |
| | | No response | 1 |
| Best motor response | To verbal command | Obeys | 6 |
| | To painful stimulus | Localizes | 5 |
| | | Flexion - Withdrawl | 4 |
| | | Flexion - abnormal (decorticate rigidity) | 3 |
| | | Extension (decerebrate rigidity) | 2 |
| | | No response | 1 |
| Best verbal response | | Oriented and converses | 5 |
| | | Disoriented and converses | 4 |
| | | Inappropriate words | 3 |
| | | Incomprehensible sounds | 2 |
| | | No response | 1 |
| | | Intubated | T |

PUPILS + Reactive - Nonreactive ± Sluggish

PUPIL GAUGE (MM)

2 3 4 5 6 7 8 9

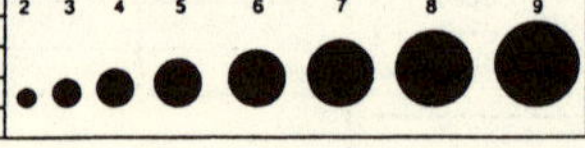

### Edema Scale

| | Depression | Return |
|---|---|---|
| 1+ Trace | Slight | Rapid |
| 2+ Mild | 1/4 in/.6cm | 10-15 sec |
| 3+ Moderate | 1/4-1/2 in/.6-1.3 cm | 1-2 min |
| 4+ Severe | 1/2-1 in/1.3-2.5 cm | 2-5 min |

### Pulse Quality

0 Absence of Pulse
+1 Doppler Pulse
+2 Moderate Impairment
+3 Normal Pulse
+4 Boudning

### Stools

1 Normal
2 Soft
3 Diarrhea
4 Impaction
5 Black Tarry

ration. Vaginal exams should include dilation, station, and effacement. And interventions include pitocin, anesthesia, analgesia, catheter, and comfort measures, including positioning the patient.

Some conditions that might alert the obstetrician of complications include:

Premature rupture of membranes
Fetal demise
Fetal distress
Toxemia
Breech position
Uncontrolled vaginal bleeding
Cesarean section
Perineal, vaginal, and cervical laceration,
Infections or fever
Eclampsia
Meconium-stained amniotic fluid
Placenta previa
Abruption
Acidosis
Anesthetic complications
Cord prolapse, knot in cord
Cephalopelvic disporportion
Arrest of dilatation
Precipitous or prolonged labor
Type and Rh

## Laboratory Values Alterations in the Pregnant Patient

Some laboratory values may be altered simply by pregnancy itself. Following is a list of normal nonpregnant lab values and normal variations caused by pregnancy.

| Value | Nonpregnant | Pregnant |
|---|---|---|
| CBC (complete blood count) | | |
| Hbg g/dl (hemoglobin) | 12–16 | 10–14 |
| Hct % (hematocrit) | 37–47 | 32–42 |
| RCV ml (red cell volume) | 1600 | 1900 |
| Plasma volume | 2400 | 3700 |
| RBC ml/mm$^3$ (red blood cell count) | 4–5.5 | 4–5.5 |
| WBC per mm$^3$ (white blood cell count) | 4500–10,000 | 5000–15,000 |

| | | |
|---|---|---|
| PMN % (polymorphonuclear) | 54–62 | N/C |
| Lymphs % (lymphocytes) | 38–64 | N/C |
| MCHC g/dl (mean cell hemoglobin concentration) | 30–36 | N/C |
| MCH (mean cell hemoglobin) | 29–32 | N/C |
| MCV mic/m³ (mean cell volume) | 82–96 | N/C |
| **Coagulation and Fibrinolytic Activity** | **Nonpregnant** | **Pregnant** |
| Factors 7, 8, 9, 10 | | I'd |
| Factors 11, 12 | | I'd |
| Protime (sec) | 60–70 | I'd |
| PTT (sec) (prothrombintime) | 12–14 | I'd |
| Bleeding Time (min) | 1–3 | N/C |
| Coagulation Time | 2–4 | N/C |
| Plt × $10^3$ (platelets) | 150–350 | |
| Fibrinogen mg/dl | 250 | 400 |
| Serum Fe ug (serum iron) | 75–150 | 65–120 |
| TIBC ug (total iron binding capacity) | 250–450 | 300–500 |
| Fe sat % (iron saturation) | 30–40 | 15–30 |
| **Blood sugar** | **Nonpregnant** | **Pregnant** |
| Fasting | 70–80 | 65 |
| 2 hr post prandiol | 60–110 | 140 |
| **Total Protein** | **Nonpregnant** | **Pregnant** |
| g/dl | 6.7–8.3 | 5.5–7.5 |
| albumin g/dl | 3.5–5.5 | 3.0–5.0 |
| globulin g/dl | 2.3–3.5 | 3.0–4.0 |
| **Bladder Capacity** | **Nonpregnant** | **Pregnant** |
| ml | 1300 | 1500 |
| RPF (∧25%) (renal plasma flow) | 490–700 | 612–875 |
| GFR (∧50%) (glomerular filtration rate) | 105–132 | 160–198 |
| BUN mg/dl (Blood Urea Nitrogen) | 20–25 | |
| Serum Creatinine mg/kg/24 hr | 257–750 | |
| **CV Determinations** | **Nonpregnant** | **Pregnant** |
| B/P (blood pressure) | 120/80 | 114/65 |
| PVR (pulmonary vascular resistance) | 120 | 100 |

| | | |
|---|---|---|
| Pulse | 70 | 80 |
| SV ml (stroke volume) | 65 | 75 |
| CO L/min (cardiac output) | 4.5 | 6 |
| whole blood | 4000 | 5600 |
| plasma renin | 3–10 | 10–80 |
| cardiac volume | | ∧70 ml |

| **EKG Changes** | **Pregnant** |
|---|---|
| $V_1$ & $V_2$ | inverted T wave |
| $V_4$ | low T |
| III | Q & inverted T |
| aVr | small Q |

### Routine Obstetrical Care

Following is the suggested protocol:

*First visit*. History and physical examination, risk evaluation, counseling, prescribed treatment (prenatal vitamins, calcium and iron supplements), appropriate labs (CBC, VDRL, HTLV III, AB screen, T&X, rubella, urine screen, pap & GC), glucose screen for patients at increased risk. Physicians have a duty to warn their patients that oral contraceptives may cause problems with the pregnancy and should not be taken while pregnant. Follow-up appointments should be scheduled monthly for the first 32 weeks, every two weeks from 32 to 36 weeks, and every week thereafter until delivery. Weight should always be checked (normal weight gain approximates 3 lb/month) and blood pressure changes noted, especially noting significant increases (30 mm systolic, 15 mm diastolic). Urine should be checked for glucose and protein. Fetal heart tones should be noted, fundal height checked, any peripheral edema, specific complaints and questions.

*16 weeks*. Alpha fetal protein (looking for open neural tube defects).

*20 weeks*. Fundal height at umbilicus. Fetal heart tones may be audible with fetascope.

*28 weeks*. Diabetes screen, Rh antibody screen, Rhogam if negative, if required.

*32 weeks*. Hbg/Hct.

*36 weeks*. Any cultures indicated, cervical evaluations, labor instructions.

*40 weeks*. Duration of normal-term pregnancy, plus or minus 2 weeks.

Of course, as with all other medical disciplines, obstetrics is an art and not an exact science; therefore individual preference, judgment calls, and local protocol will play into what treatment each individual patient receives.

A typical OB admit note will read:

This 34 yo female, G3, P1, Ab1, with an EDC {estimated date of confinement or estimated date of delivery] of ______, and FDLMP [first day of last menstrual period] ___ was admitted to labor in *(type of labor)*. Uterine contractions at ______ intervals and of ______ intensity, membranes *(intact/ruptured)*, FHT (fetal heart tones) ______, cervix dilated ______, effaced ______ %. Associated complaints: Attending physician notified. Orders written. Prenatal complications listed, if any: Anticipate *(vaginal/C-section)* delivery, with or without anesthesia. Mother to breast or bottle feed baby. A prenatal flow chart will profile the patient's history since her last menstrual period.

## High-Risk Pregnancies and Deliveries

High-risk pregnancies are those that require special attention by the obstetrical staff. These include maternal hypertension, diabetes, preeclampsia (toxemia of late pregnancy), placenta previa (the placenta is implanted in the lower uterine segment), abruptio placenta (the placenta separates itself from the uterus), and cord prolapse (compression of the umbilical cord). They are often diagnosed prior to the date of delivery.

## Fetal Monitoring

Fetal monitoring strips—graphic displays indicating fetal heart tones in response to maternal uterine contractions—will be found in the obstetrical record. From this recording the physician can determine any fetal distress. In the example provided (Figure 3.4), notice the maternal uterine contractions graphically displayed using a pressure scale/time, in mm Hg (millimeters of mercury). The fetal response shows fetal heart rates recorded in beats per minute. As a uterine contraction takes place, a corresponding increase in the fetal heart rate accompanies it.

*Baseline patterns* indicate if stress is present. Bradycardia indicates that the baby's heartbeat is less than 100 beats per minute; Tachycardia indicates that the baby's heartbeat is more than 170 beats per minute.

*Periodic patterns* indicate mechanism or cause of stress to the baby. Normal accelerations indicate an increase in the baby's heartbeat in response to uterine contractions; decelerations indicate a decrease in the baby's heartbeat in response to uterine contractions. If the deceleration appears early, it may indicate head compression; if the deceleration appears variable, it may indicate cord compression; if the deceleration appears late, it may indicate uteroplacental insufficiency.

*Variability* indicates if stress is *distress*. Normal variability is 7–14 beats per minute; illness would be indicated if variability beyond 7–14 beats per minute exists during labor.

Non Stress Testing (NST) should be performed biweekly if reactive. If NST is reactive with variable decelerations, an ultrasound should be performed.

**Figure 3.4**
**Fetal Monitoring Strips**

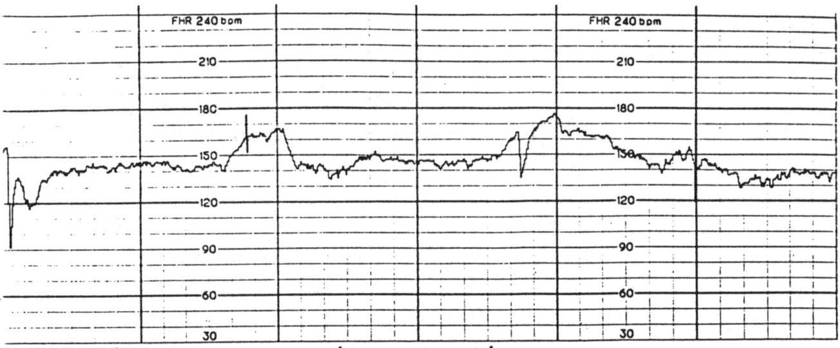


Fetal response to uterine contractions

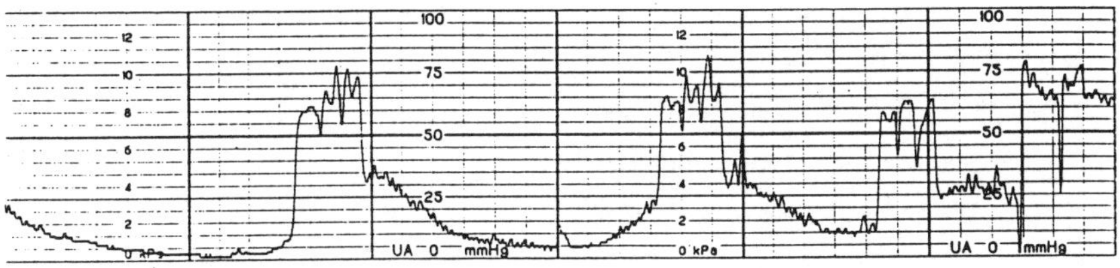


Uterine contractions

## Labor

Labor is divided into three stages: (1) Uterine contractions, causing dilation and effacement of the cervix; (2) Complete cervical dilation and expulsion of the fetus; and (3) Separation and expulsion of the placenta.

## Cesarean Section

A cesarean section should be performed when the attending staff believes that any further delay in delivery would compromise the health of the mother, the fetus, or both, and vaginal delivery cannot be safely accomplished. Common causes are cephalopelvic disproportion, abnormal fetal presentation, fetal distress, weakness of the uterus (after prior surgery), and other emergency situations. When general anesthesia is employed, it crosses the placenta and may depress the central nervous system of the fetus. Monitoring of both patients is crucial. When assurance cannot be made that the mother's stomach is empty and general anesthesia must be employed, endotracheal intubation is essential. A standard in anesthesia suggests the use of any induction agent like thiopental, with a paralyzing agent, succinylcholine, and nitrous oxide with forane. Narcotics should be delayed until the fetus is delivered and the cord is clamped.

The cesarean section itself may cause complications, such as infection, sepsis, hemorrhage, or pulmonary embolism.

### Obstetrical Anesthesia

Most women opt for relief of labor pain. Anesthesia for childbirth differs from surgical anesthesia, as two lives are at stake. The major considerations during any anesthetic undertaken during pregnancy are related to preserving fetal oxygenation. Anesthetic and sedative drugs may jeopardize the infant's respiratory system. Also, since most labors occur without much warning, the pregnant patient may have food contents in her stomach, a major risk in anesthesia due to the possibility of vomiting with aspiration. A checklist formulated by *Obstetric Emergencies*, by Cavanagh, Woods, O'Connor, and Knuppel, suggests the following:

1. Do not assume the patient's stomach is empty. Endotracheal intubation is essential with general anesthesia.
2. Give small doses of spinal anesthesia.
3. Do not give drugs you are unfamiliar with.
4. Do not use incompatible drug combinations.
5. When local anesthesia is required,
   A. Use the minimum effective concentration of solution.
   B. Always aspirate before infiltration when there is any danger of inadvertent intravenous injection.
6. Ensure adequate oxygenation is maintained throughout anesthesia.
7. Deal promptly with all emergency situations.

The American College of Obstetricians and Gynecologists suggests in its Standards for Services that the mother's blood pressure should be taken every 1–2 minutes for the first 10 minutes following an injection of anesthesia and then every 5–10 minutes during the entire period of anesthesia. Her vital signs and status should be recorded throughout labor and delivery.

Other forms of pain relief for the laboring patient include spinal anesthesia (not to be used with maternal hypertension) and paracervical, pudendal, and epidural blocks. Epidural complications include postspinal headache, hypotension, central nervous system stimulation, adverse effects on the progress of labor, and inadvertent spinal anesthesia.

### Delivery

A delivery progress note should include the following information:

Date and time of delivery

Physician performing the delivery, and any assistants

Position of the patient

Anesthesia utilized

Episiotomy if required, type utilized

Forceps if utilized

Position of the fetus

Vaginal or C-section

Description of the delivery should include suction of the infant, clamping of the cord, those present, type of delivery, delivery of the placenta, inspection of the cervix, inspection of the perineum, repairs, and type of suture and techniques used.

Disposition of the patient and infant at the end of the delivery should be listed, including APGAR scores, numerical assessments of an infant at 1 and 5 minutes after birth. (In a compromised infant, continued assessments should be taken at 10 and 20 minutes, if appropriate.)

| **Score** | **0** | **1** | **2** |
|---|---|---|---|
| Heart rate | Absent | <100 | >100 |
| Respiratory effort | Absent | Slow, irregular | Good crying |
| Muscle tone | Limp | Some flexion of extremities | Active motion |
| Color | Blue or pale | Body pink, extremities blue | Completely pink |
| Reflex (response to nasal catheter) | No response | Grimace | Cough or sneeze |

Caring for a distressed newborn involves transferring to the neonatal intensive care unit when appropriate, where the baby's environment needs to be monitored rigorously. Warming lamps are often necessary, and light may be used to treat neonatal jaundice. When the child is born without a heartbeat, blue, limp, unresponsive, or without breath, immediate measures should be taken to provide oxygen and artificial stimulation. Tiny masks and ventilation bags are made for neonotes. Intubation may be performed when indicated with a very small endotracheal tube. When the infant needs ventilation assistance and supplementary oxygen, concentrations should be lowered as soon as the child is out of danger, because oxygen can be toxic to the newborn's eyes and cause a condition known as retrolental fibroplasia.

### Obstetrical Drugs

Most women who are monitored by a physician throughout their pregnancy are prescribed prenatal vitamins. Although failure to do so does not constitute malpractice, laboratory values taken upon initial visits should reveal any anemic values that would necessitate providing iron supplements. Some fat-soluble vitamins have been linked with producing birth defects and should not be routinely supplemented. If the mother has been prescribed medically indicated medications prior to her pregnancy, they should be checked for their teratogenic (causing birth defects in a developing embryo) potential. Some drugs should not be given during the first trimester of pregnancy, when most of the embryo's major organ systems are being formed. Certain drugs like aspirin and some anti-inflammatory medications should not be given toward the end of pregnancy because of their potential to inhibit normal progress of the fetus; others have the potential to stimulate uterine contractions and bring about premature labor. Many medications should never be given during pregnancy or nursing.

A common source of labor mishaps involves the use of drugs that are given to the mother to stimulate contractions of the uterus to accelerate delivery. These drugs should not be given if the fetus exhibits any signs of fetal distress, because hard contractions that result can cause further distress to the unborn child. Oxytocin, the hormone released by the posterior lobe of the pituitary gland, stimulates rhythmic contractions of the uterus. This is how labor begins. Synthetic analogs of this substance can be injected to induce, stimulate, or enhance labor. Their use is indicated when membranes are prematurely ruptured and delivery is indicated, to stimulate labor in selected cases of uterine inertia, as adjunctive therapy of incomplete abortion, and to assist third-stage delivery and control postpartum bleeding. They are contraindicated in cephalopelvic disproportion, unfavorable fetal presentation, when surgical intervention favors the outcome for the fetus or the mother, in cases of fetal distress where delivery is not imminent, hypertonic uterine patterns, and hypersensitivity to the drug. Other forms of these drugs are oxytocin (Syntocinon and Pitocin) and methylergonovine (Methergine, for use only *after* delivery).

Magnesium sulfate is often employed to relax the muscle cells of the uterus. Adverse reactions to its use are flushing, nausea, headache, suppressed deep tendon reflexes, chest pain, and possible respiratory depression and coma with prolonged or excessive dosing.

Beta blockers are also widely employed for treating premature labor in attempt to prolong the pregnancy. Maternal side effects are significant and include hypotension, tachycardia, tremulousness, nausea, dizziness, headache, hypokalemia, hyperglycemia, and lactacidemia.

## THE DENTAL RECORD

The dental record should contain the patient's current medical history, including whether the person is under the care of a physician for any reason and

**Figure 3.5**
**The Dental Chart**

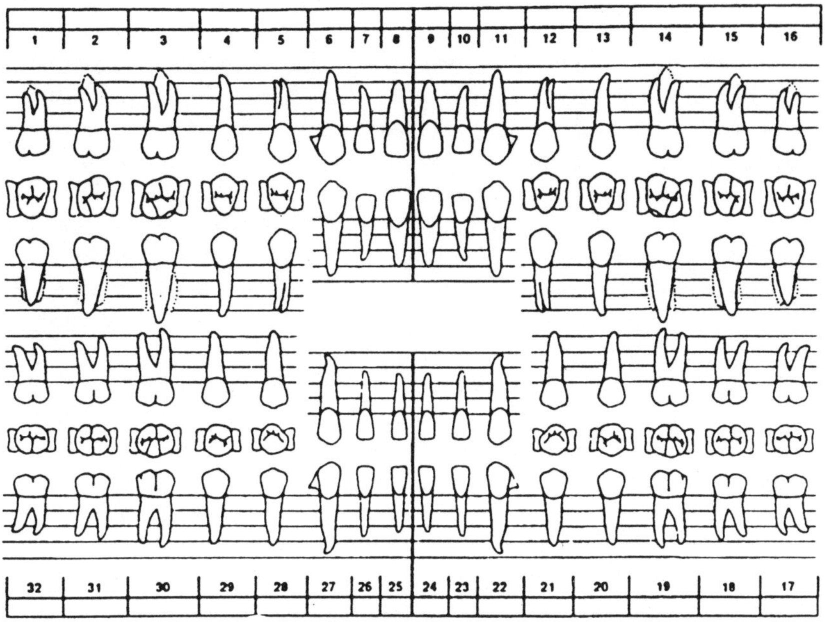


the nature of the care. The patient should be asked how long it has been since the last dental examination if he or she is not an established patient. Women should be asked if they are pregnant. Current dental concerns should be addressed, and allergies and medications should be listed on the dental record. Blood pressure should be checked and documented. Past surgeries and prosthetics should be recorded. Patients with artificial heart valves or heart disease should receive special preventive care during a dental exam. They should take prophylactic antibiotics for dental procedures because it is easy to introduce infections from the mouth directly into the bloodstream.

A soft tissue examination should evaluate the mucosa, hard and soft palates, pharynx, tongue, floor of the mouth, gingiva, lymph nodes, lips, and ridges.

Evaluation of the temperomandibular joint (TMJ evaluation) should check for joint tenderness, muscle tenderness, restriction of movement, and jaw noises.

The dental exam itself should note any crowns, bridges, appliances, fillings, and missing teeth. These will be recorded schematically, as shown in Figure 3.5.

## PHARMACOLOGY

Drugs are listed in the medical records on the ''Orders'' sheet by the name of the drug, the prescribed dosage, administration, and the prescribing physician.

Justification for the medicine may also be found in the progress notes and treatment plan in the medical records.

Practically speaking, a drug can be any molecular substance that, when introduced from outside (*exogenously*) into the body, alters the body's function by interacting at the molecular level. *Pharmacokinetics* determines the amount of drug required to produce the desired effect. The principles that govern concentration are based on what the human biological system does to the drug as well. *Pharmacotherapeutics* is the application of drugs in the prevention, treatment, or diagnosis of disease and their use in purposeful alteration in normal function.

*Toxicology* is the study of the harmful effects of chemicals, the systems and treatment of poisoning. *Toxicology*, however is a relative term; in fact, *all drugs are toxic in overdose*, yet what is toxic to one person may be therapeutic to another. Every individual has a level of responsiveness to different chemical compounds, or a level of *tolerance*. This principle is based on *potency* (degree of effect) and *efficacy*, or maximum intensity of a drug. Additional factors—dissolution, absorption, distribution, metabolism, and excretion, as well as sex, weight, and size—determine an individual's biological response to certain concentrations of a drug.

Certain drugs will be defined by their function as an *agonist*, which occupies a cell's receptors and makes it stimulate a certain physiological activity; or as an *antagonist*, which occupies a cell's receptors and blocks the action of another substance without producing a physiological effect itself.

### Drug Nomenclature

Generally drugs are commonly referred to in three ways:

1. *Proprietary or trade name*—the name provided by the manufacturer to distinguish its preparation. Examples are Bufferin and Tylenol.
2. *The generic name*—to designate pharmacological relationships among a group of drugs. Examples are aspirin and ibuprofen.
3. *The chemical name* (its genetic makeup)—refers to the chemical composition of the drug's structure (acetylsalicylic acid, or 2-hydroxybenzoic acid acetate 2-carboxyphenyl ester).

We will categorize the most commonly encountered therapeutic drugs by their intended effects, breaking them down into general subject headings, followed by the generic name and trade names.

### The Pharmacological Review

A complete medical records review is certain to list medications ordered for the patient. This guide will assist you in understanding the intended use of the drug and its administration. If questions arise concerning whether a prescribed medication was appropriate, consider the following questions:

- Was the drug a proper choice for the condition of the patient?
- Did the patient fit the description for its indications?
- Was it prescribed in the proper amount?
- Was it given by the correct means?
- Did the patient have any allergies to the medication prescribed or its contents?
- Did the patient fit any criteria for contraindications to its administration?
- Was the patient on any other medications that adversely interact with this prescription?
- Was the patient advised of possible adverse effects from the medication?
- If the patient exhibited adverse effects from the drug, were appropriate measures taken?

### Autonomic Drugs

Autonomic drugs have their effect on the autonomic nervous system, which is made up of *sympathetic* (''fight or flight'' response) and *parasympathetic* (''housekeeping'' functions) nerve fibers supplying various organs. The autonomic nervous system provides interaction of two complementary systems with independent functions. Basically sympathetic fibers excite; parasympathetic fibers relax. The organs themselves have receptors for both and respond accordingly. For example, blood vessels have the ability to constrict and dilate, as does the pupillary response in the eye. The heart increases contractility in response to sympathetic innervation, while parasympathetic fibers allow it to relax.

The sympathetic response is produced by neurotransmitters called *adrenergic*, in that the main sympathetic neurotransmitter, epinephrine, is produced by the adrenal gland. These are also called *catecholamines*. Their receptors receive norepinephrine, epinephrine, and dopamine, and they react at various sites.

The parasympathetic response is induced by *cholinergic* transmitters (acetylcholine, or ACh). These are further broken down into *muscarinic* and *nicotinic* receptors.

Autonomic drugs are exogenous substances that mimic the adrenergic or cholinergic responses at receptor sites. Some inhibit (*antagonists*); some exaggerate (*agonists*). Those that do both are called *agonist-antagonists*. Some block the uptake of transmitters that the body produces, thereby allowing it to act at the receptor site longer (*esterase inhibitors*).

*Cholinergic agonists* are used to increase the parasympathetic cholinergic response. They are used to dilate the pupil, treat glaucoma, increase gastrointestinal motility and urinary contractility, and calm the cardiovascular system. (Yet slowing the heart may cause a physiological dilation of the blood vessels. The body produces its own reflex sympathetic response by activating the adrenal gland to produce epinephrine and norepinephrine to increase the heart rate and constrict the blood vessels.)

**Acetylcholine (the prototype)**

Methacholine (Mecholyl)

Bethanechol (Urecholine)

Carbechol (IsoptoCarbechol)

**Alkaloids (naturally occurring)**

Muscarine

Pilocarpine

**Investigative**

Oxotremorine

**Male Impotence**

Yohimbine (Yocon)

**Miscellaneous**

Metoclopramide (Reglan) (an antiemetic)

*Cholinesterase inhibitors* are mainly concerned with treating the eye, the gastrointestinal tract, and the skeletal neuromuscular junction. They are prescribed in glaucoma, paralytic ileus, bladder atony, and intoxication by anticholinergic drugs. They are also used to treat myasthenia gravis, a neuromuscular disease.

Physostigmine (Eserine)

Pyridostigmine (Mestinon)

Echothiophate (Phospholine)

Pralidoxime (Protopam, 2-PAM)

Neostigmine (Prostigmin)

Edrophonium (Tensilon)

Parathion

Malathion

*Cholinergic antagonists* decrease the cholinergic response. They reduce gastric motility and gastric acid secretion and thereby are used to treat peptic ulcers, paralytic ileus, and irritable bowel syndromes. They are used to examine the retina and optic disc in eye exams, treat arrythmias, treat motion system, inhibit salivation and respiratory tract secretions, cause bronchodilation, and have been used to treat enuresis (bed-wetting).

Botulinum Toxin (release inhibitor)

Botox (local paralysis)

**Belladonna Alkaloids** (These antimuscarinic drugs have higher side effects)

Atropine

Scopolamine (Isopto Hyoscine)

Homatropine (Isopto Homatropine)

Ipratropium (Atrovert)

Methscopolamine (Pamine)

**Synthetic Derivatives**

Propantheline (Probanthine)

Cyclopentolate (Cyclogyl)

Tropicamide (Mydriacyl)

Dicyclomine (Bentyl)

*Neuromuscular blocking agents* produce relaxation of skeletal muscle and are used during surgery as an adjunct in anesthesia, in orthopedic procedures, to facilitate intubation with endotracheal tube, facilitate laryngoscopy, bronchoscopy, esophagoscopy, and to prevent trauma during electroshock therapy.

**Competitive Antagonists**

D-Tubocurarine

Pancuronium (Pavulon)

Atracurium (Tracrium)

Gallamine (Flaxedil)

Metocurine (Metubine)

Vecuronium (Norcuron)

**Depolarizing Blockers**

Succinylcholine (Anectine)

Decamethonium

*Ganglionic agents* work on ganglionic receptors to stimulate or inhibit (nicitonic receptor) response.

**Ganglionic Stimulants**

Nicotine

DMPP

**Ganglionic Blocking Agents**

Hexamethonium

Mecamylamine (Inversine)

Trimethaphan (Arfonad)

*Adrenergic receptor agonists* mimic the endogenous sympathetic neurotransmitters—epinephrine, norepinephrine, and dopamine—and are therefore referred to also as *sympathomimetics*. They have a wide variety of clinical uses. They can treat bronchial asthma and anaphylaxis. Some are used to treat hyperactive children. Some treat hypertension. There are eye drops and nose spray. Receptor sites are selective on the organ systems themselves, so the drugs know where their work is to be done. Drugs that act on alpha-1 receptors decrease bronchial congestion, can treat hypotension, control hemorrhage, and manage certain types of shock. Beta-2 drugs relax bronchial muscles, enhance insulin secretion, and can delay premature labor. They also can dilate coronary and skeletal blood vessels. Alpha-2 drugs inhibit insulin secretion.

**Catecholamines**

Epinephrine (Adrenalin, Epi-Pen)

Norepinephrine (Levophed)

Dopamine (Intropin)

Isoproterenol (Isuprel)

Dobutamine (Dobutrex)

**Noncatecholamines**

| RECEPTOR | |
|---|---|
| a-1 | Phenylephrine (Neo-Synephrine) |
| a-1 | Methoaxamine (Vasoxyl) |
| | Metaraminol (Aramine) |
| | Mephentermine (Wyamine) |
| | Ephedrine (hydrochloride) (Primatene, Quadrinal, Tedral) |
| | Ephedrine (sulfate) (Marax, Rynatuss) |
| | Amphetamine (Biphetamine) |
| | Hydroxyamphetamine (Paredrine) |
| | Methylphenidate (Ritalin) |
| | Diethylpropion (Tenuate) |
| | Phenylpropanolamine (Propadrine) |
| | Fenfluramine (Pondimin) |
| b-2 | Albuterol (Ventolin) |
| b-2 | Terbutaline (Brethine) |
| b-2 | Metapropterenol (Alupent) |
| b-2 | Ritodrine (Yutopar) |

| | |
|---|---|
| b-2 | Pirbuterol (Maxair) |
| b-2 | Bitolterol (Tornalate) |
| a-2 | Clonidine (Catapres) |
| a-2 | Guanfacine (Tenex) |
| a-2 | Guanabenz (Wytesin) |
| a-2 | Alpha-methylnorepinephrine (Nordefrin) |
| | Naphazoline (Privine) |
| | Tetrahydrozoline (Tyzine [nasal], Visine [ophthalmic]) |
| | Oxymetazoline (Afrin) |

*Adrenergic antagonists*, also known as *sympatholytics* (kills the sympathetic response), these compounds selectively inhibit responses of effector organs. They have the ability to control hypertension, treat cardiac arrhythmias, and/or dilate blood vessels.

**Alpha**

Phenoxybenzamine (Dibenzyline)

Phentolamine (Regitine)

Prazosin (Minipress, Minizide)

**Beta**

Propranolol (Inderal, Inderide)

Metoprolol (succinate) (Toprol)

Metoprolol (tartrate) (Lopressor)

Nadolol (Corgard, Corzide)

Pindolol (Visken)

Timolol (Blocadren, Timolide, Timoptic)

Acebutolol (hydrochloride) (Sectral)

Atenolol (Tenormin, Tenoretic)

**a** and **b**

Labetalol (hydrochloride) (Normodyne, Trandate)

*Neuronal agents* are categorized as adrenergic, noradrenergic, or cholinergic. These terms have to do with the type of transmitter they are and the receptors on which they act. These are used in various clinical settings (e.g., for hypertension, paralysis, depression, asthma). Some of these drugs are contraindicated in patients on monoamine oxidase (MAO) inhibitors. MAO inhibitors metabolize neurotransmitters; thus, if a patient is on a drug that inhibits MAO, neurotransmitters cannot be metabolized. The drug administered will build up to a toxic level.

**Adrenergic**

Alpha-methyl-p-tyrosine

Guanethidine (Esimil [hypertension], Ismelin)

Guanedrel (Hylorel)

Reserpine (Diopres, Hydropres, Sur-Ap-Es)

Alpha-methyldopa

Bretylium (tosylate) (Bretylol [antiarrythmic injection])

Clonidine (Catapress [antihypertensive])

Tyramine

Amphetamine (Biphetamine [CNS stimulant])

Ephedrine (hydrochloride) (Primatene [bronchodilator], Quadrinal, Quelidrine, Tedral)

Ephedrine (sulfate) (Marax, Pazo [hemorrhoid ointment])

Ephedrine (tannate) (Rynatuss [antitussive, decongestant])

Cocaine (hydrochloride)

Imipramine (Tofranil [tricyclic antidepressant])

Pargyline (Pargyline [MAOI])

**Cholinergic**

Botulinum toxin (Botox [treats eye spasms])

Black widow spider antivenom (Antivenin [neutralizes venom from bites])

Physostigmine (salicylate) (Antilirium [reverses anticholinergic response])

Neostigmine (methylsulfate) (Prostigmin [injectable])

Neostigmine (bromide) (Prostigmin [tablets])

Edrophonium (chloride) (Enlon Plus [injection], Tensilon [injectible myasthenia gravis diagnostic])

*Autacoids*, endogenous substances that are self-remedies for various physiological and pathological processes, act as local hormones, neurotransmitters, or neuromodulaters. Most have limited clinical use, but drugs have been developed to either enhance or inhibit their formation.

*Histamine receptors* are classified as $H_1$ or $H_2$. Generally, histamine 1 responds to antigen-antibody reactions and insults such as bee stings and tissue injury. The histamine 1 response includes causing vasodilation. This decreases the overall blood pressure level, thereby producing hypotension. These histamine reactors also act on the intradermal tissue, causing flushing and swelling. Histamine 2 receptors are found in cells lining the stomach, causing gastric acid secretion, so a histamine blocker, or antihistamine, will be aimed at blocking either of these two actions, while a histamine stimulator will enhance these physiological processes.

**$H_1$ Stimulators**

Morphine

Codeine

Tubocurarine

Succinylcholine

X-ray contrast media

Plasma expanders

*Antihistamines* ($H_1$ Inhibitors). These antihistamines inhibit histamine release and may be used in prophylactic treatment of bronchial asthma and allergic conditions.

Epinephrine

Cromolyn sodium (Aarane, Intal)

These antihistamines competitively block $H_1$ receptors.

*Ethanolamines* also produce marked sedation; they have anticholinergic, local anesthetic, and antiemetic actions.

Diphenhydramine (Benadryl)

Dimenhydrinate (Dramamine)

*Ethylenediamines* produce moderate sedation, dizziness, and GI side effects.

Tripelennamine (PBZ)

Pyrilamine (tannate) (Rynatan)

Pyrilamine (maleate) (Triaminic, Ru-Tuss with hydrocodone, 4–Way Nasal Spray)

*Alkylamines* cause slight sedation; they are used in over-the-counter preparations.

Chlorpheniramine (maleate) (Chlor-Trimeton, Atrohist, Dristan, Chlorafed, Comtrex, Tylenol Cold, Novahistine, Deconamine, Quelidrine, Pediacare, Sinulin, Brexin, Hycomine, Kronofed, Ru-Tuss tablets, Teldrlin, Comhist, Ana-kit [anaphalyxis emergency kit])

Chlorpheniramine (polistrex) (Tussionex Pennkinetic)

Chlorpheniramine (tannate) (Rynatan, Rynatuss)

Brompheniramine (Atrohist, Bromfed, Dimetane, Dristan Allergy)

*Piperazines* produce slight sedation and are useful for motion sickness.

Cyclizine (Marezine)

Meclizine (Antivert, Bonine)

Hydroxyzine (hydrochloride) (Atarax, Marax, Vistaril [IM solution])

Hydroxyzine (pamoate) (Vistaril [oral])

*Phenothiazines* provide the strongest antiemetic action. They also produce marked sedation and have anticholinergic and local anesthetic properties.

Promethazine (hydrochloride) (Mepergan, Phenergan)

*Piperidines* do not cross the blood-brain barrier (BBB) and therefore produce no sedation.

Terfenadine (Seldane [rapid onset, for acute symptoms])

Astemizole (Hismanal [slow onset, long duration])

**Miscellaneous**

Cyproheptadine (Periactin [moderate sedation; serotonin antagonist as well])

*$H_2$ Antagonists* inhibit gastric acid secretion. They are used for gastric and duodenal ulcers, Zollinger-Ellison syndrome (gastric hypersecretion due to pancreatic tumor), and gastroesophageal reflux disease.

Cimetidine (Tagamet)

Ranitidine (Zantac)

Famotidine (Pepcid)

Nizatidine (Axid)

*Serotonin* receptors are found in the brain, peripheral nerve endings, and vascular and nonvascular smooth muscle. Serotonin (5-hydroxytroptophan) functions as a neurotransmitter in the central nervous system, is involved with intestinal motility and respiratory response, and is also released from platelets. They have been implicated in stimulating the vascular response involved in migraine headaches, as well. Some drugs that interact with serotonin include reserpine, cocaine, and tricyclic antidepressants.

*Serotonin antagonists* are used to treat migraine headaches, carcinoid syndrome, and pruritic dermatoses.

Methysergide (Sansert)

Cyproheptadine (Periactin)

*Angiotensin* has various physiological functions involved in the cardiovascular system, central nervous system, kidney, adrenal cortex, nervous tissue, and vascular smooth muscle. Angiotensin and renin drugs are mostly aimed at controlling blood pressure and regulating water balance. Renin release inhibitors include pepstatin and *beta blockers*:

Propranolol (Inderal, Inderide)
Metoprolol (succinate) (Toprol)
Metoprolol (tartrate) (Lopressor)
Nadolol (Corgard, Corzide)
Pindolol (Visken)
Timolol (Blocadren, Timolide, Timoptic)
Acebutolol (hydrochloride) (Sectral)
Atenolol (Tenormin, Tenoretic)

*ACE inhibitors* refer to angiotensin-converting enzyme inhibitors. They assist physiology by lowering blood pressure and increasing cardiac output.

Captopril (Capoten)
Elanapril (Vasotec, Vaseretic)
Lisinopril (Prinivil, Prinzide, Zestoretic, Zestril)

**Eicosanoids**

*Arachidonic acid* is a fatty acid released by the cellular membrane, which is a precursor for several biological substances involved in the mediation of pain, platelet aggregation, vasodilation, and other physiological responses. Among these substances are prostaglandins (vasodilation, fever, pain, inflammation, promotes motility in smooth muscles), thromboxanes (platelet aggregation, vasoconstrictor, and bronchoconstrictor), and leukotrienes (vasoconstrictor, bronchoconstrictor, induces peripheral vascular permeability, and attracts mediators of inflammation). The pathways involved in their biosynthesis involve many complicated steps. Their production is necessary for many biological processes, which medical science may need to alter in certain scenarios. In this section we will deal with inhibiting steps along the path of their production.

*Glucocorticoids* inhibit the first step of this pathway. But with many steroid preparations, the side effects are numerous and far reaching. If the first step of the pathway is interrupted, *none* of the other physiological reactions is allowed to take place, so drugs are also aimed at inhibiting specific biochemical reactions later on down the path.

*Prostaglandin inhibitors* are aimed at blocking the production of certain types of prostaglandins. PGE and PGF series promote uterine contractions, thereby inducing labor:

Carboprost tromethamine (Prostin/15 M)
Dinoprost tromethamine (Prostin F2)
Dinoprostone (Prostin E2)

Neonatal application is used to maintain patency of the ductus arteriosus (a physiological opening in the fetal heart to shunt oxygenated blood) during surgery on neonates with certain rare cases of congenital heart disease:

Alprostadil (Prostin VR)

They also inhibit gastric acid secretion and stimulate secretion of bicarbonate and mucus to protect the stomach:

Misoprostol (Cytotec)

### Antimicrobial Therapy

The ideal antimicrobial agent is selectively toxic to a certain group of microorganisms, is nontoxic to the host, does not induce microbial resistance, is effective following oral administration, and is inexpensive. Also in an ideal situation, the choice of therapy can await the results of appropriate cultures and sensitivity tests. In certain life-threatening situations, however, the clinician does not have the time to wait for culture and sensitivity results and must choose an antimicrobial agent based on incomplete information. Certain organisms are more likely to cause infection in certain tissues than others. For example, pathogens that are most likely to grow in burned skin or subcutaneous tissue are *Staphylococcus aureus, Streptococcus pyogenes* (group A), and *Pseudomonas aeruginosa.* Organisms that most often cause meningitis are the viruses *Neisseria meningitidis, Haemophilus influenzae*, and certain streptococcus and staphylococcus bacteria. Pending culture results, most infectious disease specialists prefer to use a third-generation cephalosporin in adults and in children over 3 months old. Another important consideration is that the antibiotic can penetrate the targeted organ. Certain antibiotics like penicillins, cefotaxime, and moxalactam cannot penetrate into the cerebrospinal fluid without meningeal inflammation, whereas sulfonamides have excellent lipid solubility and can reach the cerebrospinal fluid without meningeal inflammation.

Bacterial organisms are identified by their microscopic appearance and their gram-staining patterns. Most clinical laboratories are equipped to test bacteria for susceptibility to antimicrobial drugs with a disk diffusion test or semiautomated methods to designate susceptibility. Certain penicillins—erythromycin, lincomycin, vancomycin, bacitracin, and clindamycin—are primarily effective against gram-positive cocci and bacilli. Aminoglycosides and polymixins are primarily effective against gram-negative bacilli. Antibiotics have different mechanisms of action that determine their effectiveness against certain organisms. Penicillins, cephalosporins, bacitracin, and vancomycin inhibit cell wall synthesis. Erythromycin reversibly inhibits intracellular protein synthesis in the 50S subunit. Sulfonamides inhibit intermediate metabolism. Some antifungals affect the function of the cytoplasmic membrane.

Microbes have their own intrinsic resistance to certain antibiotics as well. Penicillin G cannot affect certain gram-negative organisms; amphotericin B kills fungi but not bacteria; Isoniazid is effective against mycobacteria but does not affect most other bacteria. Microbes can also acquire resistance to antibiotics by converting form, producing enzymes that inactivate the agent, or by altering a metabolic pathway.

Host factors that affect the choice of antimicrobial agents include the patient's age, metabolism, defense mechanisms, genetic disorders, allergies, pregnancy, and site of infection. Renal and liver function are important variables for certain drugs as well.

Antibiotics may produce untoward side effects and toxicities, such as gastrointestinal upset, renal toxicity, neurotoxicity, allergy, hypersensitivity, and superinfection with microbes that are more difficult to treat.

Antimicrobial agents may also be combined to produce a synergistic effect, to prevent the emergence of bacterial resistance, for use in mixed bacterial infections, and when the etiology is unknown.

Common reasons for failure of antibiotic treatment include inadequate dosing (diarrhea may have an effect on dose), incorrect drug, treatment of a nonbacterial infection with an antibacterial agent, failure to drain purulent material or to remove an obstruction, defects in the patient's resistance, drug reaction, superinfection, and the duration and severity of the infection.

The following guide lists some common antibiotics you may encounter in medical records:

*Amikacin* (Amikin). A parenteral aminoglycoside used to treat infections caused by gram-negative strains that are resistant to gentamicin, tobramycin, and netilmicin, including some strains of *Pseudomonas aeruginosa*. Amikacin is generally reserved for treatment of serious infections caused by susceptible gram-negative strains known or suspected to be resistant to these drugs. It is also used concurrently with other drugs for treatment of *Mycobacterium avium* infections.

*Aminosalicylic acid* (PAS). Used in antituberculosis regimens for many years, its gastrointestinal effects cause many patients to stop taking it prematurely.

*Amoxicillin* (Amoxil). An oral semisynthetic penicillin similar to ampicillin, with better absorption and fewer diarrhea effects. Amoxicillin is at least as effective as oral ampicillin for the treatment of most infections, except shigellosis.

*Amoxicillin/clavulanic acid* (Augmentin). Has a beta-lactamase inhibitor that extends its spectrum of activity to include beta-lactamase-producing strains of *Staphylococcus aureus, Haemophilus influenzae, Moraxella catarrhalis*, and many strains of enteric gram-negative bacilli. This combination may be useful for oral treatment of bite wounds, otitis media, sinusitis, and some lower respiratory tract and urinary tract infections, but it may cause a higher incidence of diarrhea and other gastrointestinal symptoms than amoxicillin alone.

*Ampicillin* (Polycillin, Omnipen). A semisynthetic penicillin as effective as penicillin G in pneumococcal, streptococcal, and meningococcal infections, and also active against many strains of *Salmonella, Shigella, Proteus mirabilis*, and *Escherichia coli* and most strains of *Haemophilus influenzae*. Some strains of *H. influenzae*, however, are now resistant to ampicillin, and the drug is not effective against penicillinase-producing staphylococci. Rashes are more frequent with ampicillin than with other penicillins.

*Ampicillin/Sulbactam* (Unasyn). A parenteral combination of ampicillin with the beta-lactamase inhibitor sulbactam, which extends the antibacterial spectrum of ampicillin to include beta-lactamase-producing strains of *S. aureus, H. influenzae, M. catarrhalis, Neisseria*, and many gram-negative bacilli, including *Bacteroides fragilis*. Ineffective against *Pseudomonas aeruginosa, Enterobacter*, and *Serratia*. Has shown utility in treating gynecological and intra-abdominal infections.

*Azithromycin* (Zithromax). An expensive oral macrolide antibiotic that has much less gastrointestinal toxicity than erythromycin. A single dose has been effective for treatment of urethritis and cervicitis caused by *Chlamydia*. Azithromycin has been effective in treating AIDS-associated *M. avium* infections, toxoplasma encephalitis, and cryptosporidiosis.

*Aztreonam* (Azactam). A parenteral beta-lactam antibiotic active against most aerobic gram-negative infections, including *Pseudomonas aeruginosa*, but it is almost inactive against gram-positive organisms and anaerobes. Little cross-allergenicity with penicillins and cephalosporins. Pseudomembranous colitis caused by *C. difficile* has occurred in patients treated with aztreonam.

*Bacampicillin* (Spectrobid). An expensive oral agent that is rapidly converted to ampicillin in the bloodstream. Equivalent doses lead to higher serum concentrations than with ampicillin, and the drug may cause less diarrhea.

*Bacitracin*. Used to treat severe systemic staphylococci infections in the past, which are resistant to penicillin G. Now restricted mainly to topical application because of its nephrotoxicity.

*Capreomycin* (Capastat). A second-line antituberculosis drug.

*Carbenicillin* (Geopen, Geocillin). A semisynthetic penicillin used against serious *Pseudomonas, Proteus*, and some other gram-negative infections. Active against some gram-positive cocci. Often used in conjunction with other drugs to treat serious systemic infections.

*Cephalosporins*. Similar to penicillins, these drugs are the most widely used agents in the world. Most are chemically derived from a fugus. These drugs are often prescribed for patients with penicillin allergies, but there may be cross-reactions. Active against most gram-positive cocci and many strains of gram-negative bacilli. They are widely used for soft tissue, respiratory, and urinary tract infections due to susceptible organisms. These drugs are broken down into three generations based on their activity against gram-negative organisms (First generation are less effective; third generation are most effective.)

**First generation**

Cephalothin (Keflin)

Cefazolin (Ancef, Kefzol)

Cephapirin (Cefadyl)

Cephradine (Velosef, Anspor)

Cephalexin (Keflex)

Cefadroxil (Duricef, Ultracef)

**Second generation**

Cefamandole (Mandol)

Cefuroxime (Zinacef, Kefurox)

Cefonicid (Monocid)

Cefaclor (Ceclor)

Cefotetan (Cefotan)

Cefoxitin (Mefoxin)

Cefmetazole (Zefazone)

**Third generation**

Cefotaxime (Claforan)

Ceftriaxone (Rocephin)

Cefoperazone (Cefobid)

Ceftizoxime (Cefizox)

Ceftazidime (Fortaz)

Ceforamide (Precef)

The most common adverse effects of cephalosporin therapy are pain on injection or thrombophlebitis with IV use and minor gastrointestinal complaints. Bone marrow depression and thrombocytopenia have been reported. Alcohol ingestion should be avoided with the use of cefamandole, cefoperazone and cefotan because the methylthiotetrazole can cause severe reactions.

*Chloramphemicol* (Chloromycetin). Used to treat meningitis, epiglottitis, serious *H. influenzae, Salmonella typhi*, and *Bacteroides* infections. Used for anaerobic infections. This is a good choice for treating pneumococcal or meningococcal meningitis in patients allergic to penicillin. This drug may cause fatal blood dyscrasias, so should be used only for serious infections that cannot be effectively treated with less toxic agents. Hypersensitivity reactions, superinfections, and a fatal syndrome in neonates have been known to occur. Prolongs the half-life of drugs metabolized by the liver.

*Cinoxacin* (Cinobac). An oral agent used to treat urinary tract infections.

*Ciprofloxacin* (Cipro). An oral or intravenous fluoroquinolone used to treat a variety of gram-positive and gram-negative bacterial infections in adults, including methicillin-resistant staphylococci, *H. influenzae, Neisseria, Pseudomonas aeruginosa*, enteric pathogens and other aerobic gram-negative bacilli. Not effective against anaerobes. Occasionally causes central nervous system toxicity.

*Clarithromycin* (Biaxin). A macrolide antibiotic with a shorter half-life than azithromycin.

*Clindamycin* (Cleocin). A derivative of lincomycin, which can cause severe diarrhea and pseudomembranous colitis. Treats anaerobic infections outside the central nervous system. May also be used to treat some staphylococcal infections in penicillin-allergic patients.

*Clofazimine* (Lamprene). An oral agent used along with other antileprosy drugs. Can also be used to treat *M. avium* infections in AIDS patients and has been used to treat resistant strains of tuberculosis.

*Cloxacillin* (Tegopen). An oral penicillinase-resistant penicillin used to treat infections caused by strains of staphylococci that produce an enzyme that inactivates penicillin. Also effective against pneumococci and Group A streptococci.

*Colistimethate* (Coly-Mycin). A polymyxin E, used topically to treat infected wounds and external ear infections.

*Cycloserine* (Seromycin). A second-line antituberculosis drug.

*Demeclocycline* (Declomycin). An intermediate-acting tetracycline preparation for oral use. Has a broad spectrum against gram-positive and gram-negative infections. Should not be given to patients with renal dysfunction. Toxicities include gastrointestinal disturbances, sun sensitivity, depression of bone growth, tooth discoloration, and hypersensitivity reactions. Outdated tetracyclines can cause Fanconi syndrome, manifested by nausea, acidosis, proteinuria, glycosuria, and aminoaciduria.

*Dicloxacillin* (Dycill). An oral penicillinase-resistant penicillin used to treat penicillinase-producing staphylococci, pneumococci, and Group A streptococci.

*Doxycycline* (Vibramycin). A long-acting tetracycline, requiring fewer doses. This tetracycline is the safest to use in patients with renal failure, as its primary route of elimination is hepatic. Causes sun sensitivity, depression of bone growth, and tooth discoloration. Has good oral absorption, less gastrointestinal disturbance, and is least affected by food.

*Enoxacin* (Penetrex). An oral fluoroquinolone used to treat urinary tract infections and uncomplicated gonorrhea.

*Erythromycin* (Erythrocin, EES, Ilosone). A macrolide obtained from *Streptomyces erythreus*, used to treat respiratory tract infections due to pneumococci, Group A streptococci, *Mycoplasma* pneumonia, *Chlamydia trachomatis, Legionella pneumophilia*, and other gram-positive bacteria. Slightly less effective than penicillin but useful for patients allergic to penicillins. Its main side effect is mild gastrointestinal upset. Its estolate (Ilosone) can cause cholestatic jaundice. Resistance may develop rapidly in serious staphylococcal infections. Should not be injected intramuscularly, as it is extremely painful. Erythromycin decreases the hepatic clearance of thephylline and can potentiate the effects of carbamazepine, corticosteroids, oral anticoagulants, cyclosporine, and digoxin.

*Erythromycin-sulfisoxazole* (Pediazole). Combines erythromycin ethylsuccinate and sulfisoxazole acetyl for the oral treatment of acute otitis media.

*Ethambutol* (Myambutol). Used in an antituberculosis regimen. May cause optic neurotis.

*Ethionamide* (Trecator-SC). A second-line antituberculosis drug.

*Furazolidone* (Furoxone). A monoamine oxidase inhibitor, this oral antimicrobial nitrofuran is not absorbed and is recommended for the treatment of bacterial diarrhea.

*Gentamicin* (Garamycin). An aminoglycoside primarily useful for treating aerobic gram-negative infections including *E. coli, Proteus, Pseudomonas, Klebsiella, Enterobacter*, and *Serratia*. Not effective against anaerobic bacteria. Toxic to the kidney and has the ability to induce progressive destruction of the vestibular and auditory functions, as it accumulates in the endolymph and perilymph of the inner ear. Plasma measurements should be taken to avoid toxicities.

*Imipenem-cilastatin* (Primaxin). A very broad-spectrum parenteral beta-lactam used to treat serious aerobic gram-negative bacilli, anaerobic, and *S. aureus* infections.

*Isoniazid* (INH). A major antituberculosis drug. Can cause fatal hepatitis.

*Kanamycin* (Kantrex). An aminoglycoside active against some gram-negative bacilli. Used with other drugs to treat tuberculosis. Toxic to the ear and the kidney, as is gentamicin.

*Lincomycin* (Lincocin). Can cause severe diarrhea and pseudomembranous colitis. Treats anaerobic infections outside the central nervous system. May also be used to treat some staphylococcal infections in penicillin-allergic patients. Clincamycin is more effective than lincomycin.

*Lomefloxacin* (Maxaquin). An oral fluoroquinolone used to treat urinary tract infections and bronchitis. Pneumococci and other streptococci are resistant to it.

*Methenamines* (Mandelamine). Oral prophylaxis for chronic or recurrent urinary tract infections, this drug can sterilize an acid urine. Trimethoprim-sulfamethoxazole is more effective.

*Methicillin* (Staphcillin). A penicillinase-resistant penicillin for parenteral use.

*Metronidazole* (Flagyl). An agent used to treat trichomoniasis, amebiasis, giardiasis, and *Gardnerella vaginalis* vaginitis in its oral form. Its intravenous form may be used to treat anaerobic bacterial infections. *B. fragilis* infections of the central nervous system may be treated with this agent because of its ability to penetrate the blood-brain barrier. May also be used to treat pseudomembranous enterocolitis due to *Clostridium difficile*.

*Mezlocillin* (Mezlin). A penicillin used for parenteral treatment of gram-negative bacilli. When treating serious gram-negative infections, it should be used in combination with an aminoglycoside. Active against some gram-positive cocci, including streptococci and some strains of *Enterococcus*.

*Minocycline* (Minocin). A tetracycline of long duration with hepatic elimination and biliary excretion. Its gastrointestinal disturbances are less than the shorter-acting tetracyclines, but it can cause photosensitivity, depression of bone growth, discoloration of teeth, hypersensitivity, and vestibular toxicity.

*Nafcillin* (Nafcil). A penicillinase-resistant penicillin used to treat infections caused by penicillinase-producing staphylococci, pneumococci, and group A streptococci. Used parenterally. Will not be effective against methicillin-resistant *Staphylococcus aureus* or *S. epidermidis.*

*Nalidixic acid* (NegGram). An oral preparation used against gram-negative organisms that cause urinary tract infections, but these organisms develop resistance to this preparation rapidly. Adverse reactions include visual disturbances, intracranial hypertension, and convulsions.

*Neomycin* (Neosporin, Cortisporin). For topical use, this aminoglycoside is active against some gram-negative bacilli. Used over large areas of skin or any type of ingestion can cause deafness and renal damage.

*Netilmicin* (Noroxin). An oral fluoroquinolone used to treat urinary tract infections caused by *Enterobacteriaceae, Enterococcus*, or *Pseudomonas aeruginosa.*

*Novobiocin* (Albamycin). Not recommended for treatment of any infection because of the frequency of hepatic dysfunction and blood dyscrasias.

*Ofloxacin* (Floxin). A fluoroquinolone used to treat a wide variety of gram-positive and gram-negative bacterial infections in adults; similar in use to ciprofloxacin. May be used in a single-dose treatment for gonorrhea and for a seven-day treatment of chlamydial infections.

*Oxacillin* (Prostaphlin). A penicillinase-resistant penicillin, used to treat infections caused by penicillinase-producing staphylococci, pneumococci, and group A streptococci. Not effective against methicillin-resistant strains of *Staphylococcus aureus* or *S. epidermidis.*

*Penicillin.* An organic acid that interferes with bacterial cell wall biosynthesis. Widely distributed in body fluids (except prostatic tissues, intraoccular fluids and phagocytic cells), penicillin remains the drug of choice for group A streptococcal, pneumococcal, and other infections. Allergic reactions range from a mild rash to fatal anaphylaxis, due to penicillin acting as a hapten (initiates an immune response when coupled with a carrier protein). Massive doses can cause myclonic seizures and hyperkalemia in persons with renal dysfunction. Thrombophlebitis may occur following intravenous administration.

*Piperacillin* (Pipracil). A parenteral extended-spectrum penicillin used to treat gram-negative bacillary infections. Its antibacterial activity covers a wide spectrum, particularly against *Enterobacteriaceae* such as *Klebsiella* and some anaerobes including *Bacteroides fragilis.* Active against some gram-positive cocci like streptococci.

*Piperacillin/Tazobactam* (Zosyn). Combines a beta-lactamase inhibitor to the extended spectrum penicillin to widen its spectrum to include beta-lactamase-producing strains of staphylococci and many gram-negative bacilli.

*Polymyxins* (B and E-Coly-Mycin, colistemethate, colistin sulfate). Used topically to treat infected wounds and external ear infections. Usually used in combination with other antibiotics.

*Probampacin* (Polycillin-PRB). Combines ampicillin and probenecid for a single-dose treatment of uncomplicated urogenital or anal gonorrhea.

*Pyrazinamide.* Often used in the initial treatment regimen of tuberculosis.

*Rifabutin* (Mycobutin). Used to prevent and treat disseminated *Mycobacterium avium* infections in patients with AIDS.

*Rifampin* (Rafadin, Rimactane). An antituberculosis drug used with other antituberculosis drugs. Also used concurrently with other drugs to treat AIDS patients with *M. avium* infections. Also for prophylactic use in those in close contact with patients with sulfonamide-resistant meningococcal disease and in children who are in close contact with patients with *Haemophilus influenzae* meningitis.

*Rifampin-isoniazid* (Rifamate, Rimactane/INH). A fixed dose combination used to treat tuberculosis.

*Spectinomycin* (Trobicin). May be used for penicillin-resistant infections and may be used by patients who are allergic to penicillin. This is used as a single-dose treatment of urogenital or anal gonorrhea but is not effective against syphilis.

*Streptomycin.* An aminoglycoside used concurrently with other drugs to treat tuberculosis infections. It is toxic to the kidneys and inner ear and has mostly been replaced by gentamicin to treat gram-negative infections. Streptomycin is least toxic to the kidney and most toxic to the vestibular apparatus of the ear.

*Sulfonamides.* Used to treat acute, uncomplicated urinary tract infections. Also have shown effectiveness in otitis media and *Pneumocystis carinii.* Toxicities include renal toxicity, blood disorders, hypersensitivity reactions, and prenatal toxicity. They should not be used in the third trimester of pregnancy.

*Tetracyclines.* Can cause severe liver damage, especially when given in excess to pregnant women and those with renal dysfunction. Calcium and iron absorption may be interrupted with the use of tetracyclines, which should not be taken with milk or milk products. They should be taken with food, as they can cause gastric irritation. Sun sensitivity is a common toxicity. Renal and hepatic changes may occur, as may discoloration of teeth, depression of bone growth, hypersensitivity reactions, and vestibular toxicity. Outdated tetracyclines can cause Fanconi syndrome, characterized by nausea, acidosis, proteinuria, glycosuria, and aminoaciduria, but symptoms disappear within a month after cessation of therapy. Tetracyclines should not be prescribed during the last half of pregnancy or to children below age 5 years.

*Ticarcillin* (Ticar). A penicillin used to treat serious infections caused by susceptible strains of *Pseudomonas, Proteus*, and some other gram-negative organisms. Active against some gram-positive cocci as well, but not against beta-lactamase-producing strains.

*Ticarcillin/clavulanic acid* (Timentin). Combines ticarcillin with a beta-lactamase inhibitor to extend its spectrum to include beta-lactamase-producing strains of *S. aureus, H. influenzae*, and enteric gram-negative bacilli, including *B. fragilis*. Not effective against *Pseudomonas aeruginosa.*

*Tobramycin* (Nebcin). An aminoglycoside that can be used to treat *Pseudomonas aeruginosa* and is often used to treat burn patients. Like all other aminoglycosides, tobramycin is toxic to the kidneys and to the auditory and vestibular function of the ears.

*Trimethoprim* (Proloprim). An oral agent used to treat uncomplicated urinary tract infections caused by gram-negative bacilli. Frequent use has the potential to produce resistant organisms.

*Trimethoprim-sulfamethoxazole* (Bactrim, Septra). Combines a folic acid antagonist with a sulfonamide. Used to treat otitis media, traveler's diarrhea, bronchitis, urinary tract infections, shigellosis, and *Pneumocystis carinii* pneumonia.

*Troleandomycin* (TAO). Similar to erythromycin but may cause cholestatic jaundice.

*Vancomycin* (Vancocin). Used to treat endocarditis caused by *Streptococcus viridans* or *Enterococcus*, for severe staphylococcal infections, and for penicillin-resistant pneumococcal infections. Enterococci are becoming resistant to vancomycin. Vancomycin is the drug of choice to treat methicillin-resistant *Staphylococcus aureus* and S. *epidermidis* infections. Also used to treat antibiotic associated colitis caused by *Clostridium difficile*.

## Antifungal Agents

*Amphotericin B* (Fungizone). A broad-spectrum antifungal agent used to treat systemic fungal infection; administered intravenously. Its use is effectively employed in treating almost all fungal infections but is chosen as a last choice because of its high toxicity. May cause renal damage, hypokalemia, thrombophlebitis, nausea, chills, fever, and vomiting, anemia, blood dyscrasias, peripheral neuropathy, convulsions, anaphylaxis, and dysrhythmias.

*Fluconazole* (Diflucan). A broad-spectrum antifungal agent used to treat oral and esophageal candidiasis and cryptococcal meningitis. Gastrointestinal distress is one of its few side effects. In patients with AIDS, allergic rash, eosinophilia, Stevens-Johnson syndrome, and transient abnormalities of hepatic function are reported.

*Flucytosine* (Ancobon). A broad-spectrum antifungal agent, administered orally to treat serious systemic fungal infections caused by susceptible strains of candida and cryptococcus. It is well absorbed and widely distributed, even to the central nervous system. It is used in combination with amphotericin B because when used alone, fungal resistance can occur rapidly. May cause GI disturbances, hepatic dysfunction, blood dyscrasia, hallucinations, and confusion.

*Griseofulvin* (Fulvicin-U/F). A narrow-spectrum antifungal agent taken orally for the treatment of skin, hair, and nail infections caused by dermatophytes. Occasionally causes gastrointestinal disturbances and allergic and photosensitivity reactions. There are other rare effects of the blood, kidney, central and peripheral nervous system, liver damage, and lymphadenopathy. May interfere with drugs metabolized by the liver.

*Ketoconazole* (Nizoral). A broad-spectrum antifungal agent given orally to treat paracoccidiomycosis, chronic mucocutaneous candidiasis, disseminated histoplasmosis, blastomycosis, coccidioimycosis, spirotrichosis, mucormycosis, aspergillosis, and cryptococccosis. Nausea and vomiting are frequent complaints. Occasionally causes gynecomastia in men, abdominal pain, rash, itching, dizziness, constipation, diarrhea, fever, chills, photophobia, and headache. Rare cases have been reported of transient elevated transaminase, hepatitis, and fatal massive hepatic necrosis.

*Miconazole* (Monistat). Has been used intravenously to treat systemic fungal infections, but its primary use has been as a 2 percent cream in dermatophytosis and vaginal candidiasis.

*Nystatin* (Mycostatin). A broad-spectrum antifungal agent used only topically or for local effects in the gastrointestinal tract. Treats candidiasis of the skin, mucous membranes, and the vulvovaginal region.

*Potassium iodide.* The narrowest-spectrum antifungal agent. Used orally for localized cutaneous lymphatic spirotrichosis; it can cause irritation (rhinitis, coryza, sneezing).

## Antiviral Drugs

*Acyclovir* (Zovirax). Inhibits viral DNA polymerase and is used to manage initial genital herpes in patients with normal immunity and initial and recurrent mucosal and cutaneous infections in immunocompromised patients. May cause phlebitis following intravenous infusion, pruritis, rash, anemia, leukopenia, neurotoxicities, and nephrotoxicities rarely.

*Amantadine* (Symmetrel). An oral antiviral agent used in the prevention and/or treatment of influenza A viral infection and is also used for the treatment of Parkinsonism. Its central nervous system toxicity causes depression, confusion, dizziness, drowsiness, insomnia, rare hallucinations, and psychoses.

*Idoxuridine* (Herplex). A topical antiviral application for herpes simplex keratitis. May cause irritation, inflammation, pain, itching or swelling of the eyelids, and light sensitivity.

*Ribavarin* (Virazole). An antiviral drug used to treat severe respiratory syncytial virus in infants and young children.

*Rimantadine* (Flumadine). A structural analog of amantadine but with fewer central nervous system effects.

*Vidarabine* (Vira-A). May be used topically or intravenously for the treatment of herpes simplex, encephalitis, and conjunctivitis. Toxicities include nausea, vomiting, weakness, thrombophlebitis, hallucinations, psychoses, ataxia, tremor, and dizziness.

*Zidovudine* (Retrovir). Better known as AZT or azidothymidine. Is used in the treatment of the human immunodeficiency virus, which causes AIDS. May cause severe bone marrow depression, nausea, myalgias, headache, insomnia, seizures, and encephalopathy.

Chapter 4

# Medical Research

## INVESTIGATION

Most of the integral information found in a medical case will be contained in the medical records themselves. With experience, you will be able to pinpoint issues quickly for fact, research, and review.

You may encounter occasions where the validity of the medical records may be in question: times of entry in different sections may not match; signatures may differ; items may be crossed out; pages may be slipped in that do not seem to fit with the others. A medical case that contains tampered records is already won.

If you have doubts about the originality of the records, you may need to view the original documents at the hospital or clinic where they originated. You will need to contact the custodian of the medical records to find out the local procedure for viewing the original documents. The custodian will tell you what is required of you and can set up an appointment for you to view the documents. If you need to look at older records, they may have to be retrieved from a storage facility or you may need to view them on microfiche.

It is a good idea to bring your copies with you to compare to the originals. Question the use of correction fluid in a medical record. Entries should be made in ink, and any corrections should be crossed out and initialed by the writer. Some documents allow entries in pencil, but the document itself should state that pencil should be used and erasures are permitted.

Question the client-patient about any inconsistencies in the records. If something does not make sense in the case, ask. If you are dealing with a wrongful death case and the patient is deceased, ask family members. You may talk to health care providers other than those involved in the actual suit.

If you are dealing with a personal injury or products liability case involving a mishap, there are many people to investigate—anyone who may have witnessed the accident or other incident. Be industrious. Talk to anyone you can think of. If the case involved a boating accident, question witnesses at cabins on the beach and other boaters, among others. Talk to hosts and wait staff at restaurants. Sometimes you can glean the most material with intricate details from unlikely sources. Seemingly insignificant trivia could turn out to be the fact that makes your case. You never know who might shed light on the plaintiff's medical complaints as well. Talk to doctors, nurses, and technicians if the case allows. Speak with neighbors. Be resourceful.

## REGULATORY AGENCIES

There are regulatory agencies at every level in the health care profession. Their standards are set forth in their own publications. You may find out what is expected of nurses, nursing assistants, volunteer workers at the hospitals, custodians of record, pharmacy personnel, ambulance drivers, paramedics, emergency room personnel, chiropractors, dentists, hospital administrators, and others. Some of these agencies are listed below:

*NPDB (National Practitioner Data Bank)*, P.O. Box 6048, Camarillo, CA 93011–6048 (U.S. Department of Health and Human Services), (800) 767–6732. Collects information regarding the professional competence and conduct of physicians and dentists (mandatory inclusion) and other health care professionals (information from nurses in voluntary). The data bank contains information collected from peer review actions adversely affecting clinical privileges, licensing boards for incompetence or professional misconduct, and insurance companies upon settlement of malpractice claims. The information can be released only to hospitals and health care entities, state licensing boards, individuals requesting information about themselves, professional societies and researchers. Plaintiffs' attorneys can gain access to this information through the discovery process.

*JCAH (Joint Committee on Accreditation of Hospitals).* Publishes accreditation and licensure requirements of hospitals.

AMA *(American Medical Association)*, 535 N. Dearborn Street, Chicago, IL 60611, (312) 645–5000. Contains a data bank as well as annual directory of practice parameters for M.D.'s.

*AMA Division of Survey and Data Resources*, 515 North State Street, Chicago, IL 60610. Publishes the *American Medical Directory*.

*AOA (American Osteopathic Association)*, 212 E. Ohio Street, Chicago, IL 60611, (312) 280–5800. Contains a data bank and keeps practice parameters for D.O.'s.

*Federation of State Medical Boards*. Contains board action data bank (state board actions involving a physician's license).

*State board of medical examiners* in individual states. Responsible for issuing, suspending, revoking, and supervising physicians' licenses. Punitive actions may be taken for activities such as fraud, crime, malpractice, neglect, unprofessional conduct, and drug abuse.

*ABMS (American Board of Medical Specialists)*, 1 Rotary Center, Suite 805, Evanston, IL 60201, (708) 491–9091. Provides guidelines for Medical Specialties.

*American Chiropractic Association*, 1701 Clerendon Boulevard, Arlington, VA 22209, (703) 276–8800. Contains a data bank and practice parameters for chiropractors.

*American Dental Association*, 211 E. Chicago Avenue, Chicago IL 60611, (312) 440–2500. Contains a data bank and practice parameters for dentists.

*American Society of Hospital Pharmacies*, 7272 Wisconsin Avenue, Bethesda, MD 20814, (301) 657–3000. Contains practice parameters for hospital pharmacies.

*American Nurses Association*, 600 Maryland Avenue SW, #100 W, Washington, DC 20024–2571, (202) 651–7000. An organization which provides a data bank, practice parameters, and publications for nurses.

*National Council of State Boards of Nursing*. Contains a data bank involving nursing licenses.

*State board of nursing examiners* in individual states. Lists the status of individual nurses licensed to practice in that particular state.

Standards outside of the medical realm may prove just as important:

*CDC (Centers for Disease Control)*, Department of Health and Human Services, Atlanta, GA 30333, (404) 639–3311.

*OSHA (Occupational Safety and Health Administration)*, Department of Labor, 2000 Constitution Avenue NW, Washington, D.C. 20210, (202) 523–8151.

*EPA (Environmental Protection Agency)*, 401 M Street SW, Washington, D.C. 20210, (202) 260–4454.

*FDA (Food and Drug Administration)*, Department of Health and Human Services, 5600 Fishers Lane, Rockwell, MD 20857, (301) 443–2410

Additional standards pertaining to products liability cases may be found through the manufacturing company, including internal correspondence. Individual hospital by-laws cover in-house rules.

Another means by which you can obtain information is through the Medical Information Bureau, which receives its information from insurance companies. The bureau functions to determine risk and prevent fraud. It categorizes medical condition, lifestyle risk factors, and participation in hazardous activities. Patient identifiers are name, birthdate, birth state, occupation, and residency. Individuals can access this information through its Consumer Information Office, (617) 426–3660, P.O. Box 105, Essex Station, Boston, MA 02112.

## RESEARCHING THE LITERATURE

Complex medical cases often require researching medical literature. If you understand basic medical terminology and can find your way around a medical library, you are already halfway there. Medical research is certainly no more complex than legal research. Many law firms specializing in personal injury already have basic medical texts in the law library.

The following guide lists several fundamental medical sources that will get you started in any subject area.

### Drug References

The Federal Food, Drug, and Cosmetic Act regulates the manufacturing and processing of drugs within the United States. It categorizes substances within its domain as a drug, a new drug, or a device. The *United States Pharmacopoeia* is an official list of medicines and their properties. The *National Formulary* contains an official description of their ingredients.

Most prescription drugs are dispensed with product information provided by the manufacturer of the medication.

The *Physicians' Desk Reference* (Medical Economics Co.) provides an exhaustive overview of most drugs in use in the United States today. The drugs are indexed by product name, product category, and generic and chemical names. The drugs are also pictured with full-color illustrations. In the product information section, the medications are described in full: indications, usage, dosage, routes/methods/frequency/duration of administration, contraindications, adverse reactions, potential for drug dependence, overdosage, and precautions. The PDR also publishes a reference for nonprescription drugs, for generics, for ophthalmology, and for drug interactions. The PDR is revised annually, as new medications are constantly appearing on the market. Supplements are available updating the annual publication.

Since the information supplied in the PDR is provided by the pharmaceutical manufacturers themselves, it may not be as objective as *Facts and Comparisons*, which contains objective drug information, lists products by therapeutic categories and classifies them by use. Sections cover these topics:

- Group monographs and individual monographs.
- Administration and dosage.
- Actions, indications, and contraindications.
- Warnings and precautions.
- Drug interactions, adverse reactions, and overdoses.
- Patient information and cross references.

*Goodman and Gilman's Pharmacologic Basics of Therapeutics* is a textbook of pharmacology, toxicology, and therapeutics. It focuses on correlations of pharmacology with related medical sciences, drug actions and usage, and applications of pharmacodynamics to therapeutics.

*Compuserve* provides members with a reference service from the Consumer Reports Complete Drug Reference. If you are a member, type in "GO DRUGS" for access.

The *Internet* has a service listing over 4,000 drugs, with a comprehensive drug name cross-index. *http://www.rxlist.com/*

### Medicine Texts

The *Merck Manual of Diagnosis and Therapy* provides definitions and explanations of many diseases and conditions, arranged by body system. A concise text with a disease-oriented approach, it is a useful and easy reference.

The *CIBA Collection of Medical Illustrations*, prepared by Frank Netter, is unsurpassed. The CIBA series is a compilation of anatomical paintings depicting various physiological and pathological states. The text is provided by experts in their field. There are separate volumes for the nervous system, reproductive system, digestive system, endocrine system, heart, kidneys, urogenital system, and respiratory system. Not only are these informative, they make fantastic medical illustrations for presenting a case.

*Harrison's Principles of Internal Medicine* is the internist's encyclopedia. Almost every clinical problem imaginable is presented and investigated in as much depth as needed in initial review of an internal medicine case. The contents are generally broken down into the following categories:

Introduction to Clinical Medicine

Cardinal Manifestations of Disease: An Approach to Clinical Problems

Biological Considerations in the Approach to Clinical Medicine

Disorders Caused by Biological and Environmental Agents

Diseases of the Organ Systems

The *Accreditation Manual for Hospitals* by the Joint Commission for Accreditation of Hospitals discusses accreditation requirements for hospitals, quality assurance, licensure, and nonclinical aspects of health care delivery.

A reliable medical dictionary is an essential tool. *Dorland's* and *Stedman's* are the standards for most physicians. Some are illustrated. There are also medical-legal dictionaries, pocket dictionaries, medical dictionaries for lawyers, and other books.

An anatomy text is imperative to have on hand. The standard is always *Gray's Anatomy*. The *Anatomy Coloring Book* is a basic guide to anatomy. *Pansky's* is another concise, informative anatomical text. If you perform many personal injury cases, an orthopedic text would be a wise investment.

## DIAGNOSTIC CODES

Hospital medical records use standard diagnostic codes. In 1988, the Medicare Catastrophic Coverage Act made diagnostic coding mandatory. The standard manual that ascribes these codes is the *International Classification of Diseases*, published by the Practice Management Information Corporation. It is suggested for use in all clinical settings and is required for all diseases reported to any U.S. Public Health Service program. This system of coding ensures accurate diagnostic coding. Further, the diagnostic codes must support procedural codes, based on currently accepted standards of practice by the medical profession. Originally published by the World Health Organization, it continues to ascribe cause of death coding in the United States. It is updated annually in September.

The ICD classifies diseases and injuries into seventeen sections, using the following numeric codes:

| | |
|---|---|
| 001–139 | Infectious and Parasitic Diseases |
| 140–139 | Neoplasms |
| 240–279 | Endocrine, Nutritional and Metabolic Diseases, and Immunity Disorders |
| 280–289 | Diseases of the Blood and Blood-Forming Organs |
| 290–319 | Mental Disorders |
| 320–389 | Diseases of the Nervous System and Sense Organs |
| 390–459 | Diseases of the Circulatory System |
| 460–519 | Diseases of the Respiratory System |
| 520–579 | Diseases of the Digestive System |
| 580–629 | Diseases of the Genitourinary System |
| 630–676 | Complications of Pregnancy, Childbirth, and the Puerperium |
| 680–709 | Diseases of the Skin and Subcutaneous Tissue |
| 710–739 | Diseases of the Musculoskeletal System and Connective Tissue |
| 740–759 | Congenital Anomalies |
| 760–779 | Certain Conditions Originating in the Perinatal Period |
| 780–799 | Symptoms, Signs and Ill-defined Conditions |
| 800–999 | Injury and Poisoning |

Additionally, *V codes* are assigned when a person who is not sick encounters health services, for treatment for certain diseases (kidney dialysis, chemotherapy), or when a problem affects a person's health status but in itself is not a disease condition.

*E codes* classify external causes of injury and poisoning. They ascribe codes based on the specific cause of injury or poisoning. For example, E800–E848 involves accidents related to transport craft:

| | |
|---|---|
| E800–E807 | railway |
| E810–E819 | motor vehicle traffic accidents |
| E820–E825 | motor vehicle nontraffic accidents |
| E826–E829 | other road vehicles |
| E830–E838 | watercraft |
| E840–E845 | aircraft and spacecraft |

The diagnoses, codes, and specifications contained in the ICD.CM are very specific. It also contains glossaries, appendixes, indexes, and terminology. It can be obtained from: Practice Management Information Corp., 4727 Wilshire Boulevard, Suite 300, Los Angeles, CA 90010, (800) MED-SHOP.

## PROCEDURAL CODES

The CPT (*Physician's Current Procedural Terminology*), published by the American Medical Association, is a systematic listing and coding of procedures and services performed by physicians. Each procedure a physician performs on a patient, and *for which the patient is billed*, is identified with a five-digit code. These digits are broken down systemically as well:

| | |
|---|---|
| 00100–01999 | Anesthesiology |
| 10040–69979 | Surgery |
| 70010–79999 | Radiology (includes diagnostic ultrasound and nuclear medicine) |
| 80002–89399 | Pathology and Laboratory |
| 90701–99199 | Medicine |
| 99100–99140 | Anesthesiology |

These sections are divided into subsections. The terminology used has been developed to describe almost every procedure found in medical billing records. Modifiers are also used to indicate specific circumstances—for example:

- That a service has both a professional and technical component.
- A procedure was performed by more than one physician or in more than one location.
- A service has been increased or reduced.
- Only part of a service was performed.
- An adjunctive service was performed.
- A bilateral procedure was performed.

- A service or procedure was provided more than once.
- Unusual events occurred.

The CPT is available from the Department of Coding and Nomenclature, American Medical Association, 515 North State Street, Chicago, IL 60610.

## MEDICOLEGAL DECISIONS

Citation Publishing Corporation in Long Grove, IL (800) 626–5210, publishes a semimonthly newsletter encompassing 20 summaries of key issues in medical malpractice cases. The information comes from published appellate court decisions. The compilation of these summaries was initially undertaken by the American Medical Association general counsel. Now this medicolegal digest is available by subscription for $130 per year. It can also be found in libraries and through AMA published materials.

## MEDICAL LIBRARIES

Access to a medical library—found at a medical school, a teaching hospital, or a large community hospital—is essential.

To use it, go to the reference section, where you will find the most current basic texts in your area of inquiry. Ask the reference librarian for assistance in finding a reference text. Always start with general works, and narrow your search as you go along.

Although specialty texts may help to define particulars, the books and journals could send you on tangents that will draw you into minute details. Of course, some cases may require getting more detail than the general references provide. Start at the card catalog or computer, and define your search. You may have to browse the shelves to locate specific texts in a certain discipline. Make sure your time is spent wisely in the specialty texts. Focus your search. Know as precisely as possible what details you are querying.

Spend most of your time in the stacks of literature. A good medical library will have domestic and foreign journals, through which you will find the most informative and current information available. An invaluable tool found in most medical libraries is the *Cumulated Index Medicus*, published by the National Library of Medicine. This is the most comprehensive bibliography of medical literature available. Medical subject headings are assigned to each article and indexed accordingly.

If you have found an article that the local medical library does not carry, ask the librarian to check the nearest regional medical library for a loan:

New York Academy of Medicine
Greater Northeastern Regional Medical Library Program

2 East 103d Street, New York, NY 10029
(212) 876–8763; (800) 242–RML1; fax (212) 722–7650

University of Maryland Health Sciences Library
Southestern/Atlantic Regional Medical Library Services
111 South Greene Street, Baltimore, MD 21201
(301) 328–2855; (800) 638–6093; fax (301) 328–8403

University of Illinois at Chicago Library of the Health Sciences
Greater Midwest Regional Medical Library Network
P.O. Box 7509, Chicago, IL 60680
(312) 996–2464; fax (312) 996–2226

University of Nebraska Medical Center
Midcontinental Regional Medical Library Program
600 South 42d Street, Omaha, NE 68198–7606
(402) 559–4326; (800) 633–7654; fax (402) 559–5498

University of Texas Health Science Center
South Central Regional Medical Library Program
P.O. Box 20036, Houston, TX 77225
(713) 792–4875

Southwestern Medical Center at Dallas
5323 Harry Hines Boulevard, Dallas, TX 75235–9049
(214) 688–2085; fax (214) 688–3277

Health Sciences Library and Information Center at the University of Washington
Pacific Northwest Regional Health Sciences Library Service
University of Washington, SB-22, Seattle, WA 98195
(206) 543–8262; fax (206) 543–8066

Louise Darling Biomedical Library, UCLA
Pacific Southwest Regional Medical Library Service
10833 Le Conte Avenue, Los Angeles, CA 90024–1798
(213) 825–1200; (800) 669–0144; fax (213) 206–8675

If the publication is not available through any of the regional libraries listed here, contact the National Library of Medicine.

## MEDICAL DATABASES

Some libraries offer access to the computer files of the National Library of Medicine through various computer-assisted medical research tools. Some libraries have access to a local medical research database for members (i.e., TexSearch). Computer files of the National Library of Medicine, MEDLARS (Medical Literature Analysis and Retrieval System), offer access to almost 50 databases—for example:

AIDSLINE. Dates back to 1980 and discusses AIDS and related topics. Coverage includes both clinical and research information, health care policy, technical and government reports, meeting abstracts, and journal articles. Updated weekly.

BIOETHICSLINE. Covers the ethical, legal, and public policy issues surrounding health care and biomedical research. These bibliographic citations include topics like euthanasia, organ donation and transplantation, and patients' rights. Updated bimonthly.

CANCERLIT. Contains almost 1 million references and abstracts to published cancer literature. Topics include clinical and experimental therapies; chemical, viral, and other agents that cause cancer; and mechanisms of carcinogenesis.

DIOGENES. Provides access to Food and Drug Administration regulatory information regarding pharmaceuticals and medical devices. Updated weekly.

HEALTH. Covers topics in hospital administration, personnel, planning, licensure, accreditation, organization, and health care delivery. Produced by the American Hospital Association. Updated monthly.

HDA (Health Devices Alerts). Has a directory of reported medical device problems, evaluations, hazards, and recalls. Topics include problems with medical equipment, implantable devices, and disposable medical products. Derived from various medical, legal and technical literature.

HSDB (Hazardous Substances Data Bank). Covers government and technical reports, and text excerpts regarding chemical toxicity and the biomedical effects of chemicals.

MEDLINE. Contains over 7 million biomedical references to articles published in 4,000 international journals. These cover topics in medicine, surgery, dentistry, nursing, and health care management from 1966 to the present. MEDLINE is the source of the printed volumes of *Index Medicus*, the *Index to Dental Literature*, and the *International Nursing Index.*

PDQ (Physician Data Query). Publishes advances in cancer treatments and clinical trials, ongoing investigational protocols, conventional treatment, directories of physicians and organizations involved in cancer care. Designed by the National Cancer Institute.

SEDBASE. Publishes literature on every known side effect of every known drug currently in use.

TOXLINE. Updates information monthly with the toxic effects of drugs and chemicals, as well as their biochemical, physiological, and pharmacological effects.

If you have access to a computer with a modem, you can subscribe to Compuserve, which offers PaperChase (800) 638–8480, an online information service that helps you search MEDLINE, HEALTH, AIDSLINE, and CANCERLIT. References are updated weekly and are available 24 hours a day. You may perform new searches, print and reference old searches, verify references, and set up custom lists. You can search by subject, author, or journal title. You can pool references from two or more lists, scan through the references, print abstracts, or order the photocopied full-text articles.

On the Internet, you may access an HIV/AIDS literature database at: http://www.ama-assn.org.

Other information vendors that include but are not limited to medical databases are:

BRS Information Technologies, (800) 955–0406

Dialog Information Services, (800) 334–2564

National Technical Information Services, (800) 638–8480

Mead Data Central, (800) 227–4908

Strategize your search well. Organize the data you are going to query before going online. MeSH (Medical Subject Headings) for the *Index Medicus* is broken down into five major groups: (1) parts of the body, (2) plant, animal or microbe, (3) condition or disorder, (4) drug or chemical, and (5) diagnostic or therapeutic procedure.

Subheadings are used to define or qualify a search. Take a medical subject heading, followed by a slash (/), and a list of all subheadings will follow. Each subheading is given a two-letter abbreviation, assigned by the National Library of Medicine (AE = adverse effects; MX = major topic).

The search parameters progress from general to specific. Shortcuts you may use to take up less time online are to stack your commands, limit your search options, update an old search, and exclude references.

## DOCUMENTING THE CASE

Before you begin your research, you must first have a complete summary of the issues involved in the case. You may have to provide evidence to support certain medical contentions, such as advising an attorney of specific disease states that have arisen from silicone posoning, or answer what types of tests should be ordered for silicone-induced autoimmune disorder. You may have uncovered some evidence of a preexisting condition in your client that you will have to try to work to your advantage.

## AREAS OF MEDICAL SPECIALTY

When you know what type of case you are working on, begin your search generally. You should already have access to a general text to get your starting point. Next decide what type of specialty you might want to research for reference guides. Specific areas of study and subspecialty will overlap. You will find journal articles and periodicals in the following areas of specialty:

*Allergy/immunology*: Treatment of allergies and the study of immune responses.

*Anesthesiology*: The administration of drugs during surgery. Subspecialties of anesthesia include acute and chronic pain management.

*Cardiology*: The study of and treatment of heart conditions.

*Cardiovascular surgery*: Surgical treatment of heart diseases such as coronary artery bypass grafts.

*Chiropractic*: A system of therapeutics that attempts to restore function of the body through structural manipulation.

*Dermatology*: The medical specialty concerned with the diagnosis and treatment of conditions of the skin, hair, scalp and nails, including acne, funguses, parasites, moles, and skin cancers.

*Endocrinology*: The study and treatment of the body's glandular system—internal organs that secrete hormones—and the endocrine system's role in the physiology of the body.

*Family practice*: General health and wellness.

*Gastroenterology*: Study and treatment of the digestive system: oral cavity, pharynx, esophagus, stomach, liver, gallbladder, pancreas, duodenum, small intestine (jejunum and ileum), appendix, large intestine (ascending, transverse, and descending colon), and rectum. Conditions treated in this area of specialty are those that affect the digestion and absorption of food products and the elimination of wastes.

*Gynecology*: The study of the female reproductive system and treatment of diseases of the female genital tract.

*Hematology*: The study of the blood, blood disorders, and blood cell production.

*Internal medicine*: Study and treatment of disease conditions of the internal systems of the body that do not (yet) require surgical intervention.

*Neonatology*: The art and science of diagnosis and treatment of conditions affecting the newborn infant.

*Nephrology*: The study of the kidney—its anatomy, physiology, and pathology, including kidney dialysis treatment.

*Neurology*: The branch of medicine that deals with the study, diagnosis, and treatment of disorders of the nervous system that do not require surgery.

*Obstetrics*: The branch of medicine that deals with the management of pregnancy, labor, delivery, and the puerperium (the state following labor and delivery).

*Oncology*: The study of and treatment of tumors, and the treatment of postsurgical cancer patients. Oncologists provide chemotherapeutic agents for the elimination of cancer. Radiation oncology deals with the x-ray treatment of tumors.

*Ophthalmology*: Specializing in the diagnosis and treatment (optical, medical and surgical) of diseases and defects of the eye and related structures.

*Orthopedics*: A branch of surgery concerned with the skeletal system, including muscles, bones, and joints. Seeks to preserve and restore the function of skeletal structures and articulations.

*Osteopathy*: A study of manipulative medicine focusing on the interrelationships of body structure and function. This system of therapy is founded on the belief that the body will heal itself when given the appropriate therapeutic assistance. It utilizes generally accepted physical, medicinal, and surgical methods of diagnosis and therapy while emphasizing the importance of normal body mechanics.

*Otorhinolaryngology*: Most commonly known as ENT, this specialty is concerned with the medicinal and surgical treatment of the diseases of the head, ears, eyes, nose, and throat.

*Pathology*: Deals with the functional and structural changes in tissues and organs that cause or are a result of disease. A pathologist examines the gross and microscopic detail of the nature of disease. Pathologists perform autopsies.

*Pediatrics*: The branch of medicine that treats children—their development and care and prevention of disease.

*Physiatry*: A form of rehabilitative medicine utilizing physical agents such as light, heat, cold, water, and electricity, or with mechanical apparatus. The intent is to restore function and motion of the body after injury.

*Plastic surgery*: Also reconstructive surgery. Restores damaged body tissues or performs revisions of existing characteristics.

*Podiatry*: Deals with the study and care of the foot, including medical and surgical treatment.

*Proctology*: Concerned with disorders of the rectum and anus.

*Psychiatry*: The study of medicine dealing with the treatment and prevention of mental and emotional illness. Psychiatrists are involved in the treatment of chemical dependency also. This field includes the use of pharmaceutical drugs, electroconvulsive therapy, and surgery.

*Pulmonology*: A subspecialty of internal medicine dealing with the anatomy, physiology, and pathology of the lungs. A pulmonologist deals with many critical care patients.

*Radiology*: The reading and interpretation of scanning procedures including x-rays, CT scans, MRI scans, and therapeutic modalities such as radiation oncology.

*Reproductive medicine*: Deals with assisting women and couples who are having difficulty conceiving. Infertility studies are performed, along with artificial insemination, donor implantation, and new advances in conception.

*Rheumatology*: The study of disorders marked by inflammation, degeneration, or metabolic derangement of the connective tissue structures, especially the joints and related fibrous tissue.

*Surgery*: Performing operations. General surgeons perform a multitude of interventional operations and removals. Subspecialties include neurosurgery, orthopedic surgery, pediatric surgery, cardiac surgery, plastic surgery, thoracic surgery, vascular surgery, and hand surgery.

*Urology*: The study and treatment of diseases of the urinary tract in males and females and the male genital system.

Medical specialties and subspecialties have their own journals. It is a good idea to scan the journal articles before you copy them. If the information is pertinent to your inquiry, copy it. You most likely will need to quote the article later when presenting your case.

Each specialty has its own organization that board certifies its members. You may contact these organizations for their standards regarding membership. They are listed by specialty in Chapter 5.

Chapter 5

# Medical Experts and Consultants

Health care liability claims often require the plaintiff's attorney to file an affidavit attesting that a written opinion has been obtained from an expert, showing that (1) The expert is a licensed physician who has knowledge of the accepted standards of care for the diagnosis, care, or treatment of the illness, injury, or condition involved in the claim and (2) The acts or omissions of the physician or health care provider were negligent and a proximate cause of the injury, harm, or damages claimed.

It is a good practice to submit an affidavit only when you are certain to designate the expert on whose opinion the affidavit is based. When you have designated a testifying expert, rules governing their designation allow discovery of (1) the subject matter on which the expert is expected to testify, (2) the expert's mental impressions and opinions, and (3) the facts known to the expert that relate to or form the basis of his or her mental impressions and opinions through standard request for disclosure, deposition, or court-ordered report.

## USING TREATING PHYSICIANS AS EXPERTS

The most important witness you may present in a medical negligence case is often a treating physician. A treating physician with knowledge of the alleged negligence who is willing to provide evidence that a previous treating physician performed below the standards of care (plaintiff's expert) or within the accepted standards of care (defendant's expert) will be your best witness. When deposing treating physicians, particular care must be taken not to disclose sensitive, privileged information that has no relevance to the issues in the lawsuit. Confidential communication between a patient and physician (who is not a defendant in the lawsuit) is privileged. If such information is revealed, it may discredit the physician who disclosed it.

In other injury cases as well, a subsequent treating physician may become your greatest expert. In orthopedic injuries, a physician who becomes involved with a patient soon after an accident may be of immense value in describing the nature of the damage when first consulted, what treatments have been advised and/or performed, other consultations, and the extent of permanent injuries, if any.

The physician may have performed multiple procedures to try to restore the patient to the condition he or she was in before the accident. An orthopedic surgeon may testify as to what the patient's medical status was when he or she was first consulted and what further operations or follow-up care may be required as well. On the defense side, a physician may have been consulted who determined that the plaintiff had no real injuries, required no treatment, or had achieved maximum medical benefit.

Psychiatrists, therapists, and clinical psychologists may become involved in treating the patient and assessing psychological and emotional effects of the injury, if any. Neuropsychiatric tests should be conducted when appropriate. The psychological expert will report the interpretation.

As a rule, most physicians are not anxious to testify in a malpractice claim against one of their colleagues. Doctors in practice are painfully aware that someday they may become a defendant. A delicate approach may reveal any sense of hesitation the physician may harbor. A hostile expert witness will do irreparable harm.

Medical cases are often so complex that they require review by medical consultants to determine if there is a case, develop theories of liability, research medical issues, assist in understanding the exact nature of the injuries for settlement, and identify what type of expert will need to be scouted and retained.

The experts must be qualified in the topic in question. Standards of care have been established for every health care profession. The American Medical Association publishes standards for practicing physicians, the American Nurses Association publishes its own standards of care, as do the American Osteopathic Association, the American Dental Association, and others. You may have to research what standards of care emergency medical technicians are required to follow in your state if ambulance or transport care is in question.

Evaluate your experts by the following criteria:

- Their familiarity with the standards of care in the specialty.
- Their history of testifying.
- Their history of any licensure suspensions, revocations, limitations of practice, suspension of hospital privileges, and so on.
- The impression you think they would make on a jury: Put yourself in the position of

a juror. Ask yourself if you would believe what this expert was telling you if you were trying to reach an objective decision about the case.

## MEDICAL TRAINING

All physicians go to medical school after they complete their undergraduate training. Although the core curriculum varies from school to school, medical students must pass courses in the basic sciences and clinical sciences. Then they do their externships, or clinical rotations. They are granted their medical doctorate degree after this four-year process. They also must take and pass the national boards, two exams in the basic and clinical sciences before they may practice medicine. Then the physician begins an internship program and/or a residency training program in a chosen specialty. Some specialties also include fellowships in study.

Every specialty in medicine publishes its own standards of practice. Each medical specialty has at least one specialty board that certifies physicians if they meet certain criteria. First, they must be board eligible. Eligibility requires that the physician has completed a specified residency course and has the specified amount of experience required before taking a comprehensive and extensive written test about the field of practice. Questions for board examinations come from physicians who are already board certified in the field. If the written board exam is passed, then the physician may sit for the oral examination which is much more subjective. Once the physician becomes board certified, this may make him or her eligible to become subspecialty board certified.

## THE MEDICAL EXPERT

A testifying expert should be board certified in the area of concern. If the case deals with renal failure and is very complex, you should have a board-certified nephrologist. If the case deals with a misdiagnosed blood test or urinalysis by a family practitioner, which should have been detected by any reasonable treating physician as indicating renal failure, you may want to retain a board-certified family practitioner. It is unwise to overstep level of specialty. In a case claiming malpractice where a hospital pathologist performed an autopsy in question, try to find another hospital-based practitioner who performs autopsies regularly. If you locate instead a pathologist whose only experience is in a laboratory viewing urological slides, he or she may not make an effective testifying expert for a poisoning claim.

Nursing also has its own specialty certifications—for example, in psychiatric nursing, geriatric nursing, nephrology nursing, nurse anesthetists, and nursing administration. Keep your experts along the same level as the defendant health care practitioner. This is true in the practice of dentistry as well. An orthodontist would not be a first choice of experts against a general dentist.

When you are representing plaintiffs in a medical malpractice claim, the physician expert's opinion will need to convince the jury *beyond a reasonable probability* that the defendant(s) acted below the accepted standard of care.

### Finding a Medical Expert

If a treating physician cannot or will not help you out as an expert witness, ask the physician for recommendations.

Determine what the individual case needs are. It may be effective to find a local expert. A community resident may have more influence on a jury and also make it appear that you did not have to look too far to find someone willing to help. You may, however, have to consult experts at teaching institutions out of state to get the assistance you need. Some attorneys use a local physician in low-profile cases and secure a nationally known expert for a heavily-involved case, especially if the opponent is bringing in world-renowned experts in the top of their field.

After ensuring the expert has the necessary qualifications, your next goal is to determine whether he or she is credible. Someone who testifies for a living or supports his or her income as a professional expert loses a lot of credibility on the stand. You can count on opposing counsel asking what your expert is personally getting out of the deal. Teaching institutions are a good source for credible experts. Academicians do not necessarily need referrals from other physicians and may not be so leery of working with attorneys. They are also more up to date on current studies and cutting-edge technology.

### Medical Authors as Experts

In a large medical malpractice case, we will assume you have researched pertinent medical points in the medical library. If you have researched specialty texts in the topic, check with the author. Ask authors of medical articles what they think about your case. Run through the bibliographies as well. This may be your best source for an extremely reputable expert.

### Other Sources

In some cases your best strategy is to start cold, calling physicians of whom you have personal knowledge or have found in a medical directory or telephone book. Tell them the nature of the lawsuit and ask if they might be interested in reviewing your case. If not, call the next one. Persistence will often pay off, and once someone assists you, that person may be willing to be consulted on a later case.

In addition to the American Medical Association's medical directory, the American Board of Medical Specialties publishes a compendium of certified medical specialists:

American Board of Medical Specialties
One Rotary Center, Suite 805
Evanston, ILL 60201
(708) 491–9091

Individual medical specialty organizations can serve as a resource too:

American Board of Allergy and Immunology
(215) 349–9466

American Society of Anesthesiologists
(312) 825–5586

American Board of Anesthesiology
(203) 522–9857

American Association of Blood Banks
(703) 528–8200

American Chiropractic Association
(703) 276–8800

American Academy of Clinical Psychiatry
(619) 450–2675

American Board of Colon and Rectal Surgery
(313) 295–1740

American Academy of Cosmetic Surgery
(213) 459–5832

American Board of Cosmetic Surgery
(213) 653–7700

American Dental Association
(312) 440–2500

American Academy of Dermatology
(708) 869–3954

American Board of Dermatology
(313) 871–8739

American Board of Emergency Medicine
(517) 332–4800

American Academy of Facial Plastic and Reconstructive Surgery
(202) 842–4500

American Academy of Family Physicians
(816) 333–9700

American Board of Family Practice
(606) 269–5626

American Board of Forensic Psychiatry
(301) 539–0872

American Society for Surgery of the Hand
(303) 755–4588

American Academy of Hospital Attorneys
(312) 280–6601

American Board of Internal Medicine
(312) 280–6601

American Society of Internal Medicine
(202) 289–1700

American Society of Law and Medicine
(617) 262–4990

Society of Medical Jurisprudence
(914) 723–0005

American Academy of Medical-Legal Analysis
(702) 385–6886

American Society of Neuroimaging
(716) 886–3467

American Academy of Neurological Surgery
(617) 726–8581

American Association of Neurological Surgery
(713) 790–6015

American Academy of Neurological and Orthopaedic Surgeons
(702) 385–6886

American Board of Nuclear Medicine
(213) 825–6787

American Board of Obstetrics and Gynecology
(206) 547–4884

American College of Obstetrics and Gynecology
(202) 638–5577

American Academy of Occupational Medicine
(312) 228–6850

American Board of Ophthalmology
(215) 645–1175

American Association of Oral and Maxillofacial Surgeons
(312) 642–6446

American Academy of Orthopaedic Surgeons
(312) 823–7186

American Board of Orthopaedic Surgery
(312) 664–9444

American Osteopathic Association
(312) 280–5800

American Osteopathic Board of General Practitioners
(312) 635–8477

American Academy of Otolaryngology
(713) 528–6200

American Board of Pain Medicine
(708) 965–2776

American Board of Pathology
(813) 286–2444

American Academy of Pediatrics
(312) 228–5005

American Board of Pediatrics
(919) 929–0461

American Society of Hospital Pharmacies
(301) 657–3000

American Board of Physical Medicine and Rehabilitation
(507) 282–1776

American Physical Therapy Association
(703) 684–2782

American Board of Preventive Medicine
(513) 278–6915

American Board of Psychiatry and Neurology
(708) 945–7900

American Psychiatric Association
(202) 682–6000

American Board of Plastic Surgery
(215) 587–9322

American Society of Plastic and Reconstructive Surgeons
(312) 856–1818

American Podiatric Medical Association
(202) 537–4900

American Academy of Child Psychiatry
(202) 966–7300

American Board of Psychiatry and Neurology
(708) 945–7900

American Psychotherapy Association
(305) 689–3787

American Board of Radiology
(313) 645–0600

Radiological Society of North America
(312) 920–2670

American Board of Surgery
(215) 568–4000

American Board of Thoracic Surgery
(708) 475–1520

American Thoracic Society
(212) 315–8700

American Board of Urology
(313) 646–9720

American Urological Association
(301) 727–1100

*Medical Malpractice Verdicts, Settlements and Experts*, a national publication, has immense value in finding experts and evaluating medical malpractice cases. This reporter, published monthly, provides a summary of malpractice settlements (including amounts), malpractice litigation news, and experts. The reporter is listed by specialty of practice and allows you to evaluate cases similar to your own. The same company also publishes an annual directory of medical experts who appear in the previous year's issues of the reporter. A subscription to the publication runs from $226 to $247 annually. The address is 901 Church Street, Nashville, TN 37203, (800) 298–6288.

This service also provides custom searches starting at $20 per case, for a maximum cost of $250. It will find cases similar to yours and send you material on each case it has reported making a similar allegation, which will include names of attorneys and experts and give an idea of the value of the case. It will perform searches for experts and provide their testifying history. (This information may be useful in evaluating your opponent's experts as well.)

If you have exhausted your research using the methods above and still cannot find an expert, look into jury verdict services. These are published locally and identify experts used for both plaintiff and defense. Bear in mind, however, that you may run into professional experts utilizing this method. Check with your local bar association for the jury verdict service published in your area.

Another possibility is a physician consulting service, which will charge a flat rate to review the case and find an expert if they feel it warrants one. And legal publications list experts who advertise. (Remember that they are advertising.)

You should be able to provide potential consulting physicians with an oral synopsis of the situation if you have all your facts. Then they may be able to determine if they would support you. If they seem supportive, forward the case to them. It is unwise to send voluminous—and costly—medical records to bog down a physician initially. The person may spend hours reviewing your medical files, just to tell you that he or she cannot appear on your behalf—and charge a large fee for the review.

When you have found a suitable expert, provide the person with the entire medical record for review. The witness will lose credibility if he or she is unaware of any situation pertinent to his or her involvement in the case. A good expert will give you an honest opinion at all times, even when the truth may hurt your case. A great expert will help you turn a flaw into an asset. Approach your case together; the better your relationship is, the finer the presentation will be. You and your staff will spend much time with the medical expert if the case proceeds toward deposition, mediation, and trial. Do not allow surprises to catch your team unaware. Do your homework regarding your opponent's experts and expect that they have done the same. They will do all they can to discredit your expert.

## OTHER EXPERTS

Chemical exposure cases may require a toxicologist with a doctorate. Products liability cases may rely on the testimony of engineers. Economists are often consulted with regard to estimating the value of a case, determining specific damages, and establishing estimated monetary merit. Whatever your more obscure requirements might entail, the same rules apply for nonmedical experts.

When your expert has been determined, spell out the requirements of your affiliation. Define the exact scope of services you wish to be provided. Do you want a written report as part of a package deal? Will the expert require a retainer, or will he or she allow contingency payment? Outline your conditions with a detailed description of the scope of the work to be performed, when the work will be needed, how much it will cost, and how any extra costs will be billed.

Part II

# Individual Case Scenarios

## Chapter 6

# Medical Malpractice

Medical malpractice cases demand litigation savvy like no other, yet a malpractice lawsuit that is handled efficiently from beginning to end can be the most rewarding compensation in litigation for plaintiffs and the most satisfying defense work.

Claims of medical malpractice typically arise from one of the following areas: (1) missed diagnoses, (2) misdiagnoses, (3) procedural mishaps, and (4) informed consent failure. The physician's major theme in patient management is always *primum non nocere* (first, do no harm).

It is not always easy to determine which cases will make meritorious lawsuits. An experienced medical records review should be able to differentiate whether the outcome results from a doctor's action or failure to act, or if a negative result was inevitable. Analyzing cases that stem from a natural occurrence are much more difficult to opine. A good rule of thumb when making a determination is to get answers to the following questions:

1. Assuming the eventual outcome was not the result of genetics, was this a disease process that would have had a more favorable outcome with proper intervention?
2. Did the client consult help for a related problem or any associated symptom or condition? Was this treated with less than acceptable methods or against acceptable medical procedure?
3. Would a reasonable physician under the same or similar circumstances have made another diagnostic decision? Did this failure constitute a breach in the standard of care?
4. Would proper diagnosis and treatment have made a difference in the outcome?

If your medical consultant can answer yes to these four questions, you have a reasonable probability of a good malpractice case, all other factors considered.

An *untoward result* can be defined as an unfavorable outcome following a medical procedure. The patient may be dissatisfied with the result of the procedure, the patient and her or his physician may be displeased with the result, or the result may require further medical or surgical intervention. The physician's standard is measured using criteria established in a 1898 landmark case, *Pike v. Honsinger* (155 N.Y. 201, N.E. 760, 762) defining the physician's conduct:

> A physician, by taking charge of a case, impliedly represents that he possesses, and the law places upon him the duty of possessing, that reasonable degree of learning and skill that is ordinarily possessed by physicians and surgeons in the locality where he practices, and which is ordinarily regarded by those conversant with the employment as necessary to qualify him to engage in the business of practicing medicine (and surgery). Upon consenting to treat a patient it becomes his duty to use reasonable care and diligence in the exercise of his skill in the application of his learning to accomplish the purpose for which he was employed. He is under the further obligation to use his best judgment in exercising his skill and applying his knowledge. The law holds him liable for an injury to his patient resulting from want of the requisite knowledge and skill, or the omission to exercise care, or the failure to use his best judgment.

Medical negligence claims are filed far in abundance of their merit. Physicians, hospitals, and health care providers in general have good insurance coverage and liquid assets. Unmeritorious claims are sometimes filed hastily and without enough medical knowledge to carry the case through—and the costs of pursuing a malpractice claim can become astronomical. Therefore, good practice is to have a medical consultant review a potential medical malpractice claim before it is filed to avoid unnecessary costs, embarrassment, and possible sanctions or counterclaims. Some states require that an attorney filing a medical negligence claim have a physician's attestation that the claim meets certain elements required by that state to file the cause of action.

A claim for medical malpractice must contain the following elements:

1. Standards of care must be determined applicable to the incident that is alleged to have caused the injury. Standards of care are defined as the minimum acceptable level of care provided by a health care professional with similar education and training under the same or similar circumstances during the time when the incident occurred. These are established within the medical specialties. Each specialty board sets forth its own guidelines. See the AMA's *Annual Directory of Practice Parameters* for the year in question. Chapter 5 in this book lists the specialty boards. Current guidelines can also be found within applicable professional journals.
2. The standard of care must have been breached and the defendant acted below the standard of care.
3. The breach in the standard of care caused damage or resulted in an injury.
4. The extent of damages caused to the plaintiff by the defendant must be determined.

A sample attestation follows:

**Attestation**

My name is ______, M.D. I am a physician duly licensed to practice medicine in the State of ______, I am board certified in and currently practice ______, and I am familiar with the accepted standards of care for ____________. I have reviewed the entire medical records on ____________. Based upon my review of the above-identified items, my education, training and experience as a physician, and my familiarity with the accepted standards of care for conduct of physicians, it is my opinion that the acts of ____________, M.D., ______________________________, ____________ and ______________________________ were below the accepted standards of care. It is my further opinion that the acts by ____________, M.D., were the proximate cause of damages to ____________.

______________________________,
M.D.

It is up to the plaintiff to establish, by a preponderance of the evidence, that the defendant was negligent by acting or failing to act, failing to provide treatment within the accepted standards of care, or deviating from accepted medical practice in a way that was the substantial cause of the plaintiff's injuries. Determining the extent of damages—past, present, and future—is the craft of a skillful litigation team.

## INFORMED CONSENT

A cause of action may be filed due to a lack of *informed consent*, defined as requiring a physician, prior to performing a procedure, to inform and explain, in terms that the patient can understand, the foreseeable risks and results of the procedure, as well as the alternatives that a reasonable medical practitioner under similar circumstances would have made known. State laws vary in this definition and in how much weight it carries. Some states do not recognize this doctrine at all; others require only that a patient would not have elected to have a particular surgery if he or she was adequately informed of the risks involved. Causation issues that will have to be resolved are whether a prudent person in the position of the patient would have decided to proceed with the operation if sufficiently informed of the risks and alternatives.

There are also situations in which a physician advises the patient and/or family members to have a medical or surgical procedure performed and informs the person of the associated risks, and the patient elects *not* to undergo the procedure. If the operation proceeds in spite of the patient and/or family's refusal, not only is this a frank violation of informed consent, it may be considered *battery*. In this situation—if the patient elects not to have the procedure—the following type of form should be found in the medical records:

**Refusal of Treatment**

Date ____________________

Time ____________________

I, ______________, request that ______________ not be performed on me during this hospitalization, notwithstanding that such treatment, in the opinion of my attending physician, Dr. ______________, may deem necessary to preserve life or promote recovery. I hereby release the hospital, its personnel, and my attending physician from any responsibility whatever for any unfavorable reactions or any untoward results due to my refusal to permit this treatment, and I fully understand the possible consequences, explained to me by my physician, of such refusal on my part.

____________________________________

Signature of patient

______________ ______________

Witness Witness

Hospitals and clinics usually have preprinted consent forms regarding the specific operation and its risks. The health care practitioner may also make an entry in the medical records such as: "I have informed Ms. Doe of the following risks of the procedure up to and including ________ and the alternatives to the procedure. She says that she understands the risks and alternatives and still wishes to proceed."

Some cases, such as plastic surgery, may be more difficult to prove, as the procedure for the most part is viewed as elective and voluntary and wholely by choice of the patient. Defenses to these actions may be that the procedure and its inherent risks were too commonly known to require disclosure or that the patient authorized the procedure in spite of the risks.

## STATUTES OF LIMITATIONS

Most states have statutes of limitations of two years from the date of the incident or two years from the time in which the person became aware of the injury or damage he or she believes stemmed from the medical negligence. Few states have a one-year statue of limitations. In some states, obstetrical malpractice allows the delivered child 18 years in which to file suit.

Limitation periods may be challenged or appealed with sufficient cause. Cases in which the patient or the deceased patient's estate becomes aware of malpractice years after the statute has passed may be granted. A cataract operation performed in Michigan in 1963 resulted in the loss of one of the patient's eyes. He awakened during (insufficient) general anesthesia and rubbed his eye, during which some of the vitreous humor was squeezed out. The subsequent loss of his eye was not discovered to be connected to this incident until the patient reviewed his medical records in 1988. In 1989 the trial court granted summary judgment to the physician and hospital; on appeal the state supreme court reversed the decision, saying that the statute of limitations began to run not at the time of the surgery but when the error in care was discovered in 1988 (*Chase v. Sabin*, 516 N.W.2d 60 [Mich. Supreme Court, May 17, 1994]).

## LOSS OF CHANCE FOR RECOVERY

A claim for loss of chance of recovery by a physician's negligence occurs when a physician deprives a patient of a significant chance to recover more fully. In states where this doctrine is recognized, the loss of a significant chance of recovery must contain these elements:

1. The lost chance must be significant.
2. The injury resulting from the negligence must be substantial.
3. Damages should be computed proportionally to the percentage effect on the lost chance.

## PURSUING A CLAIM

The medical records of a potential plaintiff should always be reviewed before taking a medical malpractice. Sometimes attorneys file suit prematurely in order not to miss a statute deadline, but ideally they will have the case reviewed by a medical specialist before investing in it. Assessing a claim's potential assets and liabilities takes experience. The costs required to pursue the case (filing suit; obtaining records; research; attorneys', experts', and consultants' fees; trial preparation; and general overhead) must be weighed against potential recoverable damages.

Rejecting a case is not easy for the plaintiff or the attorney. And because clients have a legal right to pursue a cause of action against their attorney for failing to advise them adequately about their claim, the attorney must notify them of legal specifics when deciding not to pursue their claim.

When initiating a malpractice claim, the plaintiff's attorney will need to talk with the injured party to determine what is being alleged. In many cases this involves the death of a loved one, and the family cannot be relied on to rehash details of the event leading to the death. In any case, you must have a starting point. You have to know what you are looking for if you have stacks of medical records to weed through.

Once you have determined the basis for the claim, you must order all pertinent medical records. Sometimes the patient will already have obtained these records from the health care facility.

## THE MEDICAL SUMMARY

A good practice is to chronologize the records so you can write up a summary quickly and in order. Scan through the records to become familiar with them. Put them in an order that you are comfortable with (unless they must remain in a numerical order in which the hospital provided them to you). Have adhesive notes handy to mark significant pages with comments. Then organize them, and keep your system consistent. Organize chronologically either earliest to latest or latest to earliest, depending on your preference and the type of case. Make notes as you page through each document. Make sure you at least peruse each record. You must not miss a thing. Small items may become immensely important as the case progresses. You will be able to narrow your comments as you go along and become familiar with the nature of the case.

It is a good practice to look for entries like "allergies." Make sure the patient had no allergies to medications given. If the patient was diabetic, see if it is noted in the chart. Look to ensure vital signs were taken. In surgical cases, determine the average baseline blood pressure. The medical staff should be alerted to danger for any unexplained drop of 20 percent or more below baseline. Respiratory rate should be noted as well. If a patient suddenly has a respiratory rate of 35–40, this reading should signal an alert clinician to intubate. Note any suspicious gaps in the records. Pay particular attention to entries made around shift change times. The midnight or late shift is when a large portion of malpractice claims originate. The majority of malfeasance complaints arise between 6:00 P.M. and 1:00 A.M. on weekends and holidays, when ancillary services are least available.

Creating a quality medical chronology is an art well worth mastering. You can develop an instinctive sense of a case and apply it to your reviews. Consider yourself a historian. You are to determine what actions are significant and write them up in a summary—a succinct working copy of the medical records. There will be a discernable story, and the records themselves will become simply a reference. You will provide a road map through an otherwise intimidating mass of medical jargon.

Be specific and concise, for verbose medical summaries defeat their purpose. Every pertinent medical fact may be compressed into a brief and comprehensive abstract.

Determine the purpose for which you are writing the summary. If you are reviewing a potential claim as to its validity or the extent of injuries or to assess particular concerns, gear it accordingly. If you are working for the defense, the summary may be provided to the insurance carrier to outline injuries and chart recovery. You may be asked to invalidate a plaintiff's claim. You may be consulted once a lawsuit is well underway; the suit may have filed in hopes that the case would settle but is now scheduled for trial. Your expertise will be essential in presenting a meritorious medical case expediently.

An important aspect of your position is to remain objective in your initial review. If you can review the medical records with an open mind, items of importance will jump out of the records at you. If you have a predetermined prejudice, you may miss critical items that could become instrumental in winning the case or working a defense strategy.

### Case

A case was brought in for review by a cancer patient's husband who believed that his wife was misdiagnosed and improperly treated, leading to her death. A medical consultant reviewed volumes of medical records from numerous hospitals, cancer treatment centers, and teaching institutions. The task at hand seemed overwhelming. Determining standards of care was important, as was searching standard and experimental protocol in cancer treatment. In the course of reviewing the records, the reviewer saw that the patient, who was six months pregnant, was advised that aborting the child would be necessary in treating her aggressively for her cancer. The couple decided, with prompting by their doctor, that the only hope of a cure for her would be based on aborting the child; the possibility of one life was better than the certainty of two deaths, they decided. The child was aborted and the (experimental) cancer treatment continued. The woman eventually died.

The reader immediately was alerted, remembering the quotation from Sir William Osler, "First, do no harm." The case was presented to the attorney and worked up as a wrongful death claim in the termination of the unborn child's life without giving the parents adequate choice in the light of the circumstances. It was determined that the woman would have died anyway—the cancer was terminal—but that she could have been given the choice to live long enough to give birth to the child. The couple was not truly allowed this choice. As a result, the claim was based on the loss of life of the unborn child. The jury awarded the plaintiff father $6 million.

Picking up on particulars that make a good claim becomes a skill that sharpens with experience. You will be able to spot issues and elaborate on them with ease.

Your objectivity will be of immense value not only in determining the initial approach to take but determining the opposing counsel's argument as well. If you allow yourself to see only one side, you will not be able to foresee what approach opposing counsel might take. Good practice is to write up a list of possible defense arguments as you go along in your review so that you can later research them.

In some cases time may be of the essence. If such is the case, make sure you chronologize using the time of day. Military time will keep continuity and avoid adding A.M. and P.M. For example,

| | | |
|---|---|---|
| 2 Feb 94 | 1020 | temperature recorded as 98.6 in graphic chart |
| | 1030 | temperature recorded as normal by intern |
| | 1100 | temperature registered as 102.6 by chief resident |

## WORKING UP A MEDICAL MALPRACTICE CASE

### Case

Consider the following potential malpractice case. You are given the medical records of a 44-year-old Latin American woman suffering from severe arthritis who entered a local hospital to have hip replacement surgery performed. She was otherwise healthy. The operation was conducted with no complications. She died the following day, cause unknown. Autopsy revealed only brain hypoperfusion (the blood supply to her brain was not supplying enough oxygen to support life).

Where do you start? With a complete, exhaustive review of the medical records. Pick apart every page. Even when something appears obvious, do not assume it is. There may be hidden clues. Arrange the medical records chronologically, and start writing out every pertinent event. Go through every section, writing down the times vital signs were taken, medications were given, consultations were made. Then go through again, making the picture more complete, picking up on signs you may have missed the first time. (Your final summary will not include this unabridged information; you will hone it to include only that which becomes pertinent.) Consider these questions:

- Had she been taking any medications preoperatively?
- Were the appropriate postoperative medications ordered?
- Did the nurses follow the doctor's orders for giving the medications?
- How often were the vital signs ordered to be taken?
- How often were they actually taken?
- Did the vital signs give any clues as to action that should have been taken?

You find that vital signs were ordered every 15 minutes for the first hour after surgery, thereafter every half-hour for 2 hours, followed by every hour for the next 9 hours, after which vital signs were to be taken every 4 hours until discharge. You chart out the vital signs every place it appears in the records. You find a discrepancy 8 hours after surgery: no blood pressure is listed on the graphic chart. The next time the blood pressure reading appears, the patient's blood pressure is found to be 90/60. Preoperative and other postoperative readings average 120/100. No action was taken. You suspect that this is where a crisis may have begun. You go to the nurses' notes where over the past 3 hours the patient was "sleeping soundly." She never awakened.

You now have a starting point. Eight hours postoperatively, the patient became hypotensive. What happened? Was it significant? Should someone have been notified? If the answers do not become apparent in the records themselves, it may be time to perform some research.

Start by researching arthritis in the *Merck Manual* or *Harrison's*. You find that many arthritis patients take steroids for their inflammation. Find a good textbook of rheumatology at the library. Check *Goodman's and Gillman's* for steroid medications. You find that this patient had previously been on chronic steroids. You research contraindications to her surgery, and chronic steroid usage is listed as a risk: chronic steroid usage may cause the adrenal glands to shut down, thereby precipitating an Addisonian crisis during extreme stress (i.e., surgery). Records reveal that this patient was supposed to have been ''weaned off her steroids'' preoperatively. Information was scanty as to prescriptions she had been on in the past, however. You recall from past medical records from a visit to her surgeon months before her surgery that an interpreter had told the doctor (and he had documented) that her family members indicated that she had been going to Mexico to receive additional steroids.

Now research Addisonian crisis. Find a good anesthesiology textbook, and read up on recommended glucocorticoid administration preoperatively, operatively, and postoperatively. See if the suggested protocol had been followed in this case. You find it had not.

You are now building the case. You find that she was hypotensive postoperatively, and no action was taken. Hypotension could be an indication of adrenal failure. It appears that nobody investigated the amount of steroids she had been on before her hospital stay. She quit taking them and was given no supplementation or precautions.

Document every item of significance. Copy the references you have found. This material will be valuable in writing up your case. When you present your case and opinion, this will be the information on which the pursuit is based. The next step will be to find an expert to testify on behalf of the plaintiffs and to state that negligence may have occurred in the care of the deceased. It will now be your job to present these materials to a specialist in an area such as critical care anesthesia.

Following is a sample of an initial medical chronology assessing a potential malpractice claim.

Medical Records Summary

DOB: 6/12/89

MEDICAL RECORDS REVIEW

OF DR. H AND HOSPITAL B

| | | |
|---|---|---|
| 3 MAR 94 | 1543 | A 4½ year old male child was taken to Dr. H complaining of abdominal pain on the right, chills, fever (105.1°F), anorexia. Dr. H referred the child to Hospital B. Dr. H reported to Dr. M, in the outpatient department, that the child had an elevated white blood count with a left shift. |
| | 1558 | ''Stat'' urinalysis shows red blood cells being too numerous to count, crystals, bacteria, protein, and white blood cells in the urine. |

1636 Progress note from Dr. M indicated that upon examination, the child exhibited the physical signs and symptoms suggesting acute appendicitis, yet Dr. M also noted that the urinalysis was positive for blood. He still chose to perform an appendectomy, without pursuing the laboratory abnormalities.

Surgery was performed under general endotracheal anesthesia. The appendix was not perforated, but was found "slightly swollen" and was removed. Upon exploration, mesenteric nodes of the distal small bowel were noted to be swollen, and the diagnosis was given of mesenteric adenitis. After surgery the patient was extubated and sent to the recovery room in good condition.

2005 Anesthesia summary stated that Nurse K called the anesthesiologist on call requesting an order for mazicon, as the patient was too sleepy to take to his room. Order was given for 0.1 mg IV.

The child also experienced emesis in the PACU, although times and amounts were not annotated.

2020 Nurse K called the anesthesiologist back saying there was no effect from the mazicon, the oxygen saturation was decreasing, and she thought his pupils were dilating. The anesthesiologist ordered a stat CBC, SMAC, arterial blood gas, and chest x-ray, and had the nurse call Dr. M. and Dr. H.

2035 The anesthesiologist arrived at the hospital, and the patient appeared to be in acute respiratory distress. Pupils were fixed and dilated, with no corneal reflex. He began positive pressure ventilation with ambu bag and 100% oxygen. The patient appeared to be in pulmonary edema. He was intubated. The patient was given morphine and Lasix for the pulmonary edema. He was catheterized and had pink urine.

The next entry in the progress note indicated that postoperatively the patient was noted to have decreased oxygen saturation requiring reintubation. He had been found unresponsive with fixed, dilated pupils. Chest x-ray showed mild fluffy infiltrate. Postoperative labs showed hyponatremia (119) and hypokalemia (2.8). A consultant at University Medical Center was called, who recommended giving 4 cc/kg at 3% sodium, and an IV of normal saline with 40 meq potassium at 56 cc/hr. Records indicate that Drs. M, H, and A arrived. Repeat SMAC and ABGs were ordered.

2205 The child was transported to X Medical Center via helicopter, after manual ventilations were carried out with 100% oxygen until transport.

2300 The child was seen at UMC, assessed, and treated, without response.

3 MAR 94 1000 The patient was pronounced brain dead at 1000.

3 MAR 94 0930 Autopsy performed at 0930.

Final anatomic diagnosis: Diffuse proliferative glomerulone-

> phritis. Cause of death was listed as herniation of the brain secondary to diffuse cerebral edema.
>
> The renal pathology explained the blood and protein noted preoperatively. The pathological changes could represent Henoch-Schönlein purpura or other postinfectious glomerulonephritis.* [In complicated medical cases, it is a good idea to provide a pertinent medical glossary for legal staff with explanations of complex terms used in the body of your summary.] Active glomerular injury was confirmed via electron microscopy.

The summary gives enough information so that the records do not constantly have to be referred to when discussing the case. Note that items that were not pertinent were excluded. Paying close attention to vital signs throughout the postoperative care of the patient did not make a difference in his outcome. This was a frank misdiagnosis by Dr. M. Nursing care was not in question, nor was care by the emergency medical personnel on the helicopter.

Experience with various malpractice summaries will provide you with the insight as you proceed as to what should be included. You do not want to make the summary as cumbersome as the records. A records review that simply elaborates on them is just more to read. You want the finished product to be informative yet concise.

The next step is to determine if Dr. M acted below the standards of care in his treatment of the child, who obviously suffered injury. Some questions you will want to answer for yourself and the plaintiff's attorney are these:

1. *What type of physician was Dr. M?* Consult your state medical association's physician directory. Check with the state board of medical examiners. (Later you can check on the status of his medical license or how many claims he has had against him.)
2. *What board governed his specialty of practice?* Research the AMA's *Annual Directory of Practice Parameters.*
3. *What were the standards of care at the time?* Research current professional journals.
4. *Did he breach the standards of care by not pursuing the laboratory abnormalities? Would another physician with similar education and training under similar circumstances have performed an appendectomy?* Periodical literature would help support what becomes a judgment call.
5. *Who was responsible for his postoperative care? Should Dr. M have been present to ensure the patient was stable? Was it the anesthesiologist's responsibility?* The hospital by-laws may be of service here.

Once you have determined that this is a meritorious claim, you must press on to answer these questions and begin your pursuit of a medical expert to help

**Glomerulonephritis*—Inflammation of the kidney, specifically the capillary loops in the renal glomeruli (the functional unit at the lowest level of the kidney).

you answer them. The expert must be a physician serving in the same or similar capacity as the defendant, with the same or similar education, training, and qualifications. If you have a general surgery case, find a general surgeon as your expert, not an orthopedic surgeon, to define guidelines as to standards of care.

Use your chronology of medical care to provide a working guideline for a potential expert's initial review, relieving the person from weeding through the records as you just have. This will save you time and money while you are obtaining information. You are interviewing one another at this point. Make sure the expert knows the particulars before agreeing to take the case.

You may discuss the issues you summarized with your potential expert; if he or she can answer the questions to your satisfaction, get this person's curriculum vitae. Your goal is to find a strong, reliable expert with outstanding qualifications that will stand up to scrutiny. It is a good idea to interview a few potential experts at the onset and choose the one who serves the needs of the case best. You must be able to work well together in a respectful, professional relationship. It is not unheard of (and has devastating effects) for an expert to lose interest in or even quit a case if he or she is not appreciated and adequately compensated.

Once the expert has been retained, his or her opinion becomes open to scrutiny by opposing counsel. Before a consultant is named, however, his or her opinion is not necessarily discoverable. The expert may spend hours reviewing the records, performing research, and expending days in deposition, as well as at trial. It is obviously beneficial to try to keep the expert's involvement as pleasant as possible. When you have agreed on the terms of the relationship (hourly fee, deposition charges, trial fee) then you may send the expert the records. Your summary will not be sufficient for his or her review. The expert must base his or her opinion on the actual medical records.

Chapter 7

# Cancer Malpractice

Cancer litigation often arises out of one of the following situations: misdiagnosis, missed diagnosis, or correct diagnosis but improper treatment.

The prostate gland, for example, is a common site for cancer in older men; hence the rectal examination has become an integral part of of a physical examination when a man visits his physician. Any abnormal swelling alerts the physician to take certain steps to help diagnose the cause of the swelling or to "rule out" cancer. A physician who notices swelling and annotates it in the chart but does not take any action has breached his or her duty to the patient. If the patient has prostate cancer and a reasonable sign of the cancer was present, the physician has essentially missed the diagnosis by failing to act as a reasonable physician should. A physician who does not perform a rectal examination in the first place may or may not have breached his or her duty to the patient, depending on the reason for the visit to the physician, the presenting symptoms and their severity or urgency, the age of the patient, his past medical history, and other factors. But if the swelling is present, the physician has the duty to the patient to find the reason for the swelling.

Often a biopsy of the prostate gland is taken, with the tissue sent to a laboratory for microscopic examination by a pathologist, who will be able to tell if the prostate cells appear cancerous. Now the liability shifts to the pathology lab. Were the slides accurately prepared? Were they examined by a licensed physician experienced in viewing prostate tissue? Would another reasonable physician in the same situation have made a different diagnosis? If the results were assessed as cancerous, was this accurate? If you are dealing with a malpractice case where accurate tissue diagnosis is at issue, you must obtain copies of the tissue slides if appropriate and have them evaluated by another pathologist. This is also essential in cases where any specialist diagnoses cancer when it did not actually exist.

The last area where cancer liability may be at issue concerns treatment. Most cancer liability at this stage shifts to the treating oncology staff. Treatment of cancer may consist of cutting it out (a surgeon), radiating it (a radiation oncologist), or chemotherapy (an oncologist). This is where the most argument and controversy may arise, as treatment of cancer often entails experimental protocol. If you are trying to determine proper treatment in a cancer case, your expert should be an experienced oncologist who is abreast of all current *accepted* treatment modalities.

Another important point to emphasize in dealing with cancer litigation is outcome. If symptoms indicative of cancer were present and a reasonable physician acting with due care missed the signs, failed to make an accurate diagnosis, or failed to institute the proper treatment indicated for the cancer, *would it have made a difference?* If the presenting signs and symptoms of the cancer were already at a stage where the process could not have been arrested, and the patient would have ended up with the same outcome no matter what action was taken, the physician did not cause the damage to the patient; the cancer did.

## DEFINITIONS

*Cancer* may be defined as any malignant, cellular tumor. You might think of it as an unregulated production of cells. The normal, healthy body has regulatory mechanisms by which it controls cell growth. When these regulatory controls fail or are ignored by the cellular process, a cancer results. Another term you will encounter regarding cancer is *neoplasm,* which refers to any new, abnormal growth that is progressive and uncontrolled. When you see the term *malignancy,* it refers to the propensity for invasion.

*Carcinomas* are malignant new growths, composed of *epithelial* (cellular covering) cells, which have the tendency to infiltrate the surrounding tissues, and to *metastasize* (spread to other parts of the body).

Following are subclassifications of carcinomas:

*Adenocarcinoma.* Of glandular origin.

*Basal cell.* Epithelial tumor of the skin. Causes local destruction but rarely metastasizes.

*Bronchogenic.* Lung cancer of bronchial origin.

*Cholangiocellular.* From the bile duct cells of the liver.

*Chorionic.* From the outermost fetal membrane.

*Collois.* Mucinous.

*Embryonal.* Primitive germinal malignancy.

*Epidermoid.* Of the skin.

*Hepatocellular.* Of the liver cells.

*In situ.* Confined to the epithelium of origin.

*Large cell.* Of large bronchogenic cells.

*Medullary.* Epithelial in origin.

*Mucinous.* Glandular carcinomas producing mucin.

*Nasopharyngeal.* Arises in the nasopharynx epithelium.

*Oat cell.* Small cell.

*Papillary.* From an epithelial projection.

*Renal cell.* From tubular cells of the kidney.

*Scirrhous.* Dense connective tissue.

*Simplex.* Undifferentiated.

*Small cell.* Bronchogenic undifferentiated cells.

*Spindle cell.* Rapidly proliferating fusiform, squamous cell.

*Squamous cell.* From the cuboid squamous cells.

*Sarcomas* are cancers of a different origin, coming from embryonic connective tissue. Subclassifications of sarcomatous cancers are:

*Abernathy's.* Fatty tumor of the trunk.

*Alveolar.* The terminal end of the functional unit of the lung.

*Ameloblastic.* Forms dental enamel.

*Botryoides.* From submucosa.

*Endometrial.* Stromal.

*Giant cell.* Tumor of bone.

*Immunoblastic* (of T and B cells). Lymphomas.

*Kaposi's.* Occurs in immunocompromised patients.

*Osteogenic.* Bone.

*Reticulocytic.* A phagocytic cell type. (A phagocyte engulfs intruders.)

*Leukemias* are malignant neoplasms of blood-forming tissues. They are classified as being acute (acute lymphoblastic and acute nonlymphoblastic) or chronic (chronic lymphocytic and chronic myelocytic).

*Lymphomas* are neoplasms that arise in the reticuloendothelial and lymphatic systems. Major classifications are *Hodgkin's disease* and *non-Hodgkin's lymphoma.* Burkitt's lymphoma is a less common form.

Some cancers are genetic in origin, others viral. Some are caused by *carcinogenic* (cancer-causing) agents, and some have no known etiology. *Teratogens* are substances that, when exposed to a pregnant female, are capable of producing defects in the developing embryo. *Oncogenic* substances cause tumor formation.

Known occupational and environmental carcinogens are:

- aflotoxin
- arsenic
- asbestos
- benzene
- cadmium
- chloramethyl ethers
- chromium
- cigarette smoke
- naphthalene dyes
- nickel
- nitrites
- *Schistosoma haematobium*
- uranium
- vinyl chloride

Certain drugs and hormonal therapies have also been linked to cancers in humans, yet many are still used today.

Organ-specific cancers may occur in the brain, breast, ovary, cervix, uterus, lung, lymph nodes, pancreas, mouth, throat, esophagus, stomach, liver, testis, prostate, skin, colon, and other regions. When a cancer spreads, the fluid flows from the affected organ via lymph fluid. Therefore, regional lymph nodes are often the next area invaded by cancer cells.

*Early and accurate diagnosis is critical* because it affects outcome. If you are reviewing a case of a missed cancer diagnosis, research the presenting symptoms:

- Did the patient exhibit any of those signs, and are they documented?
- Were the appropriate studies ordered?
- What were the laboratory results?
- Who eventually diagnosed the cancer, and at what stage?
- When was treatment finally initiated?
- Most important, would early diagnosis have made a difference?

There are certain types of cancers that have minimal presenting symptoms and are not diagnosed until metastasis is already well underway. Consulting oncologists should pinpoint this critical area of causation in a medical malpractice case.

Proper management of a cancer patient depends on many factors including the type of cancer, its origin, the level of invasion, the nodal involvement (how many lymph nodes, if any, has it spread to?), and degree of metastasis. Cancers are usually *staged*—given numerical determinants that guide in establishing modes of therapy. Some are affected by hormones as well.

## TREATMENT

Cancers are treated by the following accepted modalities:

*Surgery*. Cut it out. Surgery may entail removing only the cancerous tissue itself, the cancer and surrounding tissue, the entire organ, or the organ and associated lymph nodes.

*Radiotherapy*. Irradiate the overproliferating cells. Radiation therapy is intended to kill via x-ray beams any cancerous cells that cannot be surgically removed. Dosage is determined by rads per time per specified area, over which dosage the radiotherapy is no longer efficacious. Litigation has arisen over this issue of excessive dosage that killed not only the cancer but adjacent tissues as well, causing undue suffering by the patient.

*Chemotherapy*. Drugs aimed at killing cancer cells. They are toxic to other cells as well. Cancer chemotherapy employs agents referred to as *antineoplastic* drugs, which inhibit the unregulated, abnormal growth of tissue.

A combination of these modes of therapy is often employed. A missed diagnosis requiring unnecessary treatment can have serious and far-reaching effects.

Experimental cancer treatments are often undertaken by pioneering physicians, and patients receiving these drugs are often given a sense of hope. Since the beneficial effects have not been proved or accepted by the Food and Drug Administration, physicians who employ these methods subject themselves to possible disciplinary action. In any dispute over sensitive emotional and ethical issues, there is no clear solution. It may be argued that the patient was offered only false hope, and the physician benefited monetarily from the patient's deep, fervent need; or it may be that all the patient had was hope in the end, and that any possibility for a cure was preferable to despair.

## CANCER DRUGS

Antineoplastic agents are by their nature toxic. They are designed to provide a rational combination drug regimen to eliminate micrometastases and to inhibit the development of secondary tumors following the removal of primary neoplasms with surgery or radiation.

*Oncogenes* are genes capable of inducing cellular transformation or mutations. One malignant cell can give rise to enough malignant cells to kill the host. Cancer drugs are aimed at killing these mutated cancer cells by targeting a constant percentage of the cells at any given time. Some of these agents are aimed at specific phases of the cell cycle; the actions of others are dependent on proliferation.

A major problem with chemotherapy is that malignant tumors function as large populations of cells undergoing spontaneous mutations and can therefore mutate toward drug resistance. That is why combination therapy is often employed—to achieve a synergistic effect by employing drugs with different mechanisms of action.

These antineoplastic agents produce untoward side effects. Since many are *cytotoxic* (cell killing) to proliferating cells, normal proliferating tissues such as the hair and skin, the bone marrow (*myelo*), the gastrointestinal tract, the reproductive system, the central nervous system, and the cardiovascular system can be adversely affected by these drugs as well. Some antineoplastic agents have been reported to be carcinogenic themselves. Using higher doses than recommended can produce neuropathies and toxicity to other organ systems, such as the liver and kidneys. Using different drugs with the same mechanisms of action has a tendency toward more toxicity than therapeutic usefulness.

Antineoplastic drugs can be broken down into categories.

### Alkylating Agents

These agents transfer their alkyl groups to RNA, DNA, or proteins, and are lethal to the cells. They are not cell-cycle specific.

*Nitrogen mustards* basically function to bind and deactivate macromolecules.

*Mechlorethamine* (Mustargen). The most rapidly acting of the class, and must be administered intravenously. Major toxic manifestations are myelosuppression, hair loss, nausea, and vomiting. It is contraindicated in pregnancy or in breast-feeding mothers as it can cause fetal abnormalities.

*Cyclophosphamide* (Cytoxan, NEOSAR). Probably the most useful of the alkylating agents. It has a broad spectrum of antitumor activity and can be administered orally, intravenously, or intramuscularly. Spectrum of toxicity includes hair loss, nausea and vomiting, myelosuppression, and sterile hemorrhagic cystitis.

*Chlorambucil* (Leukeran). The slowest-acting nitrogen mustard, which can be administered orally. It can produce myelosuppression but is moderate, gradual, and easily reversed.

*Melphalan* (Alkeran). Can be administered orally. Spectrum of toxicity is similar to the other alkylating agents; nausea and vomiting are infrequent.

*Thiotepa* (Thioplex). Used to treat adenocarcinoma of the breast and ovary, localized serosal neoplasms, papillary carcinomas, and others. Bone marrow suppression is the major complication. Administered parenterally.

*Estramustine* (Emcyt). Can be taken orally. This antineoplastic agent combines nornitrogen mustard with estrogen to treat metastatic and/or progressive prostate cancer. This drug should not be used in those with hypersensitivity to estradiol or nitrogen mustard; those with thromboembolic disorders should avoid its use as well, and patients with cerebral vascular or coronary artery disease should use it with caution. Milk products and calcium interfere with its absorption. Gastrointestinal effects can occur, as well as breast tenderness and enlargement. Fluid retention often occurs. Poorly metabolized in those with impaired liver function and may affect certain liver function tests.

*Nitrosureas* are used to treat a broad spectrum of human malignancies. They are highly lipid soluble (can dissolve in fat) and can cross the blood-brain barrier, making them useful in treating brain tumors. They can cause profound cumulative myelosuppression, limiting their therapeutic value. Long-term treatment can produce renal failure. The nitrosureas are mutagenic and carcinogenic as well.

*Carmustine* (BCNU, BiCNU). Administered intravenously. Causes delayed bone marrow suppression, which may not reach maximal depression until six weeks of therapy. Cytotoxic effects have been observed in the liver, kidney, and central nervous system. Useful for treating meningeal leukemia and brain neoplasms as it has the ability to cross the blood-brain barrier.

*Lomustine* (CCNU, CeeNU), *Semustine* (Methyl-CCNU). Rapidly absorbed from the gastrointestinal tract and administered orally. The spectrum of therapeutic usefulness and toxicity is similar to carmustine.

*Streptozocin* (Zanosar). Administered intravenously or intra-arterially. Treats islet cell carcinoma and malignant carcinoid tumors. Its major dose-limiting toxicity is renal damage (nephrotoxicity).

*Alkyl sulfonates* are one type of myelosuppressive alkylating agent.

*Busulfan* (Myleran). Active orally, used in the treatment of chronic granulocytic leukemia. No significant pharmacological action other than myelosuppression is noted.

*Triazenes* are another form of alkylating agent, which kills cells slowly.

*Dacarbazine* (DTIC-Dome). Employed for the treatment of malignant melanoma. Administered intravenously. Toxicity includes nausea and vomiting and moderate myelosuppression.

### Antimetabolites

These compete with naturally occurring compounds required for nucleic acid metabolism, thereby interrupting cell growth.

*Folic acid analogs* are antimetabolites which function like the essential dietary factor folic acid (derived from tetrahydrofolic acid) which metabolically transfers carbon units.

*Methotrexate.* An S-phase-specific antimetabolite that irreversibly inhibits DNA synthesis. Commonly used in combination therapy of acute lymphoblastic leukemia, Burkitt's lymphoma, trophoblastic choriocarcinoma, breast carcinoma, and metastatic carcinomas. Major side effects are bone marrow suppression, nausea, vomiting, anorexia, oral ulcers, hair loss, and hepatic damage.

*Pyrimidine analogs* mimic pyrimidine metabolites and thereby exert their effect of impeding nucleic acid synthesis in the cell. They treat various DNA containing viruses, neoplastic diseases, and infections.

*Fluorouracil* (5–FU, Efudex, Fluoroplex). Interferes with the processing and function of RNA, producing an imbalance in growth and thus cell death. Administered parenterally for the treatment of breast and gastrointestinal carcinomas, as well as cancers of the ovary, cervix, bladder, pancreas, prostate, and oropharyngeal tissues. The spectrum of toxicity includes myelosuppression, nausea, anorexia, diarrhea, and hair loss.

*Cytarabine* (cytosine arabinoside, Cytosar-U). Competitively blocks DNA polymerase. Used for the treatment of acute leukemia and granulocytic leukemia (in combination with thioguanine and daunorubicin). Potently myelosuppressive.

*Purine analogs* function to inhibit cellular DNA production, thereby killing the cell.

*Mercaptopurine* (6–MP, Purinethol). Inhibits several key steps in purine synthesis and disrupts RNA and glycoprotein synthesis and chromosomal replication. Useful in the treatment of acute leukemia, chronic granulocytic and lymphocytic leukemias, lymphomas, and a wide variety of carcinomas. Major toxicity is bone marrow suppression, nausea, vomiting, anorexia, and hepatic necrosis. Azothioprine, a derivative of 6–MP, is an immunosuppressive agent used to treat organ transplant rejection.

*Thioguanine* (6–TG). Similar to 6–MP and particularly useful for the treatment of acute granulocytic leukemia in combination with cytarabine.

*Plant alkyloids*, derived from the periwinkle plant (*Vinca rosea*), block mitosis with metaphase arrest, inhibiting the formation of micritubules, resulting in cell death. They are administered intravenously.

*Vincristine* (Oncovin). Used as part of a regimen in the treatment of Hodgkin's lymphoma and is the drug of choice for the treatment of acute lymphoblastic leukemia in children. Peripheral neuropathy is its most common untoward effect: numbness, weakness, loss of reflexes, foot drop, ataxia, and hair loss.

*Vinblastine* (Velban). Potently bone marrow suppressive. Most commonly used in combination with bleomycin and cisplatin to treat metastatic testicular tumors, various lymphomas, Kaposi's sarcoma, and breast carcinoma.

### Antitumor Antibiotics

*Dactinomycin* (Actinomycin D, Cosmegen). Inhibits rapidly proliferating normal and neoplastic cells. Administered parenterally. The most important clinical use is in the treatment of rhabdomyosarcoma and Wilms' tumor in children. Myelosuppression is its major limiting toxicity.

*Doxorubicin* (Adriamycin, Rubex), *daunorubicin* (Cerubidine). Mutagenic and carcinogenic. They can combine with cellular membranes and alter the fluidity and affect ion channels. These drugs are administered intravenously only. Their clinical usage is limited by cardiac toxicity, which is related to the total dose and is often irreversible. They also produce bone marrow suppression and total loss of hair. Daunorubicin treats acute leukemia, and doxorubicin treats a variety of carcinomas of the breast, endometrium, ovary, testicle, thyroid, and lung. It is also useful for hematologic cancers, neuroblastoma, osteosarcoma, Ewing's sarcoma, and rhabdomyosarcoma.

*Mitomycin* (Mutamycin, Mitomycin). A non–cell cycle specific alkylating agent, used in combination with bleomycin and vincristine for the treatment of adenocarcinomas of the stomach, pancreas, long squamous cell cervical carcinoma, and metastatic colon cancer therapy. Parenteral administration. Major toxicity is myelosuppression.

*Bleomycin* (Blenoxane). Synergistic with vinblastine and cisplatin in the treatment of testicular carcinomas. Also used in squamous cell carcinomas of the head and neck, cervix, skin, penis and rectum, and in combination therapy of lymphomas. Causes little bone marrow suppression. Its most serious adverse effect is dosage-related pulmonary toxicity; 5 to 10 percent of patients develop pulmonary toxicity, which is fatal in 1 percent of cases.

*Idarubicin* (Idamycin). An antileukemic drug, intended for intravenous use only. Functions by inhibiting nucleic acid synthesis. It has a tendency for severe myelosuppression when used at therapeutic dosages and is toxic to the heart.

### Hormonal Agents

*Adrenocorticoids.* Have the ability to suppress mitosis in lymphocytes and are therefore used in the treatment of acute leukemias in children and malignant lymphoma. Major side effects include fluid retention, hypertension, diabetes, and abnormal fat distribution.

*Aminoglutethimide* (Cytadren). Inhibits adrenocortical steroid synthesis and also inhibits an enzyme in fat responsible for conversion to an estrogenic steroid; therefore it is used for some estrogen-dependent breast cancers and adrenocorticotropic hormone (ACTH)-producing tumors. It is administered with replacement hydrocortisone therapy. This drug also diminishes the effects of coumadin and warfarin.

*Tamoxifen* (Nolvadex). A potent antiestrogen important for the treatment of breast cancer. It is slowly absorbed after oral administration. Major toxicities are bone pain, hypercalcemia, hot flashes, and nausea.

*Leuprolide* (Lupron). A synthetic amino acid peptide analogue of gonadotropin-releasing hormone, which stimulates and then inhibits the pituitary release of FSH (follicle-stimulating hormone), and LH (luteinizing hormone), causing a decrease in testicular androgen production. Used to treat metastatic prostate cancer. Sometimes initially worsens the symptoms, usually manifested by an increase in bone pain.

*Flutamide* (Eulexin). An androgen inhibitor. Inhibits testosterone binding to its receptor. Used for the treatment of prostate cancer, in combination with leuprolide.

### Cytotoxic Agents

*Carmustine* (BiCNU). Used in brain tumors, multiple myeloma, Hodgkin's disease, and non-Hodgkin's lymphoma. Its major toxicity is bone marrow suppression and therefore should not be given more frequently than every 6 weeks.

*Lomustine* (CeeNU). Used for brain tumors and Hodgkin's disease. Toxic to the bone marrow and should not be used more frequently than every 6 weeks.

*Cyclophosphamide* (Cytoxan, NEOSAR). Employed to treat various malignant diseases. It is potent but also toxic to many organ systems such as the reproductive and digestive systems, the skin, blood-forming organs, and the urinary and respiratory systems.

*Hydroxyurea* (Hydrox). Treats myeloma as well as resistant chronic myelocytic leukemia, and persistent or metastatic ovarian cancer. Its major toxicity is bone marrow suppression. Blood status, bone marrow, liver, and kidney function studies should be evaluated while on its use.

*Doxorubicin* (Adriamycin, Rubex). A cytotoxic agent.

*Estramustine* (Emcyt). A cytotoxic nornitrogen mustard/estradiol combination drug.

*Altretamine* (Hexalen). A second-line drug used to treat recurrent ovarian cancer. Bone marrow depression and neurologic toxicity are its major adverse effects.

*Ifosfamide* (IFEX). A third-line chemotherapy of germ cell testicular cancer. Should be used with a prophylactic agent for hemorrhagic cystitis, its major toxic effect.

*Interferon* (Intron A, Roferon A). Belongs to a family of naturally occurring small proteins that bind to receptors on the cell membrane, suppressing their replication. These agents are employed to treat certain leukemias, human papilloma virus, AIDS-related Kaposi's sarcoma, and chronic hepatitis. Its administration may produce burning, itching reactions at the injection site. Interferon toxicities include blood and endocrine disorders, cardiovascular effects, gastrointestinal system effects, and flulike symptoms.

*Procarbazine* (Mutalane). Should not be used in combination with sympathomimetics, tricyclic antidepressants, or foods with high tyramine content, or it may cause hypertensive reactions and psychic disturbances. Inhibits DNA, RNA, and protein synthesis, is a component in the treatment of Hodgkin's disease, and is used to treat small cell carcinoma of the lung, non-Hodgkin's lymphomas, myeloma, melanoma, and brain tumors. Major toxic effects include myelosuppression, nausea, and vomiting.

*Busulfan* (Myleran). An alkylating agent used for the palliative treatment of chronic myelogenous leukemia to relieve the clinical symptoms of the disease. Bone marrow suppression is severe and prolonged. Pulmonary effects are rare but important to mention.

*Mitoxantrone* (Novantrone). An intravenous, DNA-reactive agent used in combination with other drugs for the initial therapy of acute nonlymphocytic leukemia. Severe myelosuppression is very common; therefore, hematologic monitoring and adjunctive therapies should be employed.

*Carboplatin* (Paraplatin). Related to cisplatin and intended for use in the initial treatment of advanced ovarian cancer. Bone marrow suppression is its major toxicity.

*Cisplatin* (Platinol). A heavy metal complex indicated for use in metastatic testicular and ovarian tumors as well as advanced bladder cancer. Renal insufficiency is its major toxicity and is dosage related. Myelosuppression also occurs. Toxic to the eyes and ears. Gastrointestinal effects include marked nausea and vomiting.

*Paclitaxel* (Taxol). An injected antimicrotubule agent indicated for use in metastatic ovarian cancer and relapsing breast cancer (if prior therapy failed). Patients receiving Taxol should first be administered corticosteroids and $H_2$ antagonists due to a propensity for histamine-mediated hypersensitivity reactions. Myelosuppression is a toxicity, as are cardiovascular and nervous system effects. Taxol may also leach polyvinylchloride (PVC) from containers used to store it. Solutions should be stored in glass bottles or plastics other than PVC.

*Teniposide* (Vumon). A potent drug for injection in combination for induction therapy in patients with refractory childhood acute lymphoblastic leukemia. Blood counts and renal and hepatic functions tests should be carefully monitored. Hypersensitivity reactions may also occur.

*Streptozosin* (Zanosar). Inhibits DNA synthesis in patients with metastatic islet cell carcinoma of the pancreas. Because of its inherent toxicity to the kidneys, its usage should be limited to those with symptomatic or progressive metastatic disease.

## Antimetabolites

*Fludarabine* (Fludara). An injected substance indicated for the treatment of patients with B-cell chronic lymphocytic leukemia for those that have not responded to another alkylating agent. Toxicities are dosage dependent and can cause a syndrome characterized by delayed blindness, coma, and death. Patients should be monitored for hematologic toxicity.

*Floxuradine* (FUDR). Injections are indicated for the palliative management of incurable gastrointestinal adenocarcinoma metastatic to the liver. Selected patients should be capable of receiving the agent to the treatable site via a single artery. Contraindicated in those with a poor nutritional state, depressed bone marrow function, or serious infection. This drug is highly toxic, with only a narrow margin of safety.

*Plicamycin* (Mithracin). Used only in the hospital setting for patients with malignant testical tumors in whom other means of treatment is not possible. Should not be used in those with depressed bone marrow function or bleeding disorders. Major toxicity is a bleeding syndrome.

*Thioguanine* (Tabloid). An oral tablet indicated for acute nonlymphocytic leukemias and other neoplasms. Bone marrow suppression is its major dosage-related toxicity.

## Hormonal Substances

These should not be used by women who suspect they are pregnant.

*Medroxyprogesterone* (Depo-Provera). A progestational agent used for breast malignancies.

*Estradiol* (Estrace). An estrogen indicated for the palliative treatment of metastatic breast cancer and advanced androgen-dependent prostate cancer.

*Megestrol* (Megace). A synthetic progestational drug indicated for the palliative treatment of advanced breast or endometrial carcinoma.

*Octreotide* (Sandostatin). Similar to the natural hormone somatostatin, which inhibits growth hormone, insulin, and glucagon. Indicated for the use of carcinoid tumors, where it inhibits some of the symptoms. Also used to treat acromegaly to reduce growth hormone levels. Adverse effects include biliary tract abnormalities, cardiac conduction abnormalities, and hypothyroidism.

*Diethylstilbestrol* (Stilphostrol). An estrogen indicated for the palliative treatment of advanced prostatic carcinoma. Long-term usage may cause other neoplasms.

*Testolactone* (Teslac). A synthetic androgen similar to testosterone. Indicated for the palliative treatment of advanced breast cancer; contraindicated in men.

*Goserelin* (Zoladex). A synthetic analog of luteinizing hormone releasing hormone, used to manage advanced prostate carcinoma palliatively.

## Steroids

*Betamethasone* (Celestone). A synthetic glucocorticoid; used for palliative management of leukemias and lymphomas.

## Immunomodulators

*Aldesleukin* (Proleukin). A highly purified protein, which mimics the biological activity of the native human interleukin-2, enhancing immune function. Used in adults with metastatic renal cell carcinoma.

## Other

*Mitotane* (Lysodren). An oral chemotherapeutic agent indicated in the treatment of inoperable cortical carcinoma. Adrenal insufficiency may result from its usage, so adrenal steroid replacement therapy should be considered. Patients on anticoagulants should be monitored closely as it tends to accelerate the metabolism of warfarin. Gastrointestinal disturbances, central nervous system side effects, and skin toxicity are not uncommon.

*Etoposide* (VePesid). Treats refractory testicular tumors and small cell lung cancer. May cause myelosuppression, gastrointestinal toxicity, transient hypotension, baldness, and occasional allergic reactions.

*Intravesical* (Theracys BCG Live). A freeze-dried bacterium that, when administered to the urinary bladder, promotes an inflammatory reaction, which sometimes reduces cancerous lesions. Since it contains bacteria, it should not be used by immunosuppressed patients.

*Vinorelbine* (Navelbine). Interferes with microtubule assembly and is used alone or with cisplatin to treat unresectable, advanced non–small cell lung cancer. It should not be used in patients with pretreatment granulocyte counts below 1,000 cells/mm$^3$. Bone marrow suppression is its most common adverse effect.

*Leukovorin calcium.* A folic acid derivative used after high-dose methotrexate therapy in osteosarcoma. Diminishes the toxicity of methotrexate and treats folic acid deficiency caused by megaloblastic anemias when oral therapy is not feasible. The clinician should make sure that the anemia is not due to the lack of vitamin $B_{12}$. Allergic reactions have been reported.

*Aspariginase* (Elspar). An enzyme of bacterial origin that inhibits protein synthesis in neoplastic cells; used to treat acute lymphocytic leukemia in children and certain lymphomas. Can cause nausea, fever, and allergic reactions. Chronic use can cause liver toxicity, pancreatitis, and depression.

## Adjunct

*Filgrastim* (Neupogen). Stimulates human granulocytes in patients undergoing myelosuppressive chemotherapy, bone marrow transplants, and those with severe chronic neutropenia.

*Ondansectran* (Zofran). Reduces the nausea and vomiting in patients receiving cancer chemotherapy.

*Sargramostim* (Leukine). Stimulates human granulocytes and macrophages. Indicated for use in patients undergoing bone marrow transplants and for those in whom transplant is delayed or has failed.

*Levamisole* (Ergamisol). An immunomodulator used only in combination with fluorouracil after surgical resection in patients with colon cancer (Dukes' stage C).

*Pilocarpine* (Salagen). An oral parasympathetic cholinergic agonist. Functions to counteract the dry mouth effects suffered by patients undergoing radiation therapy of the head and neck.

*Dexrazoxane* (Zinecard). Used in conjunction with doxorubicin (in breast cancer patients) to protect the heart from its adverse effects. May add to the myelosuppressive effects, however.

*Strontium-89* (Metastron). Injected to relieve the bone pain suffered by patients with skeletal metastases.

*Granisetron* (Kytril). A serotonin receptor antagonist used to prevent the nausea and vomiting associated with cancer chemotherapy.

*Gallium nitrate* (Ganite). Inhibits calcium resorption from bone and is used to treat cancer-related hypercalcemia that has not responded to hydration. Should not be administered to patients with severe renal impairment.

Chapter 8

# Products Liability, Chemical Exposure, and Toxic Torts

A good portion of chemical exposure and products liability cases need the expertise found in standards set forth by federal agencies. These agencies publish guidelines for the prevention of toxic exposure, hazardous products, and environments. You may seek information as to whether the organization in question has been following standards set forth nationally.

Centers for Disease Control (CDC)
Department of Health and Human Services
Atlanta, GA 30333
(404) 639–3311

Environmental Protection Agency (EPA)
401 M Street, SW
Washington, D.C. 20460
(202) 260–4454

Food and Drug Administration (FDA)
Department of Health and Human Services
5600 Fishers Lane
Rockwell, MD 20857
(301) 443–2410

National Institute for Occupational Safety and Health (NIOSH)
Department of Health and Human Services
2000 Independence Avenue, SW
Washington, D.C. 20201
(202) 472–7134, (800) 356–4674

Occupational Safety and Health Administration (OSHA)
Department of Labor

2000 Constitution Avenue, NW
Washington, D.C. 20210
(212) 523–8151

## PRODUCTS LIABILITY

Products liability lawsuits are cases wherein a product, drug, or device has allegedly caused harm to the claimant. Medical cases involving products liability may center around a birth control intrauterine device or any other medical device that, when inserted into the body, has the propensity to cause harm.

These cases should allege that the manufacturer of the product performed adequate safety testing of the device, and if there was a propensity for harm from the product, it should not have been offered to the public; or if the product was allowed to go on the market for public sale, then the manufacturer had a duty to warn the public adequately of the risk of such a device.

Often products liability cases, as well as chemical exposure lawsuits, have multiple plaintiffs represented en masse by a single team of attorneys. These class action suits are based on the assumption that all of the individual plaintiffs experienced the same or similar symptoms as a direct result of the substance they are claiming harmed them. Individual cases are also commonly filed. If the cases are filed in district court, the rules governing submission of documents will vary somewhat from lawsuits filed in state courts.

Let us say that a chair breaks at a restaurant while a patron is taking his seat for an expensive business dinner. He slams to the floor, breaking his coccyx bone. The table is knocked over, red wine is spilled over one of the business associate's Armani suits, and the business negotiations never take place, as the plaintiff is whisked off to the emergency room. In this case the plaintiff might allege that the manufacturer of the chair was negligent:

- The manufacturer failed to provide a safe, secure, product that was free from causing harm.
- The product was not free from causing harm and was therefore defective.
- The manufacturer did not adequately warn the purchaser of the product that the chair was unsafe.
- The manufacturer did not perform sufficient safety studies of the chair under stress and other conditions.
- The manufacturer had a duty to provide a chair free from causing harm to the public for which it was intended.
- The user of the chair was not abusing the chair in any way. The plaintiff was using the product for its intended purpose.
- As a result of using the chair for its intended purpose and because of its defect in failing to support its intended purpose, the plaintiff was injured.
- As a result of the injuries, the plaintiff suffered physical and emotional damage.
- As a result of the physical injuries, the plaintiff was unable to perform his husbandly

duties to his wife. (The wife therefore also becomes a plaintiff in this suit for loss of consortium.)

- As a result of the defective product and the resulting accident, the plaintiff's business transaction did not materialize. Not only did he lose a potential multimillion dollar business deal, his professional reputation suffered as well.

In this type of case it is important to show individual damage and how it affects every aspect of the plaintiff's life, present and future.

An example of a products liability class action lawsuit is the large group of women who had silicone breast implants placed in their bodies. These women believed the products were safe. Their physicians introduced these foreign objects into the women without adequate knowledge of their potential for harm. As a result of the placement of the silicone implants, many women experienced problems that they believed were due to the silicone in their bodies. Affected women returned to their physicians numerous times complaining of symptoms that were similar to autoimmune diseases. Over the years, evidence mounted that perhaps these products were unsafe. Some of the implants had ruptured, extruding their contents into the systems of these women, who seemed to experience related symptoms. Laboratory examinations of their blood and tissues were revealing similar abnormalities. Women were having to undergo multiple surgeries to remove extruded silicone from their bodies, replace implants, and restore and rebuild damaged breast tissue, often leading to disfigurement. Eventually medical studies were performed, the results of which led to the belief that silicone implants were not safe. Medical literature was mounting that there was a link between silicone and a multitude of autoimmune conditions.

Investigation into the safety practices of the companies responsible for inventing, manufacturing, and distributing breast implants into the medical community was begun. It was revealed that perhaps adequate studies were not performed or that safety studies that revealed that silicone introduced into the body had a potential for untoward effects were treated as confidential.

Class action lawsuits were initiated nationwide. Citeria were established for causation. Medical evidence was exhibiting common links as well. What became particularly important in these cases was the *similarity of symptoms* displayed by the plaintiffs. Physicians working with these women had to be fully aware of the possibility of these effects, what tests should be performed, how to establish a diagnosis, and how to follow and treat these women. Teams of doctors worked with the courts to establish criteria by which a positive diagnosis could be established in women who had breast implants placed and who experienced autoimmune-type symptoms. This was especially difficult because their symptoms waxed and waned; blood factors were abnormally elevated in some women, but others were normal.

In spite of the inconsistencies in symptomatology, standards were established for proper evaluation of these patients.

When working up cases such as these, it is imperative that the attorney and the treating physician work closely together, especially in the light of the fact that the determination for what constitutes silicone implant–related autoimmune disease has essentially been a legal one. Attorneys must make the examining doctors aware of what laboratory studies and positive findings the courts have required to establish a firm diagnosis. It is further necessary that the attorney ensure that the claimant be sent to doctors with experience with patients who have contracted this disease.

Another important fact in working up any products liability case—and in particular a medical device case such as breast implants—is that identification of the product is extremely important. There must be evidence that the product was manufactured by the defendant. With breast implant litigation, you must obtain the identification sticker, which can be obtained from the medical records. Sometimes the operative report will state the name of the manufacturer of the implants as well; nevertheless, the label that the plastic surgeon removes from the breast implant package must be placed within the medical records. This label states the manufacturer of the implant, the size, the style, the catalog number, and the identification number. This evidence will quell any questions as to who fabricated the offending product.

## CHEMICAL EXPOSURE

Claims of toxic exposure may also be filed as class action suits. For example, there was an ammonia leak in a chemical plant where workers were exposed to toxic fumes. There may be hundreds of people who were exposed at once, suffered the same or similar signs and symptoms, and went to local physicians. It is important to document the history of the chemical leak, the exposure to the substance, and who was affected.

Physicians who treat these patients should document their presenting signs and symptoms, any diagnostic procedures performed, and treatment modalities rendered. If you are presenting these claims, *consistency of symptomatology* becomes very important. Do not go chasing after reports of a leg laceration when reviewing the medical records, unless it was directly caused by the person's trying to get away from the fumes. You will encounter many misleading findings in reviewing numerous medical records from multiple plaintiffs. Locate every related finding, and present it in chronological form for each individual plaintiff.

Individual cases are handled in much the same manner as cases presented for global settlement.

### Case

You have a chemical exposure case wherein the claimant was supposedly exposed to a chemical substance producing effects similar to Agent Orange while disposing of tools returned to his company after an overseas conflict. He developed cancer. Research the short- and long-term sequelae of Agent Orange exposure. Find similar cases that have set precedent in these cases. Document the exposure, onset of symptomatology, and all medical interventions.

Document individual case specifics while remaining consistent. Before you begin, write out the specific questions you will explore.

- What are the chemical components of Agent Orange?
- In what other toxins are these chemicals found?
- What are the possible side effects—long- and short-term—of these compounds?
- How have these disorders been treated in the past?
- The client seems to have a long psychiatric history with evidence of paranoia, and opposing counsel claims he is fabricating. How can I counteract this?

Approaching a research project in this manner will allow you to begin your search broadly, then narrow it down as you go along. Not only will you have answers to your questions, you may find other sources to pinpoint issues you had not yet unveiled.

You may begin at the library by asking the head of reference for texts on chemical exposure, specifically Agent Orange. You continue your search by reviewing the *Cumulative Index Medicus* or do a MEDLINE search. You may have to branch beyond the medical realm in chemical cases and research TOXLINE or HSDB. As you read journal articles that pertain to Agent Orange, you find out that it has been linked to the type of cancer that your client has. You discover that Agent Orange has also been linked to neurological damage, which has manifested as symptoms including psychosis and paranoia. Now your defense becomes an asset.

The function of this medical records review is to summarize the patient's medical history, taken directly from the medical records, emphasizing whether deleterious signs and symptoms he exhibited might be linked to chemical exposure.

**Medical Records Review**

Date of Birth:

SSN:

The plaintiff is a 49-year-old male who served in Vietnam from 5/8/66 to 1/24/67. He does not smoke, and only occasionally has a beer with his friends. His past medical history is negative, except for an appendectomy at the age of 13. Family history is negative as well. He is employed by Air Defense, and has been since 1982. Following is the plaintiff's medical summary which will reveal medical symptoms and problems which he believes are due to exposure to toxic chemicals during his employ with the Air Defense. The plaintiff's job has been to clean helicopters which have been recently recovered from storage after their Vietnam use. He was not required to use any protective covering, clothing, mask, or gloves. The following excerpts are taken directly from the plaintiff's medical records, which are attached.

11/19/82 The plaintiff was seen for heart palpitations and atypical chest pains. His past medical history was negative for hospitalizations and surgeries. He did not smoke and only drank occasionally. He was married and had 2 children. He had experienced frontal headaches recently with some dizziness. Occasionally he experienced ringing in his left ear, and tightness in his neck. There were some genitourinary symptoms, and occasional left shoulder pain.

*neurological effects*

*hearing changes*

*genitourinary effects*

*musculoskeletal changes*

9/6/84 The plaintiff consulted a doctor on his health plan with an onset of chest palpitations, tachycardia, and occasional skipped beats. Heart rate was found to be slightly irregular with 2–4 extra systoles per minute. An EKG showed one premature ventricular contraction. He was prescribed Centrax for anxiety, and scheduled for further workup.

*cardiovascular effects*

10/10/84 Follow-up visit. The plaintiff still was experiencing palpitations. An echocardiogram was normal, but a Holter monitor revealed frequent PVCs. The treating physician consulted a cardiologist, who recommended a treadmill test.

*cardiovascular symptoms*

1/12/87 The plaintiff had a health summary report performed by a computer health testing program. The health profile revealed that the plaintiff had a heart murmur, he was often depressed, he had been short of breath during the last five years. He had hayfever or chronic sinus problems. He had experienced chest pains, stomach pains, chronic indigestion, constipation, and painful urination. He had a skin rash, severe back problems, weak spells, and excessive fatigue. He had headaches and dizzy spells, as well as dental problems. There was no known cause. He was referred to a psychiatrist.

*respiratory effects*

*gastrointestinal symptoms*

*genitourinary system*

*psychiatric effects*

*neurological problems*

*skin changes*

*musculoskeletal symptoms*

*cardiovascular effects*

12/22/93 The plaintiff consulted a general practitioner with pain in his right elbow, which he had been experiencing for about four days. He had experienced episodic pain and swelling in his elbows and knees. He also experienced neck and shoulder pain, tightening in his neck, and difficulty sleeping. Past medical history revealed only evidence of some double vision in the past. The general practitioner began treating the plaintiff for chronic pain.

*musculoskeletal system involvement*

*neurological symptoms*

*visual changes*

12/29/93 The plaintiff called a physician at the Neurological Clinic. He had been very weak and tired, and was wondering where these symptoms might be coming from. He had felt this way in the past, but never this severe. He didn't know if he could work.

*neurological symptoms were experienced*

3/30/94 The plaintiff consulted a physician with a sore throat and fever that had been present for four days. His throat was red and irritated, and lymph nodes were swollen.

*respiratory system effects*

*endocrine system effects*

4/5/94 The plaintiff's doctor sent the plaintiff for further workup at a cancer clinic, where he was found to have throat cancer.

It is well documented that the toxic agents with which the plaintiff came in contact, specifically Agent Orange, affect the respiratory and genitourinary systems, have psychiatric effects, and lead to visual problems, cardiovascular symptoms, gastrointestinal problems, and endocrine, neurological, and skin alterations, all of which the plaintiff has experienced, as evidenced by his medical history. The well-documented links of Agent Orange as a carcinogen have previously been presented.

The italicized text in the medical records review represents medical documentation presented in the research literature. These are the known effects of the chemical components of Agent Orange. The important thing to emphasize here is how unrelated symptoms have materialized and have been documented by various health care providers. Many cases could be presented in the same manner; the importance is the consistency in findings and their relationship to the toxic exposure.

Chapter 9

# Workers' Compensation Claims

Workers' compensation claims are filed for injuries, accidents, or disabilities that occur on the job. The claims are presented through the state workers' compensation system, a program for administratively following medical care and rehabilitation, and providing for disability and death benefits. The actual compensation is supplied by an insurance company.

The validity of the claim depends on whether the claimant can prove that the injuries are work related and the accident or injuries occurred within the scope of employment.

The assessments are accomplished through an impairment evaluation. A causal relationship must be established between the injury and the duties the claimant performed within his or her employment to warrant a valid claim.

Each state has its own system for evaluating workers' compensation claims. Typically the claimant is assigned a case worker, who is employed by the insurance company and follows the administration of the claim. Since these systems are state run, confidentiality is not maintained. The injury reports are subject to investigation, which allows the system information necessary to create safe working environments in the future. In addition, individuals applying for insurance are required to sign a release of information that allows the insurance company access to their medical files. These authorizations may remain valid for an indefinite period of time.

The process begins by filing a report that initiates the claim. Thereafter the patient is followed and monitored throughout his or her medical treatment. The case worker will help determine which medical care is appropriate to the alleged injury. Determinations must be made for allotting disability benefits, rehabilitative care and physical/occupational therapy, even transportation and death benefits. Finally, a determination must be made as to when the patient has reached maximum medical improvement, and assessing when the claimant may return to work in a limited or full capacity and evaluating the extent of impairment.

Payments are made when a claim is approved, and fall into three categories:

- Payments to the claimant for lost wages due to temporary total disability.
- Payment of medical bills.
- Payment to the claimant for permanent disability, partial or total.

## MEDICAL EVALUATION

Independent medical examinations are normally requested in a worker's compensation claim in addition to the patient's treating physicians. Since the claimant has already been to physicians of his or her choosing, typically it will be another party requesting the independent medical examination. The employer may request that another doctor assess the claimant. In addition, the carrier for the employer may have a list of physicians who evaluate claimants. The independent medical examinations in these cases are conducted by a physician upon whom both parties agree.

The issues involved in a workers' compensation claim vary, depending, for example, on state rules, whether there is an attorney involved, and how much money is in question. Also, the claim may need to follow rules in accordance with federal agencies, admiralty laws, railroad workers, international companies, and other bodies. You will need to research the individual governing bodies pertaining to the specific claim. Check Chapter 8 for a list of sources for federal agency standards.

The American Medical Association provides *Guides to the Evaluation of Permanent Impairment*, a reference framework within which treating and evaluating physicians assess and report medical impairment. These guidelines serve as a technical reference for evaluating limitations to body systems and functioning of body parts by applying precise medical and scientific determinants. Accordingly, distinctions are made between the terms *impairment, disability*, and *handicap*:

*Impairment.* An alteration in the patient's health status, determined by medical methods (e.g., The patient has lost motor control over her lower extremity from the accident.)

*Disability.* An alteration in the person's ability to meet the needs of his or her personal, occupational, or social demands. This assessment is determined by using nonmedical methods. (e.g., She can no longer walk without assistance.)

*Handicap.* An alteration in health or ability that limits the person in performing activities of life or work, which creates a record of such impairment that regards the person as having such an impairment. (e.g., The paraplegic woman will not regain use of her lower extremity.)

Employability considerations must be made administratively and medically. *Administrative considerations* concern the person's capacity to travel to and from work, to be present at work, and to perform the tasks and duties assigned, and for which the employer is willing to pay wages. *Medical considerations* include whether the physical limitations prevent the performance of the tasks and duties assigned. These are evaluated by parameters such as limitations in motion, sensory loss, and other disorders. These limitations are further evaluated by percentage loss. Total losses for permanent disabilities are also made, such as loss of sight and amputations. These awards are independent of the individual's capacity for work. Whatever the medical conditions involved, the evaluation protocol is very explicit so as not to allow for much individual variability of the evaluating physician's role.

*Aggravation and causation* in the legal sense is a nonmedical determinant, defined as a factor that not only *can* cause an impairment but *did* cause the impairment. In order for an aggravation to have the legal impact of a causation, it must be substantial and permanent, not merely speculative.

*Aggravation* can be broken down into five types:

1. Occupational disorder aggravated by a supervening nonoccupational disorder.
2. An occupational disorder aggravated by a supervening other occupational condition arising out of and in the course of employment by the same employer.
3. An occupational disorder aggravated by a supervening other industrial condition arising out of and in the course of employment by a different employer.
4. An occupational disorder aggravated by a preexisting nonoccupational condition.
5. An occupational disorder aggravating a preexisting nonoccupational condition.

*Permanent impairment* is described as an impairment that has become static or well stabilized with or without medical treatment or is not likely to remit despite medical treatment of the impairing condition. This is a medical determination.

*Permanent disability* may be medical or nonmedical. It refers to when the degree of capacity becomes static or well stabilized and is not likely to increase in spite of continuing medical or rehabilitative measures.

The medical assessment of impairment involves a thorough medical evaluation with specific regard for the history of the medical condition. Then, clinical evaluation is observed by the appropriate protocol, which will lead the physician to the proper evaluation and diagnostic procedures. They are laid out by chapter in the AMA's *Guides to the Evaluation of Permanent Impairment*:

1. Concepts of Impairment Evaluation
2. Records and Reports
3. Extremities, Spine, and Pelvis
4. The Nervous System

5. Respiratory System
6. Cardiovascular System
7. Hematopoietic System
8. Visual System
9. Ear, Nose, and Throat
10. Digestive System
11. Urinary and Reproductive Systems
12. Endocrine System
13. The Skin
14. Mental and Behavioral Disorders

There is also a glossary and an appendix on pain.

After the history of the condition has been taken, the clinical and laboratory findings are analyzed to determine the extent and nature of the loss. Then these results are compared with criteria specified for that particular body function, part, or system. Then the person is rated "as a whole," and given an appropriate impairment rating.

For example, if a worker lost his right thumb at the metacarpal-phalangeal joint in a machinery accident, the history of the accident and loss would be taken and the physician would be directed to Chapter 3. By following the evaluation criteria, the doctor would assess the patient with a loss of 100 percent use of his thumb, and thus 40 percent loss of his hand, 36 percent loss of the upper extremity, and 22 percent impairment of the whole person.

When dealing with neurological disorders and pain, the system becomes less reliable, as the conditions are more subjective.

Symptoms are described by *intensity* and *frequency*. Intensity is described by four levels:

1. *Marked.* The symptoms preclude any activity that brings them on.
2. *Moderate.* The symptoms would cause marked performance impairment in an activity that precipitates them.
3. *Slight.* The symptoms can be tolerated but would cause some impairment in performance of an activity that precipitates them.
4. *Minimal.* The signs and symptoms constitute an annoyance but do not cause any impairment in performing a particular activity.

Frequency is broken down into four areas as well:

1. *Constant.* The symptoms occur between 75 and 100 percent of the time when awake.
2. *Frequent.* The symptoms occur between 50 and 75 percent of the time when awake.
3. *Occasional.* The symptoms occur between 25 and 50 percent of the time when awake.
4. *Intermittent.* The symptoms occur less than 25 percent of the time when awake.

## THE MEDICAL REPORT

The medical evaluation must include a narrative history of the medical conditions: onset, course, findings on previous examinations, treatments, and responses to treatment; results of clinical evaluation, laboratory studies, and other diagnostic procedures; assessment of current clinical status, with plans for future treatment; diagnoses or clinical impressions; and the estimated expected date of recovery.

The report should be addressed to the case worker in most instances, and provide the patient's name, case number, and date of injury. It should then follow this format:

1. Past Medical History (obtained from:)
   a. Medical Office Records
   b. Hospital Records
   c. From Patient
   d. From Other Source
2. Clinical Evaluation
   a. Physical Examination
   b. Laboratory Tests
   c. Special Tests and Diagnostic Procedures
   d. Specialty Evaluations
3. Diagnosis
   a. Primary
   b. Secondary
   c. Tertiary
4. Stability of the Medical Condition

   _____ The clinical condition is not likely to improve with further active medical treatment or surgical intervention. Medical maintenance care only is warranted.

   _____ Employability is not likely to improve with further active medical treatment or surgical intervention.

   _____ The degree of impairment is not likely to change more than 3 percent within the next year.

5. Impairment Evaluation—AMA Guides. Provide and attach a complete report of findings with narrative comments for each body part or system, describing Protocol Section Number and Table Number.

This patient has been under my care from _____ to _____

[*or*]

I have not provided care for this patient. I have seen this patient ____ time(s) for the purpose of evaluating medical impairment.

______________________________

Signature of evaluating physician

In evaluating impairment ratings, you will often come across the Activities of Daily Living (ADL) scale. It assesses an individual's ability to perform certain activities and restrictions in those activities. They are broken down into nine sections:

1. Self-care and personal hygiene (eating, dressing oneself, combing hair, brushing teeth, bathing, urinating, defecating).
2. Communication (writing, speaking, hearing, seeing, typing).
3. Normal living postures (standing, sitting, lying down).
4. Ambulation (walking, climbing stairs).
5. Travel (driving, riding, flying).
6. Nonspecialized hand activities (grasping, lifting, tactile discrimination).
7. Sexual function (having normal sexual function and participating in usual sexual activity).
8. Sleep (restful nighttime sleep pattern).
9. Social and recreational activities: (ability to participate in group activities).

Chapter 10

# Personal Injury Claims

Personal injury lawsuits include a multitude of causes and circumstances. No matter what the individual occurrence—a motor vehicle accident, a slip and fall, an injury in a neighbor's pool, or a hit in the head by a worker's loose hammerhead—the personal injury claim must establish that:

1. There were injuries.
2. The injuries were caused by the defendant in whole or in part. (The claimant may be found partially responsible for the injuries received, due to contributory negligence).
3. The extent of the injuries.

Counsel may send the plaintiff to physicians with whom he or she has worked in the past, some of whom accept letters of protection or guarantee from the plaintiff's attorney, agreeing to pay for costs incurred on settlement of the case. The physician's office will then coordinate with the attorney's office regarding the status of the injury and state of treatment as the case moves along.

When the plaintiff's condition is in controversy, the defense attorney may request an independent medical examination by a physician other than the plaintiff's treating doctor. This is allowed under Federal Rule of Civil Procedure 34. The attorney for the defendant will choose the doctor or psychologist, schedule the examination, and pay for the visit.

A personal injury expert will focus on the occurrence itself—the incident causing certain injuries—and the extent of those injuries.

## INJURIES

The injuries suffered in the alleged accident should be adequately documented in the medical records. There should be supporting reports from treating physicians when applicable. Make sure your descriptions are backed up with adequate exhibits. Photographs depicting physical disfigurement, temporary or permanent, make a more substantial impact than verbose descriptions.

## DAMAGES

Damages include the actual physical damages from destroyed or damaged property and injuries suffered by the plaintiff that required medical, surgical or dental treatment, physical or occupational therapy, specialist care, prescription medications, psychotherapy and so on. These actual monetary damages are rarely disputed, as they should be accompanied by genuine and tangible medical bills for services rendered.

A sample medical bill itemization follows:

| ITEM NUMBER | DATE | DESCRIPTION | PURPOSE | AMOUNT |
|---|---|---|---|---|
| Exhibit #1 | 4/11/95 | Methodist Hospital | Hospital stay | $ 3,672.45 |
| Exhibit #2 | 4/15/95 | Dr. Leholtz | Hand surgery | $ 1,314.07 |
| Exhibit #3 | 4/15/95 | Methodist Anesthesia | Anesthesia | $ 857.43 |
| Exhibit #4 | 5/25/95 - 9/14/95 | Physical Therapy Assoc. | Ongoing therapy | $ 934.78 |
| CURRENT | RUNNING | TOTAL | - | $ 6,778.73 |

Damages also include monetary compensation for physical pain, mental suffering, physical disfigurement, loss of household services, loss of consortium, and other losses that the claimant suffered as a result of the injury. Let the patient tell you how his or her life has been altered by the event. How has it affected work, home life, relationships, self-esteem, sexual relations, household services? How has the pain altered the person's ability to enjoy life?

Physical disability covers limitations in activities of daily living, personal care, vocation, and avocation that the claimant was able to perform prior to the incident. See the list of ADLs in Chapter 9.

## LOST WAGES AND LOSS OF EARNING CAPACITY

The plaintiff will most likely be asked to provide as proof of income copies of tax returns for the five years previous to the incident. Employment records as well may become open to scrutiny by opposing counsel and become general knowledge. Although this information may be sensitive to some who may feel violated in disclosing amounts, it is necessary to verify the amount of income and time lost from actual work due to the injury. If the claimant lost 240 hours of regular pay and 32 hours of overtime, this can easily be multiplied by his or her hourly wages. Economic losses are calculated by determining the actual time and resulting money lost from active employment.

Future projections are made by extrapolating this amount forward to age 65, or to an average age of life for services other than economic, determined by using statistics found in the Life Tables published by the U.S. Department of Health and Human Services, *Vital Statistics of the United States*. Then take the current economic loss (calculating back to the time of the injury), and discounted by a difference of −1.25 percent, between the thirty-year historical growth rate of average U.S. hourly wages (say 5½ percent) and, taking the present value of the dollar and a thirty-year average ninety-day U.S. Treasury bill rate (say around 6 percent), project this amount forward times the number of working years remaining. This will approximately determine the amount of future lost wages. Benefits must be calculated as well. This process may require the services of an economic consultant.

Loss of earning capacity is calculated from disability determinations. The earning capacity prior to the accident is compared with the plaintiff's earning capacity since the accident, which is subtracted and presented in the same manner.

## FUTURE DAMAGES

*Future damages* pertain to monetary expenditures expected to be put forth after settlement of the case and to last a certain amount of time into the future, up to and including death. These damages may be physical, psychological, complications from the injury, alterations in lifestyle because of the injury, future surgeries, medications required because of the injury, psychiatric fees, and so forth. These damages often cause dispute because they seem speculative.

A good practice is to base future damages on treatment already rendered. If a client has required two reconstructive surgeries in the past because of the injuries and has at least two more to go, base the demand for future damages on the amounts expended in the past, including surgeons', anesthesiologists', and radiologists' fees, hospital bills, prescription medication, and recuperative time. Most physicians will provide an estimate of their bills beforehand. If not, find out through a health insurance company what customary charges are for like treatment.

When a medical condition develops because of the accident in question, you must estimate what it will take to treat this medical condition for the rest of the plaintiff's life. Physicians can provide a narrative of treatment required, from which you can extrapolate future costs.

Describe the treatment required, the purpose for the treatment, the frequency of the treatment, the estimated unit cost, the annual cost, and the vendor providing the service.

## LIFE CARE PLAN

A life care plan is a program for a victim of a serious disability, such as loss of extremities or spinal cord injuries. This guide or table includes costs required to modify the environment of the victim to restore him or her to an acceptable level of functioning. This should incorporate product replacement, prosthetic supplies, wheelchairs, home modifications for accessibility, future medications and evaluations, surgeries, revisions, and other services. Specialized clothing may be required, as well as modified eating utensils, driving aids, and vehicle modifications. Projected evaluations, therapeutic modalities, diagnostic testing assessment, aids for independent functioning, future medical care, architectural renovation, and any potential complications should be addressed too.

Rehabilitation and occupational therapy consultants can assist in working up a life care plan for a client. It might include these items:

- Introduction, background, and current status.
- Conclusions drawn.
- Future expected routine and nonroutine medical care.
- Equipment.
- Supplies.
- Medications.
- Wheelchair needs.
- Aids for independent function.
- Attendant care.
- Home services.
- Transportation.
- Projected therapeutic modalities.
- Architectural renovations.
- Counseling.
- Case management.
- Potential complications.
- Summary of costs.
- Records reviewed.
- Resources used.

When you are encountering a severe disability, the medical expert employed should be able to answer questions regarding the level of injury, the resultant disability and limitations, whether the condition is temporary or permanent, what life care plan, environmental modifications, and medical and rehabilitative treatment should be employed, and whether these assessments are usual and customary in determining long-term needs. Vocational limitations should be covered as well as limitations in activities of daily living

The American Amputee Foundation, located at Hillcrest Station, Little Rock, Arkansas 72225, (501) 666–2523, publishes newsletters, resource books, and videos to assist with presenting how a life may be altered by the loss of limbs.

## SETTLEMENT BROCHURE

Many law offices prepare a settlement brochure when all assessments for damages have been established. A sample settlement brochure should include a description of the accident or incident in dispute; a section on causation with supportive clinical correlations; a personal statement by the plaintiff(s) as to how his or her life has been changed by the incident and resulting injuries; medical expenses past, present, and future, including any life care expenses; any physical disability or disfigurement; lost earning or earning capacity; physical pain, mental suffering; loss of consortium; and other items. This should be supported by all documentation you have obtained up to this point, including economists' statements, consultants' reports, medical records and bills, and a list of ongoing treatment costs.

The damage summary should include a statement such as:

Based on the evidence provided, it is our opinion that a jury of this state would award at least the following amounts for each element of damages suffered by the plaintiffs:

| | |
|---|---|
| Medical Expenses | $ |
| Prescription Medications | $ |
| Future Medical and Life Care Expenses | $ |
| Lost Earnings and Earning Capacity | $ |
| Physical Pain and Mental Suffering | $ |
| Physical Disability | $ |
| Physical Disfigurement | $ |
| Loss of Consortium | $ |
| TOTAL | $ |

CONCLUSION

We hereby make demand on behalf of Mr. and Mrs. Doe to settle their lawsuit for $ ________ .

Sincerely,

Attorney for the Plaintiffs

# Part III

# The Lawsuit

Chapter 11

# Initiating the Lawsuit

The litigation process begins by notifying the opposing side that you intend to file a lawsuit. Local county, state, and district courts have rules governing how the *pleadings* (documents drawn up and presented to the court) are to be submitted. Most lawsuits are filed and followed through state trial courts in the county where the defendant resides. In class action suit, or cases where citizenship or venue is in question, the suit may be filed in district court. *Jurisdiction* is the power the court has to hear and render decisions in a particular case. The court must have jurisdiction over the subject matter and over the parties involved in the lawsuit.

A minor cannot sue in his or her own name, nor can someone deemed mentally incompetent. The corporate status of all agencies involved as *parties* (participants) to the suit should always be investigated to determine their status as a legal entity.

The first pleading involved in initiating a lawsuit is the *complaint*. This document is submitted to (filed with) the court and is issued a cause number. This is how the court will refer to the case and how it will be cited or referenced. The complaint is also served on the defendant with an accompanying summons, usually by a U.S. marshal. The *summons* is a notification of the filing of the lawsuit and instruction to the defendant to answer the complaint. If the defendants do not answer the complaint, they may be subject to judgment by default.

## LIABILITY

One of the primary roles of a lawsuit is to determine who is responsible and who shares the liability. Dramatic modifications are taking place in the realm of health care delivery and will continue to change. This dynamic area of reform has far-reaching effects on the litigator. Years ago, a negligent surgeon may have been listed as the one and only defendant in a medical malpractice claim. With the political realm of health care providers in a state of flux, who is responsible?

The myriad of relationships that have been developing make the answer to this question much less clear. A surgeon may perform his craft in his own office with his own staff in attendance. The operation may have been conducted in an outpatient surgical center. It may have included attendance of consulting assistants. A hospital-based operation may have employed an in-house anesthesiologist, that of a separate group, or a *locum tenens* contractor to provide anesthesia in the case. Consider the staff at the hospital, including nurses and technicians. The hospital itself may be owned by a national corporation.

Then we have the insurance companies, preferred provider organizations (PPOs), and health maintenance organizations (HMOs), which screen physicians before allowing their service as independent contractors. The HMOs and PPOs also restrict and limit the type and amount of procedural care that physicians working on their plan can perform, thereby assuming some responsibility for care of the patient.

As you can see, the liability in a health care claim is continuing to evolve as the relationships change. The constant still remains, however, that the standards of care must have been breached in a medical negligence case.

*Vicarious liability* allows the physician to share the responsibility for the alleged action with:

- Other physicians, nurses, and medical personnel.
- The hospital at which the alleged incident occurred (for the negligent acts of its employees). The hospital as an entity may be held liable based on the theory that the hospital owed a duty of care to its patients, or that the hospital is held liable based on the relationship (employer/employee, principal/agent) with the negligent parties' actions.
- A health care business responsible for the actions of those within its domain.

Some legal theories that support this shared responsibility include:

- agency
- joint venture
- partnership
- respondent superior
- single business enterprise
- subcontractor liability

It is wise to consider these relationships when evaluating a claim for medical negligence. Here are some questions that may assist you in determining which defendants to include:

- Was there a physician-patient relationship?
- Was the physician an independent contractor or subcontractor?
- Was the physician a caregiver for a health care plan? Does this make the health care plan partly responsible?
- Was the physician hospital based?
- Was a referring physician responsible for the acts of a specialist or nonspecialist?
- Was a physician responsible for other physicians under his or her supervision?
- Did the patient suffer injuries resulting from negligence of personnel employed by a physician or the hospital?
- Is the hospital privately owned, publicly owned, or a corporate business?
- Is the physician a member of a group, and does the group itself have a relationship with the hospital?

When suit is filed, it is recommended to allow for the later inclusion of additional defendants as they become known.

## DRAFTING THE COMPLAINT

The complaint is drafted according to local court guidelines, but most include certain elements:

- Caption (the title of the case and name of court).
- The cause number (to be issued by the court).
- Identification of all known plaintiffs and defendants.
- Court jurisdiction.
- Statements of facts alleging that the plaintiff sustained damages (what, when, where, and how) and that the defendant(s) are responsible for causing those damages.
- Specific clauses according to the nature of the claim. Each allegation must be stated separately.
- Prayer for damages.
- Signature of the attorney for the plaintiff.

Commonly referred to as the plaintiff's original petition, the following medical malpractice complaint serves as an example of the pleading that initiates a lawsuit.

CAUSE NUMBER ______

| | | |
|---|---|---|
| JOHN DOE | ) | IN THE DISTRICT COURT OF |
| JANE DOE | ) | |
| and BABY DOE | ) | YOUR COUNTY AND STATE |
| | ) | |
| vs. | ) | |
| | ) | |
| DOCTOR SMITH | ) | |
| NURSE JONES | ) | |
| and GENERAL HOSPITAL | ) | ____JUDICIAL DISTRICT |

PLAINTIFFS' ORIGINAL PETITION

COMES NOW JOHN DOE, JANE DOE, and BABY DOE, Plaintiffs herein, and makes and files this their Plaintiffs' Original Petition, complaining of DOCTOR SMITH, NURSE JONES, and GENERAL HOSPITAL, Defendants, and for cause of action, would respectfully show unto this Honorable Court as follows: [For some courts and in some cases you may want to insert a fictitious name clause, allowing for inclusion of additional defendants at a later time: "The true names or capacities, whether individual, corporate or otherwise, of defendant DOES I through ____, inclusive, are unknown to the plaintiffs at the date of this filing, and plaintiffs therefore sue defendant DOES by such fictitious names, and will ask leave of this court at a later date to amend this complaint to include such defendants when their names, capacities, and any negligence performed by defendant DOES have been ascertained."]

I

Plaintiffs, JOHN DOE, JANE DOE, and BABY DOE are presently, and were at all times material herein, a resident of (County and State).

Defendant, DOCTOR SMITH, is presently and was at all times material herein, a licensed physician, having offices located at ______, at which address defendant may be served with process.

Defendant, NURSE JONES, is presently, and was at all times material herein, a licensed registered nurse, employed by GENERAL HOSPITAL, and residing at ______, at which address defendant may be served with process.

Defendant, GENERAL HOSPITAL, is presently, and was at all times material herein, a medical hospital facility, a corporation doing business in County and State, located at ______, at which address the Hospital Director may be served with process.

II

Defendant DOCTOR, NURSE, and HOSPITAL have received notice of this pursuant to State Statute ______.

III

[Here you set forth the facts and allegations of the case:]

JOHN DOE and JANE DOE are parents and legal guardians of BABY DOE. BABY DOE was a patient of DOCTOR SMITH on September 9, 1995.

BABY DOE was admitted to the care of DOCTOR SMITH at GENERAL HOSPITAL on September 9, 1995.

NURSE JONES was an employee of GENERAL HOSPITAL on September 9, 1995 and served on the eleven P.M. to seven A.M. shift, on the pediatric intensive care unit, where BABY DOE was a patient.

DOCTOR SMITH examined and treated BABY DOE, and wrote out orders for NURSE JONES to provide supplementary feedings and medications to BABY DOE at GENERAL HOSPITAL on September 9, 1995, orders which NURSE JONES never carried out.

IV

As a patient of and under the care of DOCTOR SMITH, NURSE JONES, and GENERAL HOSPITAL, on September 9, 1995, Plaintiffs JOHN DOE, JANE DOE, and BABY DOE assert that Defendants DOCTOR, NURSE, and HOSPITAL owed to them a duty to exercise ordinary care in the diagnosis, and treatment of Plaintiff, BABY DOE.

V

Defendants failed to exercise such ordinary care as would responsible and prudent persons in the same or similar situation, and by their failure to act, breached their duty owed to the plaintiff; and that failure has proximately caused serious and grievous injuries to the Plaintiffs.

VI

By failing to act as would any reasonable or prudent persons in the same capacity and in the same or similar situations, the defendants were negligent in their duty.

VII

Plaintiffs seek for damages provided by law for injuries inflicted during the period on or about 9/9/95 during which time Defendant DOCTOR and NURSE, were the agents, representatives, servants, or employees of defendant HOSPITAL, and they were acting in the scope of their authority as agents, servants, or employees of defendant HOSPITAL. Defendant HOSPITAL is jointly and severally liable for all negligence by its employees, representatives, or agents under the principles of derivative liability.

VIII

As a proximate result of defendant DOCTOR, NURSE, and HOSPITAL's negligence, the Plaintiffs have suffered serious injuries. Such injuries have caused physical pain and mental anguish to the Plaintiffs in the past, and in all reasonable probability, will continue to cause physical pain and mental anguish to the Plaintiffs for the remainder of their lives, for which the Plaintiffs seek recovery of damages herein.

IX

As a proximate result of the Defendant DOCTOR, NURSE, and HOSPITAL's negligence, the Plaintiffs have expended funds in the past for their care and treatment, loss of wages and earning capacity, and in all reasonable probability, will be required to expend funds in the future for which the Plaintiffs seek the recovery of damages herein.

WHEREFORE, PREMISES CONSIDERED, the Plaintiffs pray that the Defendants be cited to appear and answer herein; that upon final trial hereof, they have judgment against the Defendants, jointly and severally, as follows:

1) Judgment against the Defendants for actual damages in the amount in excess of the minimum jurisdictional limits of this Court, together with pre-judgment interest at the lawful rates;

2) For sums incurred and to be incurred for medical and psychological treatment, in conformity to proof, as allowed by law;

3) The mental anguish that Plaintiffs have suffered and will suffer;

4) The loss of wages and earning capacity in the past and future in conformity to proof;

5) Judgment against the Defendants for post-judgment interest at the lawful rate until paid;

6) Punitive damages against the Defendants as allowed by law;

7) Costs of suit;

8) Costs of court;

9) Such other and further relief, both in law and in equity, general or special, which Plaintiffs may show themselves justly entitled.

Respectfully submitted,

______________________________

Attorney for Plaintiff

This document is filed with the court and served on the defendants, who then must file an answer through their attorney to the court. The answer, which contains the same cause number and heading, must be typed, filed, and served with the court by the specified number of days (usually up to 30). This is only the norm; there are exceptions. Also an extension may be requested in which to file answer, or a counterclaim may be filed. The answer is in the form of a legal response, usually denying the allegations set forth in the complaint.

Motions may be submitted to the court during the course of the lawsuit to request, for example, dismissal of the case; striking of defective parts of pleadings; nonsuit defendants (remove as parties to the suit); transfer of venue; summary judgment; continuance; and so forth.

A defendant may file a motion for summary judgment, wherein a supporting affidavit must be submitted to the court negating specific element(s) of the plaintiff's cause of action. Then the plaintiff has the burden of providing evidence (through an expert), to demonstrate evidence of the standards of care, familiarity with the standards of care, and specifically why the defendant's treatment fell below the standards of care.

Chapter 12

# Fact Investigation and Discovery

Now that the lawsuit is filed, gathering facts and information becomes the primary target of the lawsuit. The entire process is referred to as *discovery*. This is where most of the medical information is obtained, research is performed, and evidence is analyzed. This will also be where most of your actual labor is performed.

There are numerous ways information can be obtained from the other side in a lawsuit. The process of discovering tangible evidence involves subpoenaing medical records, tissue slides, photographs, tapes, x-rays, films, and medical bills, but first you must become aware of their existence. Aside from information gleaned from your client and witnesses, there are means by which the opposing side must give you information that you request. Not all information is discoverable; that is, some information remains privileged and is protected by the rules of discovery.

The vehicles by which you can obtain information in the process of discovery are:

- *Interrogatories.* Written questions one side asks of the other.
- *Requests for production of documents and things.* The adverse party must make available certain objects for your perusal.
- *Requests for admission.* Written statement of fact, asking for agreement that such facts are true.
- *Depositions.* Opportunities for counsel to ask questions to sworn witnesses. This testimony is recorded by a court reporter, and written transcriptions are provided to the parties for later scrutiny.

Informal fact investigation may be performed by a number of methods, for example, interviewing and obtaining statements from witnesses or reviewing hospital records, patient charts, and pharmacy records. Some of this information requires no formal method to obtain; other critical data may have to be secured via subpoena or court order.

Rule 26 of the Federal Rules of Civil Procedure governs the scope of discovery, requiring each party to make certain disclosures. These requirements are subdivided into three categories:

1. *Initial disclosures* (due 10 days after the meeting of the parties). During this phase of discovery, evidence required to be disclosed includes:
   - Name, address, and telephone number of each individual likely to have discoverable information relevant to disputed facts alleged with particularity in the pleadings, identifying the subjects of the information.
   - A copy of or a description of, by category and location, all documents, data, and tangible things in the possession, custody, or control of the party that are relevant to disputed facts alleged with particularity in the pleadings.
   - A computation of any category of damages claimed by the disclosing party, including any documents or other evidentiary material not privileged or protected from disclosure, making available for inspection and copying the material on which such computation is based, including materials bearing on the nature and extent of damages suffered.
   - Any insurance agreement under which an insurance business may be liable to satisfy part or all of a judgment.
2. *Disclosure of expert testimony* (due 90 days before trial). This section requires the disclosure of the identity of any testifying expert witness, including a written report, prepared and signed by the witness, which:
   - States all opinions to be expressed and the basis therefore.
   - Identifies exhibits to be used as summary or support for the opinion.
   - Sets out the witness's qualifications, including authored publications, compensation received for testifying, and a list of other cases for which the witness has testified.
3. *Pretrial disclosures* (due 30 days before trial). This section requires discovery of the name, address, and telephone number of each witness not previously identified; the designation of witnesses whose testimony is expected by means of deposition, and a transcript of pertinent portions; and appropriate identification of other exhibits or documents the party intends to offer or may offer if the need arises.

## INTERROGATORIES

*Interrogatories* are written questions one party asks of another party in the case. They are submitted in the form of a pleading and must be answered to the posing party through the court. The federal rules of evidence require that each party serve no more than 25 interrogatories, without special exception. These questions are typically numerous and lengthy, so as to not leave anything unasked. Developing the questions becomes easy once you reason them out. Ask yourself what you are attempting to discover about the party involved or the incident in question.

Draft interrogatories that are specific to the facts in your case. Law firms often have draft interrogatories in a database, where you can pick out the appropriate questions to ask. Following is a sample interrogatory for a physician defendant:

CAUSE NUMBER ______

| | | |
|---|---|---|
| JOHN DOE | ) | IN THE DISTRICT COURT OF |
| JANE DOE | ) | |
| and BABY DOE | ) | YOUR COUNTY AND STATE |
| | ) | |
| vs. | ) | |
| | ) | |
| DOCTOR SMITH | ) | |
| NURSE JONES | ) | |
| and GENERAL HOSPITAL | ) | ______JUDICIAL DISTRICT |

PLAINTIFFS' FIRST SET OF INTERROGATORIES TO DEFENDANT JOHN SMITH, M.D.

TO: John Smith, M.D., by and through his attorney of record ____________
Pursuant to Rule _____ of the State Rules of Civil Procedure, John Doe, Jane Doe, and Baby Doe, Plaintiffs herein, request that John Smith, M.D., Defendant herein, answer separately and fully in writing, under oath, the following Interrogatories within thirty (30) days of service hereof and thereafter supplement the answer as required by law.

Respecfully submitted,

Attorney for Plaintiffs

CERTIFICATE OF SERVICE

I hereby certify that a true and correct copy of the foregoing was delivered to all counsel of record in accordance with State Rules of Civil Procedure on the _ day of _____, 1995.

Attorney for Plaintiffs

INTERROGATORIES

1. State the full legal name, current address, date of birth, social security number, driver's license number, medical license number(s), which state(s) issued, title, and occupation of the Defendant, John Smith, M.D.

2. Identify all persons with knowledge of facts relevant to any claim or defense of any party to this lawsuit.
3. Please describe in complete detail your qualifications to provide care to the plaintiff in the alleged occurrence.
4. Are you employed by the hospital in which the alleged occurrence took place? If so, please state your title, the capacity in which you are employed, and the inclusive dates of your employment in that capacity.
5. Please describe where you received your education and training which qualifies you to practice medicine.
6. Have you at any time and for any reason whatever been suspended from any place of practice during your career? If so, please set forth where, when, and for what reason.
7. Has your license to practice medicine ever been suspended, probated, or revoked for any reason? If so, please set forth where, when, and for what reason.
8. Please list all positions you have held in your present capacity as a medical doctor from your present position back to your medical training.
9. Please describe the nature and scope of your duties and responsibilities with regard to the care and treatment of Baby Doe.
10. Please identify any and all persons who worked with you in the care and treatment of Baby Doe.

[Information obtained by the answers to these interrogatories can obviously assist as to which tack you will take in making your case.]

Interrogatories to the plaintiff by the defendant will ask such pertinent questions as:

1. Please provide the addresses of all residences you have ever held.
2. Please provide the names and addresses of all employers for whom you have ever worked.
3. Please list any and all health care providers that you have ever seen for any reason, the dates, the addresses, and the reason for which you sought care.

Information obtained through answers to interrogatories will provide the defendants with information to subpoena the medical records from other health care providers to determine if there was, say, an underlying condition that was not due to the defendant's negligence. Be creative in your requests while still adhering to the rules of discovery.

Not all questions asked in interrogatories warrant answers. Some questions may be objected to because the details requested may be protected by the the rules of discovery. The answers are written down on a document called "Answers to Interrogatories," which usually will include the questions asked followed by the responses.

## REQUESTS FOR PRODUCTION OF DOCUMENTS AND THINGS

These requests are submitted in the same manner as and usually accompanying the interrogatories. They are a tool whereby opposing sides are entitled to ask each other for documents and tangible things. Typically the list of items they want to review will be exhaustive: curriculum vitae, medical licenses, job records, hospital bylaws, medical records, tax records, x-rays, pathology slides, photographs, a damaged car seat, statements, pamphlets, tape recordings, and so on.

Requests for production from expert witnesses should include notes and markings on any medical records and depositions reviewed by the expert.

CAUSE NUMBER ______

| | | |
|---|---|---|
| JOHN DOE | ) | IN THE DISTRICT COURT OF |
| JANE DOE | ) | |
| and BABY DOE | ) | YOUR COUNTY AND STATE |
| vs. | ) | |
| | ) | |
| DOCTOR SMITH | ) | |
| NURSE JONES | ) | |
| and GENERAL HOSPITAL | ) | _____ JUDICIAL DISTRICT |

PLAINTIFFS' FIRST REQUEST FOR PRODUCTION OF DOCUMENTS TO DEFENDANT JOHN SMITH, M.D.

TO: John Smith, M.D., by and through his attorney of record______________

Pursuant to Rule _____ of the State Rules of Civil Procedure, John Doe, Jane Doe, and Baby Doe, Plaintiffs herein, request that John Smith, M.D., Defendant herein, provide responses to the following Request for Production of Documents within thirty (30) days of service hereof and thereafter supplement the answer as required by law.

Respecfully submitted,

Attorney for Plaintiffs

CERTIFICATE OF SERVICE

I hereby certify that a true and correct copy of the foregoing was delivered to all counsel of record in accordance with State Rules of Civil Procedure on the _ day of _____, 1995.

Attorney for Plaintiffs

REQUEST FOR PRODUCTION OF DOCUMENTS

1. All documents regarding, discussing, or pertaining in any way to your professional relationship with any other Defendant.
2. All documents regarding, discussing, or pertaining in any way to your medical licensing in the state of ______, or your accreditation with any hospital association or health care association.
3. A copy of all medical bills, statements, invoices, medical records or other tangible material regarding, discussing or pertaining to health care provided to Baby Doe or costs, charges, or expenses charged to Baby Doe.
4. All documents regarding, discussing, or pertaining in any way, to any policy or procedure manuals pertaining to any care, procedure or medication administered to Baby Doe.
5. Any and all personal notes or log books kept by any physician, nurse, or member of the hospital staff who treated or provided any medical care to Baby Doe.
6. All documents that reflect or relate to any insurance policies which may possibly cover any judgment in this cause of action.
7. All correspondence putting carrier on notice regarding this incident.
8. A copy of the work schedule for JOHN SMITH, M.D., for the entire month of September 1995.
9. Policies and procedures relating to medical records and standards of care.
10. Please produce any chart entry, order, or request signed by you pertaining to Baby Doe.
11. Please provide a copy of your application for staff privileges at General Hospital.

You may go on to ask questions about any person whom the defendant expects to call as an expert in the trial of this cause, information pertaining to the regulatory bodies governing the defendants, information that might identify another defendant, and so forth. You will be able to strategize depending on the nature of the case.

When a hospital is named as a defendant, it is advisable to request information concerning and copies of policies and procedures to verify information regarding granting staff privileges to physicians at their facility; written qualifications for staff membership; descriptions of background investigations regarding a defendant physician; and copies of disclosure forms the hospital sent to the Federation of State Medical Boards (FSMB), the American Medical Association's (AMA's) physician master file, and the National Practitioner Databank pertaining to the defendant doctor. If the hospital cannot or will not provide the information, *only* then can the plaintiffs' attorney request it from the FSMB.

## REQUESTS FOR ADMISSIONS

These requests involve undisputed facts and issues as the case evolves that if agreed on do not need to be argued at trial. They also may be grounds for a summary judgment.

## DEPOSITIONS

*Depositions* are oral examinations and cross-examinations of any party, witness, or expert who may have information relative to the legal action. Federal rules limit each side to the taking of 10 depositions, without special exception. Only one attorney is allowed to act as counsel during a deposition (although many may be present). The attorney and client may not hold private conferences during the deposition.

Deposition testimony is taken out of court, usually at the office of the attorney requesting the deposition. A court reporter is usually engaged to administer the oath and transcribe the testimony. Most court reporters now use computer-aided transcription, which can be purchased on disk. You may then use a laptop computer and software that allows you to search for key names, words, dates, and so forth so depositions do not have to be summarized. Depositions are often videotaped as well. The two may be combined so you have a computerized videotape recorder connected to the court reporter's transcription machine. Your word search will then be able to advance the computerized VCR to your computer screen, with text.

The deposition may be held at any time after the lawsuit is initiated and until it is set for trial. Sometimes the requesting party will issue a subpoena *duces tecum* to the individual being deposed, requiring that the witness bring or produce certain documents at the time of the deposition. These requests should be submitted well in advance of the deposition date to ensure compliance.

Educate yourself on the subject matter by reading the literature and talking with consultants. Investigate the deponent before the deposition. When deposing a medical doctor, read any literature he or she has written, and prepare questions on it. Explore the limits of his or her knowledge on relevant subjects, as well as any lack of expertise on the care in question. When deposing a defendant medical doctor, have the person read all of his or her entries in the medical record to secure them. Find out the doctor's relationship with other providers, the hospital, and so on. Get his or her recollection of conversations with family members and other treating physicians or nurses, and try to get him or her to take a position against a codefendant. Ask questions that will tie the physician to what he or she believes constitutes a breach in the standards of care. Ask about relevant entries made by other treaters, telephone conversations, who was present at which critical events.

A lawyer may need a medical assistant present during deposition of a medical expert. The attorney should elicit questions from medical staff to pose to a deposed physician or an alleged injury victim who is being deposed. It may be necessary to review and summarize the written transcription of a medical witness's deposition testimony, when transcribed, to find any inconsistencies with any other facts that have become apparent during the case or to pursue new avenues for research. It is advisable to have someone with medical knowledge skim through the contents, condense and index pertinent facts, uncover inconsistencies in the testimony, and assist the attorneys in unveiling details that should be developed before trial. The information uncovered by a thorough review of the deposition testimony may be invaluable during trial. The opposing parties' witness may testify to events that contradict testimony during his or her deposition. It is one of the most effective methods to discredit a witness.

Although deposition testimony is the preferable discovery method for many witnesses, it is time-consuming and expensive. Additionally, if you demand appearance of an uncooperative witness, the person may become defensive and belligerent and may waste the time of all those involved.

When setting a deposition would be impractical or inefficient or when a non-party witness resides out of state, deposition by written questions may be requested of the witness. This procedure is often used when "proving up" medical records and bills. Certain questions will be presented to the custodian of medical records and bills, and he or she will be required to answer them under oath.

Deposition summaries should be written sequentially with reference to the page and line number of the original document:

Page 113, line 16: Doctor Smith was actually in the call room when Baby Doe went into respiratory arrest.
Page 114, line 7: He slept through the Code Blue.

If a party fails to comply with any stage of recovery, the opposing counsel may apply to have the court enforce compliance with an *order to compel*. If the other side still fails to submit, *a motion for sanctions* may be filed.

## SETTLEMENT

When the information requested has been obtained by all parties through the process of discovery, it may be time to attempt settlement. Some states require that the case be scheduled for *mediation* or *arbitration*, an informal hearing involving parties to the suit, their attorneys, and an impartial mediator or arbitrator. This is an attempt to bring the parties together to discuss their case and come to an agreement as to what it would take (monetarily) to avoid bringing the case to trial. A medical consultant may be asked to be present at this hearing to assist the attorney with any medical issues that arise.

## SUBROGATION

When settling a claim for medical negligence or personal injury, the attorney must be aware of whether any third party is owed compensation or any rights to settlement proceeds. These may be in the realm of:

- Medical liens.
- Health insurance policies with a contractual right of subrogation.
- Hospital liens.
- Social security income and disability benefits.
- Medicare and Medicaid liens.
- Attorney's fees.

These all must be taken into account when settlement negotiations are underway. A substantial offer may be drastically diminished when subrogation liens are subtracted from the settlement funds.

Chapter 13

# Trial Preparation

After discovery is complete and all pretrial motions have been fulfilled, either party may request that the case be set for trial. This is usually preceded by a pretrial conference, wherein the parties list facts, witnesses, legal issues, and exhibits to be utilized.

When a trial date is requested, the clerk of the court will notify counsel. It will be imperative to structure the remaining time before trial well and make sure the client, witnesses, and experts are available.

By this point, your groundwork will have been laid. Your pleadings, discovery, research, and depositions have paved the way for an effective trial presentation. The actual trial setting is the forum by which you will demonstrate your litigation savvy. This is the culmination of your team's preparation. Muster every weapon in your arsenal to overwhelm your opponent. This includes technological and demonstrative evidence on top of the documentation you have already presented. By this point you have created a story on paper. Now you must convince 12 jurors that this story is true.

## TRIAL ORGANIZATION

Medical evidence that will be presented at the trial includes your research, presentation, medical illustrations, and testimony of medical experts. (Some experts require a retainer for their time at trial.)

The trial plan notebook should contain plans for case presentation, opening statements, *voir dire* and jury selection, legal research, questions for witnesses, and closing arguments.

**Pleadings Notebook**

A folder or notebook containing all pleadings and motions, arranged chronologically, should contain an index with tabs in front of each pleading for easy reference during trial.

If you have access to a document management system, you may have every document generated to this point saved on a floppy disk, hard drive, or CD for easy retrieval during trial.

**Evidence**

An exhibit folder should contain all original documents you intend to use and present at trial. (Note that federal rules of evidence set the standards for admissibility of medical records for evidence at trial. Generally the rules require that all evidence be relevant to the facts and circumstances.) Make sure these are labeled, dated, and indexed.

You may also put together a witness folder for filing deposition summaries, investigative reports, witness statements, and other pertinent material.

Original medical records and bills will have been meticulously combed through, tabbed, and summarized by this point. Depending on the extent of medical records that you have obtained in each case, you may have numerous binders containing medical records. You must know precisely what is contained in these records and be able to find any document promptly. An effective method to arrange extensive medical exhibits at trial is as follows:

1. Complete medical chronology and summarization with references to exhibits that prove the medical case. (You may have additional diagnostic tests and consultants' write-ups here as well.) Place these exhibits (copies of your original records) directly behind the medical summary, indexed and tabbed for easy reference.
2. Medical research—a summary of the medical issues you have researched to prove your case with published journals, periodicals, and medical texts that have been researched. Behind your summary should be placed copies of the documents you have referenced, indexed, and tabbed for easy reference.
3. Medical records notebook with the original documents indexed and tabbed.
4. Medical specials folder containing medical bills that have been obtained, as well as any reports pertaining to monetary damages, worth calculations, lost wages, earning capacity charts, future income loss projections, special care required, and expert economists' reports.
5. Depending on what type of medical illustrations, photographs, and charts you will utilize, you may have a folder containing exhibits, a screen, or an easel.

Another effective weapon is to use deposition testimony against your opponent. For example, a nurse's testimony may differ on the stand from her testimony during deposition. If you have access to a videotaped deposition via laser disk, you may play back the prerecorded portion that contains the conflicting information immediately after the controverted statement given on the stand. If opposing counsel has hired a medical expert with a large bibliography, read and compare the information gleaned from the medical articles against the deposition summary. This is an effective method to reveal contradictory testimony, thereby discrediting their expert to the jury. Use any contradictory information you have uncovered from the deposition transcripts against other witnesses and parties to the lawsuit as well.

Research the background of the opponent's experts. Question how much she or he is being paid for testifying. Ask how many cases she or he has testified for before and for which side—plaintiff or defendant. (You may want to perform a custom search from *Medical Malpractice Verdicts, Settlements and Experts* to unveil the expert's testifying history.)

## DEMONSTRATIVE EVIDENCE

There is no more effective means of presenting your case than by visual media because people are are more impressed by what they see than by what they hear. Jurors in particular remember what you show them rather than what you tell them.

Demonstrative evidence is extremely persuasive. Technological advances have made convincing video and computer-assisted equipment available for presenting evidence. You may have access to a television screen to present the video or computer-generated graphics images as well. Here are some hints:

- Still photographs can depict any stage of the victim's recovery and rehabilitation. These should be large enough so the jury can see details. Mount them on poster board for added effect. Pass them around to the jurors as well.
- Enlarge and display medical documents to the jury.
- Medical illustrations can create a dramatic effect, recreating different events in the patient's medical history. Medical illustrations can be found at schools with instruction in medical illustration. Some software companies also carry medical illustration software for your computer. Make sure these are flexible and can be adjusted to your specific needs.
- Medical slides can be purchased or borrowed. CIBA-Geigy is an excellent source of numerous medical slides, which are used for instruction in many medical schools. Check their libraries. CIBA-Geigy, P.O. Box 18060, Newark, New Jersey 07191–8060, also publishes a catalog of almost 5,000 35–mm projection slides (including spinal injuries, maxillofacial injuries, and low back pain). Review your local medical library's audiovisual section for additional presentation material.
- Computer-generated images may be produced using any graphics or imaging software. These may be printed and blown up or displayed on a computer monitor to the jurors.
- Videotapes can make an impact. Illustrate what a day in the life of the plaintiff is like.

For example, show modifications of the home to accommodate wheelchair access in the bathrooms.

- Use actual medical devices like a full body cast, a Harrington rod, a metal plate placed in a complainant's scalp, or a ruptured breast implant in a products liability claim.

Handle favorable objects carefully and close to your body. When presenting unfavorable objects, hold them away from your body as you present them.

## JURY SELECTION AND *VOIR DIRE*

Plan your case presentation. Introduce yourself, your client, and any cocounsel. Introduce opposing counsel and client as well. During *voir dire* the message you want to convey to the jury is that (1) you have confidence in your case and expect to win; (2) you believe your case is true and just; (3) you and your client are a team, and the outcome matters deeply to both of you; and (4) you are sensitive to each juror's need for privacy and will respect their concerns during *voir dire*. This is generally a lengthy process in a malpractice case. Try to utilize the principle that the jurors will best remember what they hear first. You must project a favorable image to the jurors. Favorable characteristics that should be projected are honesty, sincerity, credibility, competency, and trustworthiness. Refer to your client by name, not by "my client."

One of your most important tasks will be in selecting jurors you think will most favorably view your case. There are experts in this field for hire who take a scientific approach in selecting favorable jurors. Actually, the scientific approach is a commonsense approach as well. If the case involves a claim against a pediatrician for medical negligence wherein an infant child suffered irreversible brain damage, plaintiffs' attorneys are going to choose those whom they believe would be most sympathetic to their plight: mothers of small children, mothers, parents, grandparents, and teachers. Defendants, on the other hand, would prefer a single, young, male, medical resident whose father is a physician or a successful businessman without close family members, who is far removed from a small infant. Explore relations to a doctor, nurse, or lawyer.

You may explore jurors' attitudes through practical questions like, "Is there anyone who has seen, heard, or read articles about what is termed the liability crisis?" ". . . and if you believed the statement, could that play any role in your decision in this case?" Open-ended questions are helpful as well, "What do you think about the idea that . . . ?" Encourage answers that require more than a simple yes or no.

You can sometimes get an instinctive sense of who has a sympathetic disposition. Look at the dress, the posture, and interaction with others. You can spot a hard-natured, cooler personality by noting a certain aloof and unapproachable air. Do not mistake shy and reserved for indifference, however. Try to identify and disqualify jurors with attitudes, opinions, or backgrounds that may lead them to champion the cause of the opposing side during jury deliberation.

When the jury panel has been chosen, it is over. You have no more control over who will be deciding the case. Work with the jury you have. If there are members you are concerned about, strive to make eye contact with them specifically. Demonstrate your compassion to the jury and your interest in fairness and justice.

## THE PERSUASIVE PROCESS

During your opening statement, try to humanize and personalize your client, show association between you and your client, and stress facts you wish to present as though you were testifying, in the form of a story. Plaintiff's counsel should emphasize the concept of negligence and address damages in the opening statement. First, get the jury's complete attention. Studies have demonstrated that 80 percent of jurors make up their minds in the case during the opening statement. Much of this is based on impressions more than actual content. An example of a theme might be where a patient on Medicaid received substandard care at the same hospital where a patient with full health insurance received more complete workups, additional laboratory studies, and more physician referrals.

A case theme is one of the most effective methods of encompassing and projecting your side of the story. The case theme should be a simple, unique motif that embraces the central elements of your case and projects them in a mode that jurors will remember and support. The theme should seek empathy from the jurors, not pity.

The impact of the verdict should be discussed, with particular emphasis on how the verdict will affect the defendant, the plaintiff, and the industry (medical, manufacturing, chemical, etc.).

Build up to a dramatic crescendo. Be expressive and plead your case. Make the jury feel what your client is feeling. Create a mood, and transmit it to the jury. Simplify your verbiage, and use appropriate inflections (lower your tone for impact; lower the eyes and pause for dramatics). Apply visual aids for specific impact. Ensure your visual, vocal, and physical behaviors are consistent. The jurors will believe the physical behavior first; therefore, nonverbal messages have a subtle yet dramatic effect. Keep your gestures controlled and purposeful. When communicating positive verbal messages, use the palm-up gesture. When referring to the opponent, use the palm-down gesture, which communicates disapproval. The palm-outward gesture expresses rejection of an idea. A pointed finger indicates recognition (but never point at jurors). A clenched fist expresses earnest intensity. Use animated facial gestures and eye contact. Maintain an alert yet relaxed posture. Combine simple and direct logic with emotional content and impact. This combination approach keeps the style of delivery lively, entertaining, and memorable.

The medical and consulting experts who will be presenting supporting medical evidence for your case will normally resort to their most comfortable habit of talking above the jury. This has proven to be ineffective. The typical juror will not be impressed by an attitude of "I know more than you do." All medical information and scientific research can be simplified and presented at the level of the audience, no matter who they are. Practice methods to clarify complicated data and keep it at a basic level. Pretend that you are trying to convince a ninth-grade class of the pertinent and convincing medical information. Keep it friendly. When the information becomes boring, jurors no longer listen.

As the attorney presenting the case, you become the most important witness in the trial; you will be addressing the jury, and they will be trying to assess your credibility as well as that of other witnesses.

A very effective practice is to have staff members present during the trial—both those experienced in trial practice and those who are not. If you cannot expend members of your staff, ask a friend whose opinions you trust. When evidence is being presented, have them watch the jurors. View their response to your presentation and that of your opposition. You can read their eyes, facial gestures, and body language. If they like your medical expert's testimony, they will pay attention to it. You will see them leaning forward in their seats and occasionally nodding. If they do not buy it, they will be looking down or away and will lose interest. If they frankly disagree with the testimony, they will exhibit sour expressions. They may acquire a mental impression when opposing counsel presents evidence, which can be diffused only through immediate objection. During recesses, talk with your staff about their impressions. You will be able to press forward with your present method if it is effective or shift gears if it is not. When presented with jury bias and prejudice during the trial, confront it immediately to lessen the impact.

The closing argument is your opportunity to tie together all the preceding evidence. It is not the time to try to salvage your case or to discharge prejudice, but to put it to rest.

Part IV

# Medicine for Lawyers

Chapter 14

# Introduction to Medicine

The study of medicine can seem intimidating because medical professionals speak their own language. Most medical terms stem from Latin and Greek, but they also consist of other languages, so taking a course in basic Latin will not teach you medical terminology. This basic method of introducing medical concepts with core word components will also provide a systems approach to human anatomy and physiology, providing clinical diagnosis and treatment by major organ systems. From it you will learn enough to be able to deduce the contents of almost any medical report.

## THE BASICS

Generally the human organism exists to try to remain the same physiologically. Its primary function is to achieve and maintain *homeostasis* in a constantly changing environment.

*home(o)*—the same, unchanging

*stasis*—a state of equilibrium

This constancy pertains to temperature, fluid level, acidity, electrolyte balance, and so on. External forces (ingesting food, urinating, encountering viruses, sustaining injuries) continually act on the body to change its normal physiological state. Whatever the disruption, the body has a tendency to stabilize itself. A good physician will attempt to work with the body's ability to adapt in the face of *disease*, to restore its normal function and structure.

*dis*—reversal or separation
*ease*—a state of freedom from pain or discomfort
*idiopathic*—a disease process of unknown origin

Malpractice occurs when a physician fails to render proper care or services, through ignorance or negligence. This may involve disrupting homeostasis in an attempt to alleviate a disease process.

*mal*—wrongful
*practice*—skill through experience

The word element *-iatrics*, as in *pediatrics* or *geriatrics*, pertains to medical treatment, or treatment by a physician. Since we are concerned with malpractice, another important definition to become familiar with is *iatrogenic*—a condition, state, or adverse reaction resulting from medical treatment by a physician, as when a patient undergoes an operation that introduces a systemic infection into the patient's body. This would be an iatrogenic cause. *Nosocomial* infections are those that originate in a hospital.

The body consists of:

*cells*—the fundamental structural unit of a living organism. In medicine a cell is typically described as a *cyte*, used as a suffix following the root word (*osteocyte*—bone cell).

Organized together to perform certain specialized functions, the cells form:

*tissues*—an aggregation of similarly specialized cells to perform a certain function (*adipose tissue*—connective tissue made of fat cells; *lymphoid tissue*—formed from lymphatic cells, or *lymphocytes*). Together tissues construct organs.
*organs*—somewhat independent structures that perform specialized functions.

Most organs are contained within cavities in the thoracic, abdominal, or pelvic areas, or the brain and spinal column. The skin is also technically an organ, with the largest surface area. The skin functions to protect the internal environment from potential insults from the external environment. The adjective *cutaneous* means "pertaining to the skin."

*epi*—around
*dermis*—skin

The skin is composed of the *corion* (or dermis) and the *epidermis*. Commonly the term *epidermis*, meaning "around the skin," will be used alone to represent the entire structure. Contained within the two layers of skin are hair shafts and follicles, papillae, sweat and oil glands, cutaneous blood vessels, and nerve fibers sensitive to pain, pressure, temperature, and touch.

The word element *dermato-* refers to skin. *Dermatitis* refers to any type of skin inflammation, usually described with an adjective. *Contact dermatitis* is skin inflammation due to contact with an irritating substance.

Most medical conditions can be referred to as either *acute*—that is, short-lived, with symptoms usually running a limited course—or *chronic*—persisting over a long period of time.

## BODY SYSTEMS

The human body has been broken down into individual systems of organs, which interact to make the total body function and survive. These systems also have become specific disciplines or specialties within the practice of medicine. Oftentimes medical terminology in the records will consist of positional definitions (see Figure 14.1) and anatomical definitions (Figure 14.2) which are better represented pictorially than by confusing terminology.

**Figure 14.1**
**Positional Definitions**

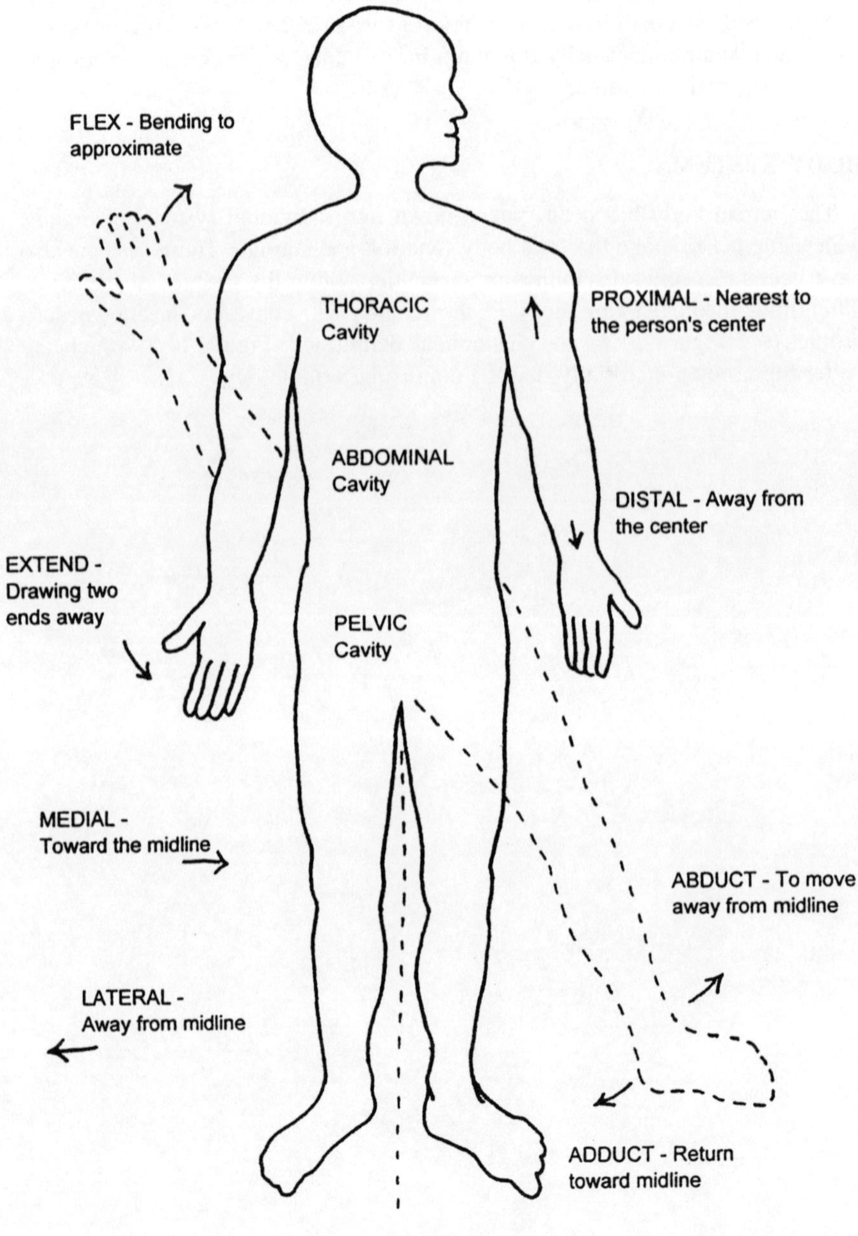

**Figure 14.2**
**Anatomical Definitions**

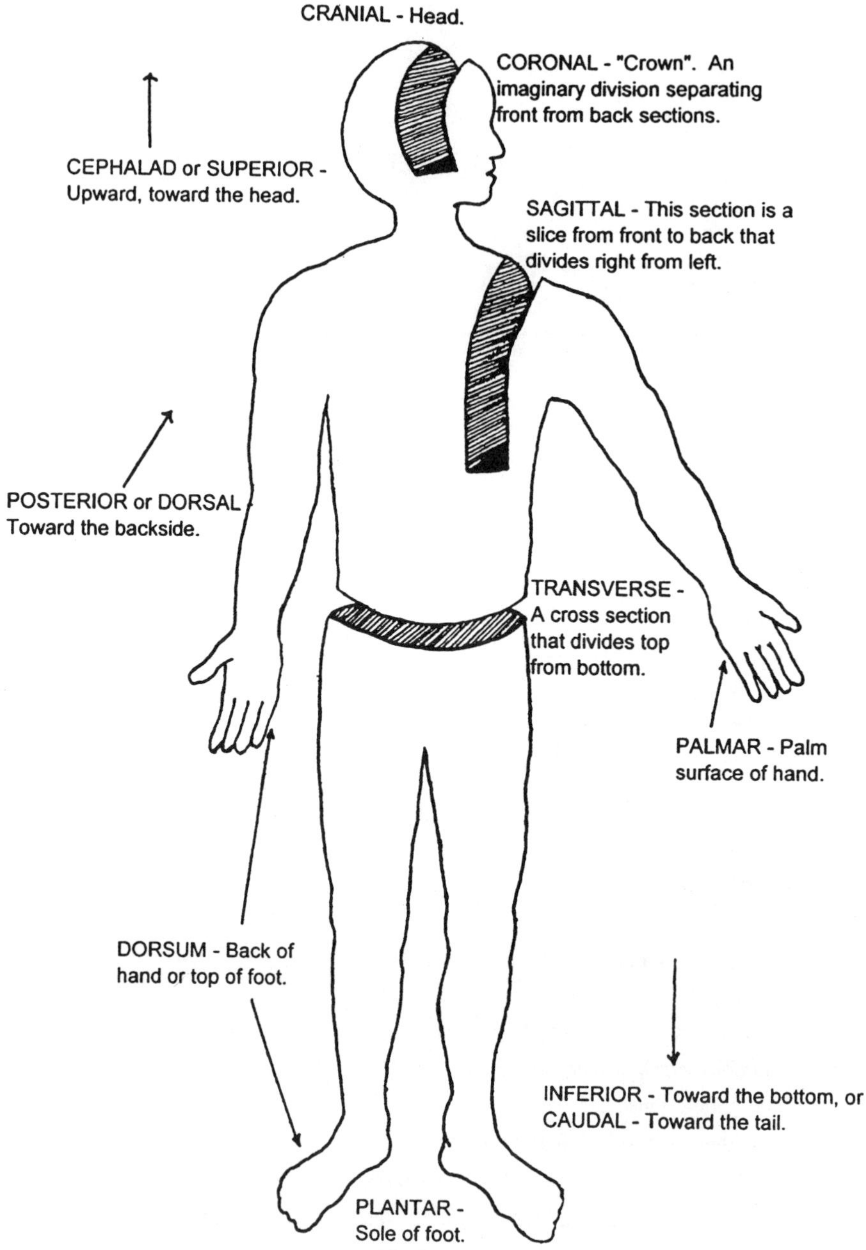

Chapter 15

# The Cardiovascular System

**Disciplines**

Cardiology

Hematology (blood)

Cardiovascular surgery

Internal medicine

*cardio*—heart

*vascular*—pertaining to blood vessels or blood supply.

The cardiovascular system is comprised of the heart, the pump that delivers blood through vessels and transports the components of blood to the body cells. The heart is an organ approximately the size of a fist.

## CARDIAC ANATOMY

*peri*—around; the outside protective covering

*epi*—upon or over; the most superficial layer

*myo*—the middle muscular layer

*endo*—the internal layer, lining the inside

*atrium* (left and right)—upper, receiving chambers of the heart

*tricuspid valve*—a valve composed of three cusps between the right atrium and ventricle

*mitral valve*—a valve composed of two cusps, shaped like a miter, between the left atrium and ventricle

*ventricle* (left and right)—the lower, pumping chamber of the heart

*pericardium*—tissue surrounding the heart

*epicardium*—outside surface of the heart

*myocardium*—middle muscular layer

*endocardium*—the inner lining of the heart chambers

The heart's natural pacemaker is a small mass of cells referred to as the *sinoatrial* node, which transmits impulses that cause the heart to contract. The impulses travel to the *atrioventricular* node, down to a wall between the ventricles, the *interventricular septum,* and then divide into right and left halves. ECGs can detect any of these transmission abnormalities.

Pulse rates are taken to determine how fast the heart is pumping blood. *Palpable* (those you can feel) pulses may be felt at the carotid, brachial, radial, femoral, popliteal, dorsalis pedis, and posterior tibial arteries. If abnormal, rates will be described as:

*arrhythmia*—abnormal rhythm

*bradycardia*—slow heart rate

*tachycardia*—fast heart rate

Heart sounds will be *auscultated* (listened to) with a stethescope. They will be described as $S_1$, $S_2$, $S_3$, or $S_4$. Heart rhythms will be determined using ECGs. The patterns will be described as exhibiting waves, identified as P, QRS, T waves. From these patterns, certain heart abnormalities can be discovered. Some of these may be described with terms such as:

*paroxysmal*—sudden

*hypertrophy*—abnormally large

*infarct*—a deadened area

*flutter*—continuous, rapid sequence of waves

*fibrillation*—rapidly erratic waves

They will be further described by their location, such as:

*sinus arrythmia*—abnormal rhythm originating from the sinoatrial node

*multifocal atrial tachycardia*—fast rate originating all over the atria

*paroxysmal ventricular tachycardia*—sudden rapid rate from the ventricles

A heart attack, or *myocardial infarction*, is characterized by *angina pectoris*, or strangling chest pain. Often an atherosclerotic vessel occludes part of the blood supply to the heart muscle itself, which becomes *necrotic* (dead tissue.) When this process reaches a critical level, certain stressors will produce this debilitating chest pain, which sometimes radiates to the left arm, neck, and jaw. Emotional stress and excitement, physical exertion, cold weather, or consuming cigarettes or a big meal can bring on this pain. Another diagnostic sign is *diaphoresis*—profuse sweating.

A patient diagnosed with this disease process may sometimes be managed with diet and exercise; usually drugs are employed as well. Sometimes surgery is required to reroute the blood supply by transferring a vessel (usually from the leg) to supply the heart muscle. This operation is called a coronary artery bypass graft, or *CABG* (pronounced "cabbage"). Balloon angioplasty is another treatment, whereby the artery is dilated with an artificial device attempting to restore function.

## THE VASCULAR SYSTEM

Blood vessels are broken down into the following components:

*arteries*—carry oxygenated blood away from the heart. The *aorta* is the main artery leaving the heart. In the thoracic cavity it is called the *thoracic aorta*. In the abdomen it becomes the *abdominal aorta*. Vessels supplying blood to the heart muscle are called *coronary* arteries. The walls of arteries are relatively thick and are made up of three layers (outer, middle, inner). *Arterioles* are small arteries. (See Figure 15.1.)

*veins*—carry "used" blood back to the heart. The largest and main vein is the *vena cava*, (vein cavity), which is separated into the *superior* (toward the top) and *inferior* (toward the bottom). *Venules* are small veins. Veins are thinner than arteries and have valves that keep blood flow in one direction: toward the heart.

*capillaries*—resembling a hair. These minute vessels connect the smallest arteries (arterioles) to the smallest veins (venules).

Blood flow can be interrupted through an *embolism*—the sudden blocking of an artery through the lodging of foreign material. This may be due to air, fat, infection, plaque, or a dislodged heart valve prosthesis.

*Exsanguination* means the extensive loss of blood through internal or external *hemorrhage*, or bleeding. A *hematoma* is a localized collection of blood from a break in the wall of a blood vessel.

Blood pressure is taken with a cuff called a *sphygmomanometer*. Blood pressure readings are broken down into *systolic* and *diastolic* pressure or tension. Systole is the pressure recorded through the ejection phase of the ventricles as they are pumping out blood, and diastole is the recorded pressure as the ventricles dilate and fill with blood. They are commonly referred to with two numbers: systolic and diastolic. From these readings the patient's blood pressure is described as normal, *hypotensive* (low pressure), or *hypertensive* (high pressure). The prefix *ortho-* means "straight, correct, or normal." Often blood pressure will be described as *orthostatic*, which pertains to standing erect. *Orthostatic hypotension* would mean a drop in blood pressure when the patient stands up.

**Figure 15.1**
**The Cardiovascular System**

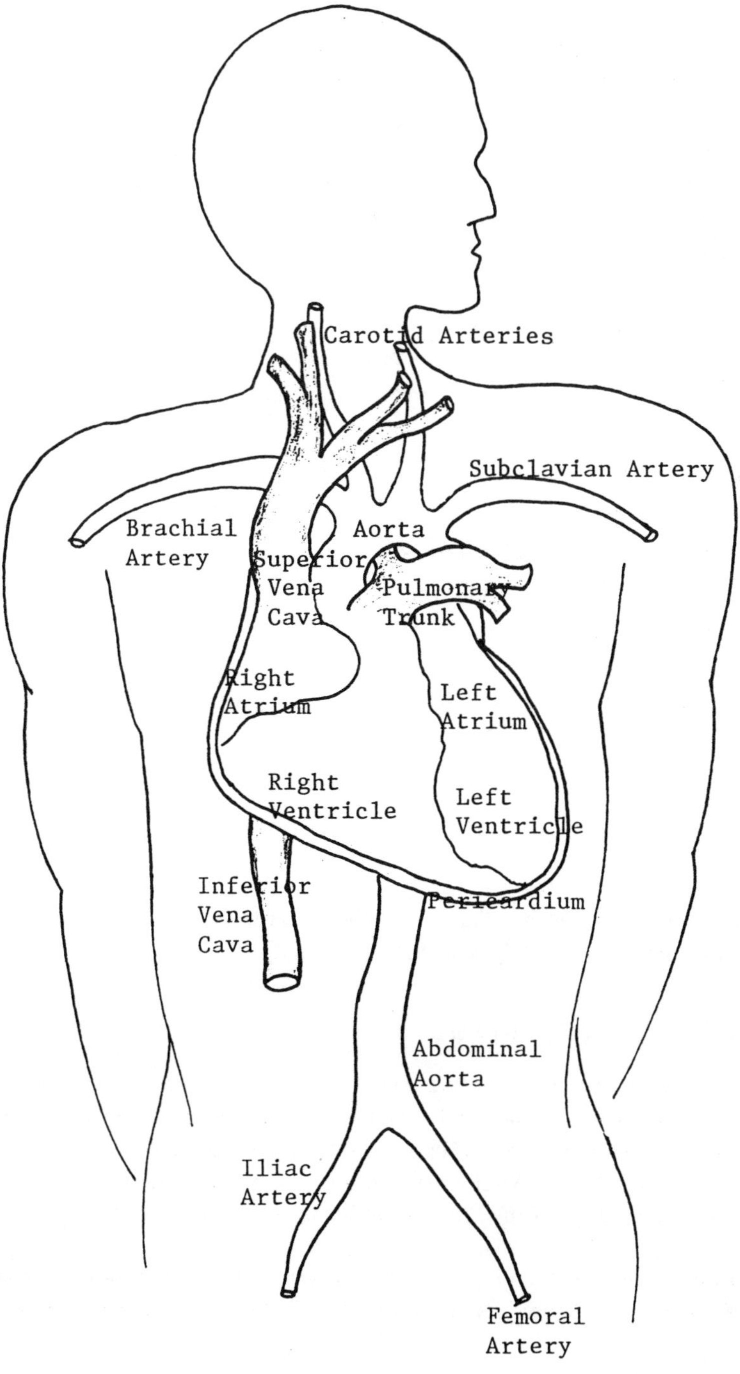

*hypo*—less than normal

*hyper*—more than normal

Blood cells are formed in the *hematopoietic* system, which is responsible for developing components of the blood: red and white cells. These organs consist of the *bone marrow*, the *spleen (lien)*, the *liver*, and the *lymph* nodes. White blood cells are referred to with the word element *leuk-*. A *leukocyte* is a white blood cell. *Erythro* means "red." An *erythrocyte* is a red blood cell, which transports oxygen (picked up in the lungs) to the rest of the body. *Hemoglobin* is its protein, made up of substances like iron.

*-emia*—blood condition

*-oma*—tumor or neoplasm (cancerous growth)

*-osis*—a condition usually denoting pathology (too much)

*-penia*—a suffix meaning deficient

*anemia*—less than the normal amount of a certain component of blood

*erythrocytosis*—increase in the red blood cell mass

*leukemia*—a blood disease affecting blood cells

*leukopenia*—not enough white blood cells

*lymphoma*—a cancer of the lymphoid tissue

*heme*—a word element representing the oxygen-carrying properties of the hemoglobin molecule. As far as we are concerned, however, when used as a prefix in the form of *hem-*, *hemo-*, or *hemato-*, it will mean *blood.*

*hemanalysis*—analysis of the blood

*hematuria*—blood in the urine.

*hemocyte*—a blood cell

*Hemi*, however, means "half." Cerebral *hemisphere* means half the brain. *Hemianalgesia* means analgesia on one side of the body.

## DIAGNOSTIC PROCEDURES

Examination of heart disorders should always begin with the most noninvasive procedures. The least invasive technique to determine what sort of abnormalities may be present in the heart consists of auscultation with a stethoscope. An astute clinician can thereby detect signs of heart enlargement, friction rubs, murmurs, valvular problems, rhythm abnormalities, and some pulmonary problems as well.

Radiological examination of the heart is very important in proper diagnosis and management of heart disorders. Major radiological techniques consist of:

Plain chest films (views are anteroposterior, posterioanterior, lateral, oblique, inspiration-expiration, decubitus)

Fluoroscopy

Radionuclide imaging

Echocardiography

Invasive techniques might consist of:

Venous cutdown or cannulation

Central venous pressure measurement

Pulmonary artery catheterization

Cardiac catheterization

Angiography

Pericardiocentesis

Surgery

These techniques have associated risks and contraindications because of their invasive nature. Introducing any foreign substance into the body should not be attempted unless less invasive measures have proved inadequate. The patient should always be warned of the inherent risks and dangers of a procedure before consenting to its execution.

## ANTICOAGULANT THERAPY

When we bleed, various blood elements are activated to coagulate the blood so we will not bleed to death: platelets, thrombin, thromboplastin, fibrinogen, fibrin, and various other blood factors. Like many other physiological processes, they can become pathological. Anticoagulant therapy is directed to therapeutically arrest clotting, or the formation of a *thrombus* (an aggregation of blood factors). Thrombi cause embolic events; a blood clot lodges someplace it is not supposed to, like the lungs, heart, or brain. When this happens, fresh oxygenated blood cannot reach its target organ and the organ may die.

Drugs developed to arrest this process include those that prolong clotting time. Called *anticoagulants*, they inhibit stages in clotting synthesis. Normal prothrombin times should be established before starting warfarin. The objective of therapy is to induce an anticlotting effect without causing a significant bleeding event. Side effects include bleeding, rebound thrombosis at cessation of treatment, and, rarely, coumadin-induced skin necrosis. Management of bleeding should include stopping the anticoagulant, administering blood or plasma, or vitamin K injection. Clinical indications are:

Acute pulmonary embolism

Deep vein thrombosis

Arterial embolism, mitral valve disease, atrial fibrillation, artificial heart valve implants

Postmyocardial infarction treatment

Prophylaxis in surgical patients

Cerebral ischemia

**Anticoagulants**

Heparin (sodium) (Heparin)

Heparin (calcium) (Calciparine, Coumadin)

Warafin

Protamine sulfate

*Thrombolytic therapy* is aimed at activating plasminogen and plasmin, which dissolve formed fibrin clots. In general, thrombolytic agents are aimed at salvaging myocardial function by restoring circulation postmyocardial infarction. Thrombolytic therapy is intended to dissolve any forming thrombus to reperfuse the ischemic area soon after the onset of chest pain. Bleeding is a major disadvantage of these agents. There is often an underlying vascular injury on which superimposed anticoagulant therapy results in a defect in hemostasis (the process of arresting bleeding) by reducing fibrinogen, impairing platelet aggregation, and forming breakdown products with their anticoagulant activities.

**Thrombolytics**

Streptokinase (Streptase)

Urokinase (Abbokinase)

APSAC

rt-PA

Recombinant pro-urokinase

*Hemostatics* is the term used to denote drugs that arrest the bleeding process. Drugs in this category also include antifibrinolytic agents. They enhance hemostasis when fibrinolysis contributes to bleeding. Some may enhance the body's own hemostatic mechanisms. This may be needed following surgical complications or severe trauma, to counteract anticoagulant activity, or for patients with hemophilia, clotting defects, or von Willebrand's disease. They should not be administered without a definitive diagnosis.

**Hemostatics**

Aminocaproic acid (Amicar)

Tranexaminic acid (Cyklokapron)

Desmopressin acetate (DDAVP)
Phytonadione (Konakion)
Factor IX complex (Konyne 80)
Aprotinin (injection) (Trasylol)

*Hemostats* may be used in the surgical setting as well, to control bleeding during an operation.

**Hemostats**

Microfibrillar collagen hemostat (Instat)
Collagen-absorbable hemostat (Instat)
Absorbable gelatin (Gelfoam, Gelfilm)
Oxidized regenerated cellulose (used only as an adjuvant in gynecological pelvic surgery to reduce postoperative pelvic adhesions) (Surgicel, Interceed)
Thrombin (Thrombogen)

Patients receiving anticoagulant therapy should be monitored for their bleeding time and clotting status. *Bleeding time* is a general measurement and will be prolonged in patients with low platelet counts or following aspirin ingestion. More specific coagulation tests include prothrombin time (PT), used to monitor oral anticoagulants, and partial thromboplastin time (PTT), used to monitor heparin therapy.

## CARDIOVASCULAR DRUGS

Cardiovascular disease is a major cause of death in our society. Clinical and medicinal management is aimed toward alleviating the causes: hypertensive heart disease, myocardial ischemia/infarction, and rhythm abnormalities. The major functions of a healthy heart that we are concerned with preserving are contractility, rate, and rhythm. Possible etiological factors that may contribute to the development of cardiac arrhythmias are:

Hypertensive heart disease
Viral heart disease
Degenerative states such as coronary artery disease
Congenital abnormalities
Congestive heart failure
Disturbances in other organs
Infections and toxic states
Malnutrition and anemia
Electrolyte disturbances

*Angina* is pain resulting from myocardial ischemia. This condition develops when the demands of the working heart exceed the capacity of the coronary circulation to provide oxygen and remove metabolites.

Treatment of cardiovascular disease will be aimed at increasing contractility, normalizing rate and rhythm, decreasing the workload of the heart, and increasing blood flow to the heart muscle.

## Inotropics

Cardiac glycosides are steroid-based agents that increase cardiac contractility by inhibiting sodium/potassium/ATPase. This very important group of drugs, often responsible for saving lives, has also been responsible for causing deaths by producing abnormal heart rhythms in patients who are vulnerable. It is necessary for patients who are receiving digoxin to have their blood levels monitored closely.

**Digitalis**

Digoxin (Lanoxicaps, Lanoxin)

Digitoxin (Crystodigin tablets)

Cardiotonics increase cardiac contractility through sympathomimetic and nonsympathomimetic mechanisms.

**Sympathomimetics** (includes beta-1 agonists)

Dopamine (Intropin)

Dobutamine (Dobutrex)

**Nonsympathomimetics**

Amrinone (lactate) (Inocor [injection])

Milrinone

Theophylline

## Antidysrythmic Drugs

Antiarrythmic agents fall into four separate classes of drugs that generally depress the electrical activity of the heart or alter its circuitry.

*Class I antiarrhythmic agents* function as sodium channel blockers. This action changes the cardiac action potential.

Quinidine gluconate (Quinaglute Dura-Tabs)

Quinidine polygalacturonate (Cardioquin)

Quinidine sulfate (Quinidex)

Procainamide hydrochloride (Procan)

Disopyramide phosphate (Norpace)

Lidocaine (for IV emergencies)

Phenytoin (Dilantin)

Tocainide hydrochloride (Toconard)

Mexilitine (Mexitil)

Encainide

Flecainide acetate (Tambocor)

Propafenone hydrochloride (Rythmol)

Moricizine hydrochloride (Ethmozine)

*Class II antiarrhythmics* are beta blockers:

Propranolol (Inderal, Inderide)

Metoprolol (Toprol, Lopressor)

Nadolol (Corgard, Corzide)

Atenolol (Tenormin, Tenoretic)

Acebutolol (Sectral)

Pindolol (Visken)

Sotalol

Timolol (Blocadren, Timolide)

Esmolol (Brevibloc [injection])

*Class III antiarrhythmic drugs* prolong the action potential duration and block potassium repolarization (these are changes you can note on the ECG):

Bretylium (Bretylol [injection])

Amiodarone (Cordarone)

Sotalol

*Class IV antiarrhythmic drugs* are calcium channel blockers, which alter the action potential of cardiac muscle.

Verapamil (Calan, Isopten)

Diltiazem (Cardizem)

Miscellaneous drugs include:

Adenosine (Adenocard)

Digoxin (Lanoxicaps, Lanoxin)

### Antianginal Drugs

Antianginal drugs are used to treat the causes of chest pain. They are primarily aimed at decreasing the workload of the heart and increasing the blood flow to the heart muscle.

*Nitrates* are vasodilators useful for acute relief or prevention of anginal attacks. They relax vascular smooth muscle.

Amyl nitrite (Isoamyl nitrite)

Nitroglycerin (Deponit, Minitran, Nitro-Bid, Nitrodisc, Nitro-Dur, Nitrolingual, Nitrong, Nitrostat, Transderm, Tridil)

Isosorbide dinitrate (Ditrate, Isordil, Sorbitrate)

Erythrityl tetranitrate (Cardilate)

Pentaerythritol tetranitrate (Peritrate)

*Beta blockers* are primarily used for prophylaxis, due to their adverse cardiac effects. They decrease heart rate, blood pressure, and contractility, reducing the myocardial oxygen demand.

Propranolol (Inderal, Inderide)

Metoprolol (Toprol, Lopressor)

Nadolol (Corgard, Corzide)

Atenolol (Tenormin, Tenoretic)

Acebutolol (Sectral)

Pindolol (Visken)

Sotalol

Timolol (Blocadren, Timolide)

Esmolol (Brevibloc [injection])

*Calcium channel blockers* are also used for prophylactic treatment of angina. They function by inhibiting calcium influx in vascular smooth muscle. This process dilates the coronary arteries, thereby increasing oxygen supply. It also reduces myocardial oxygen demand and prevents vasospasm.

Verapamil (Calan, Isoptin, Verelan)

Diltiazem hydrochloride (Cardizem, Dilacor)

Nifedepine (Adalat, Procardia)

Isradipine (DynaCirc)

Nimodipine (Nimotop)

Amlodipine (Norvasc)

Felodipine (Plendil)

Bepridil hydrochloride (Vascor)

All vasodilators relax vascular smooth muscle, but they vary in their site of action. Vasodilators useful for hypertension primarily relax smooth muscle of arterioles. Vasodilators useful in angina may relax venous smooth muscle, while those used for congestive heart failure generally combine relaxation of venous and arteriolar smooth muscle to achieve an overall increase in cardiac output.

Hydrazaline hydrochloride (Apresoline, Apresazide, Sur-Ap-Es)

Minoxidil (Loniten, Rogaine)

Diazoxide (Hyperstat, Proglycem)

**Nitrates**

Amyl nitrite (Isoamyl nitrite)

Nitroglycerin (Deponit, Minitran, Nitro-Bid, Nitrodisc, Nitro-Dur, Nitrolingual, Nitrong, Nitrostat, Transderm, Tridil)

Isosorbide dinitrate (Ditrate, Isordil, Sorbitrate)

Erythrityl tetranitrate (Cardilate)

Pentaerythritol tetranitrate (Peritrate)

**Adrenergic Blockers**

Prazosin hydrochloride (Minipress, Minizide)

Guanethidine monosulfate (Ismelin, Esimil)

Terazosin hydrochloride (Hytrin)

Guanadrel sulfate (Hylorel)

Phenoxybenzamine (Dibenzyline)

Daxazosin mesylate (Cardura)

Labetalol hydrochloride (Normodyne, Trandate)

**Converting Enzyme Inhibitors**

Captopril (Capoten)

Captopril with a diuretic (Capozide)

Enalopril maleate (Vasotec)

Enalopril with a diuretic (Vaseretic)

Enaloprilat (Vasotec IV)

Quinapril hydrochloride (Accupril)

Lisinopril (Prinivil)

Lisinopril with a diuretic (Prinzide, Zestoretic, Zestril)

Ramipril (Altace)

Benazepril hydrochloride (Lotensin)

Fosinopril (sodium) (Monopril)

Antihypertensives fall into a number of categories, including those listed above. They all have in common the ability to lower blood pressure by decreasing cardiac output, decreasing total peripheral resistance, or perhaps some other mechanism.

**Other coronary vasodilators**

Erythrityl (Cardilate)

Isosorbide dinitrate (Dilatrate, Sorbitrate)

Isosorbide mononitrate (Ismo)

Pentaerythritol tetranitrate (Peritrate)

### Hypocholesterolemic Drugs

These drugs attempt to lower plasma levels of triglyceride and cholesterol, thereby reducing the risk of clinical coronary heart disease. Cholesterol has been implicated in forming atherosclerotic plaques, occluding and damaging vessel walls and interfering with blood flow. Cholesterol levels are broken down into categories:

VLDL—very low-density lipoprotein

LDL—low-density lipoprotein (the "bad" cholesterol)

IDL—intermediate-density lipoprotein

HDL—high-density lipoproteins (the "good" cholesterol)

Diet, of course, should also be modified accordingly. Changing diet and lifestyle can cause regression of atherosclerotic lesions. The mechanisms these drugs employ vary. Some bind bile acids in the gut, preventing reabsorption of fatty acids; others inhibit enzymes necessary for the biosynthesis of cholesterol.

**Fibric Acid Derivatives**

Clofibrate (Atromid)

Gemfibrozil (Lopid)

**HMG-CoA Reductase Inhibitors**

Lovastatin (Mevacor)

Pravastatin sodium (Pravachol)

Simvastatin (Zocor)

**Nicotinic Acid**

Niacin (Niocor, Nicobid, Nicolar)

**Bile Acid Binders**

Cholestyramine (Questran)

Colestipol hydrochloride (Colestid)

Probucol (Lorelco)

## Chapter 16

# The Respiratory System

**Disciplines**

Pulmonology

ENT (Ear, Nose, Throat)

Internal medicine

Allergist

The word element *-pnea* means ''respiration'' or ''breathing.'' So if you see a word containing *-pnea*, such as *dyspnea*, it pertains to the respiratory system.

*a*—a negative prefix (without)

*dys*—difficult

*pnea*—breathing

*apnea*—not breathing

*dyspnea*—difficulty breathing

The respiratory system consists of the body's breathing apparatus (See Figure 16.1). It is the process by which we exchange used carbon dioxide from the cells for new, oxygenated blood.

## RESPIRATORY ANATOMY

The *nose (rhino)* inhales air through the *nasal* cavity, where it is filtered, warmed, and cooled as needed. This filtered air passes through the nasal *sinuses* (four air cavities—the frontal, ethmoid, sphenoid, and maxillary sinuses) to the

**Figure 16.1**
**The Respiratory System**

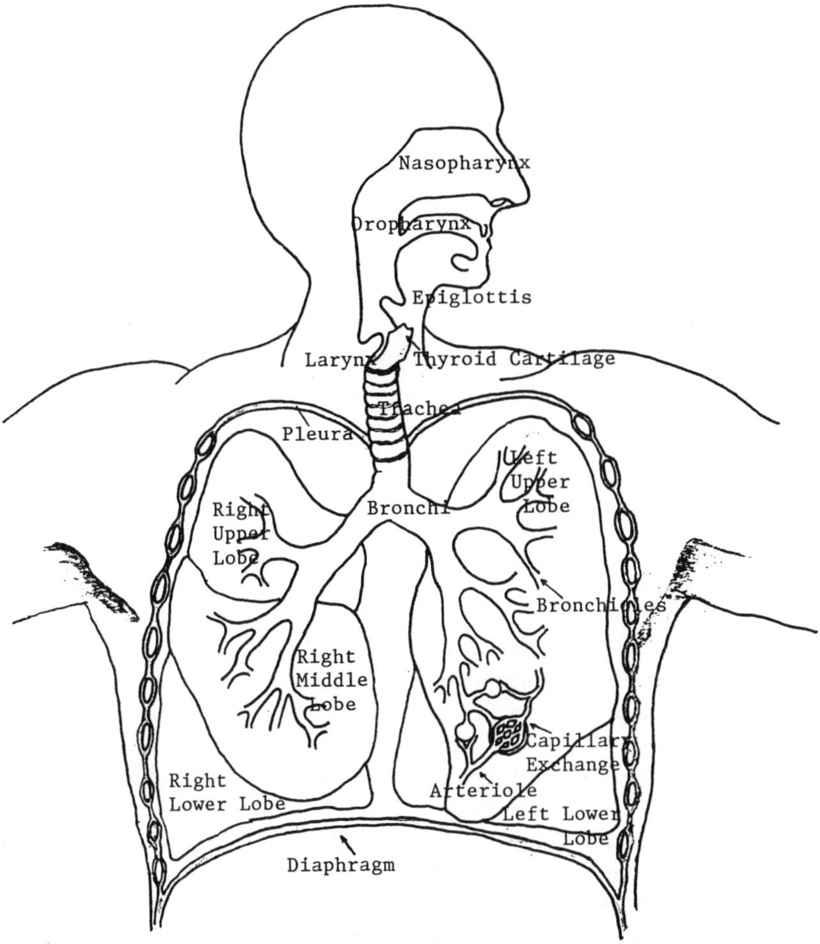


back of the sinus cavity, where it encounters the *nasopharynx*. The *pharynx* is the anatomical throat, a cavity behind the nose, mouth, and larynx. It is subdivided into the *nasopharynx* (the connection to the nose or nasal cavity), the *oropharynx* (the connection with the mouth), and the *laryngopharynx* (the lowest portion communicating with the larynx. The nasopharynx is the part of the pharynx behind the nasal cavity.

*rhinorrhea*—nasal discharge

*rhinitis*—inflammation of the nasal cavity

*Tonsils* are small, round, masses of lymphoid tissue on the side walls of the pharynx. These are often inflamed (*tonsillitis*) and have to be removed by their surgical excision (*tonsillectomy*).

The *larynx* is the voice organ, which contains the vocal cords. The larynx separates the pharynx from the trachea and is made up of nine cartilages. When the larynx becomes inflamed, *laryngitis* results.

*laryngo*—larynx
*itis*—inflammation

The *trachea*—the "windpipe"—is a cartilaginous tube that carries the air from the larynx to the bronchi. This structure is anterior to (in front of) most other organs in the throat; therefore if there is an obstruction to breathing superior to (above) the trachea, often a *tracheotomy* or *tracheostomy* must be performed to provide oxygen to the system.

*trachea*—the windpipe
*-otomy*—creating an incision
*-ostomy*—creation of an opening

The *bronchi* (plural of *bronchus*) are a system of small tunnels that convey air from the trachea into the lungs themselves. The right bronchus is more vertical than the left; it is therefore more susceptible to lodging of foreign objects. The bronchi get progressively smaller as they branch toward the lung itself and are called *bronchioles* (small bronchi). The inspired air ends its inward journey at the *alveoli* (plural of *alveolus*). These are saclike structures whose opening is the end of the bronchioles. These cavities within the lung are where the actual gas exchange occurs with capillaries. After the transaction is made, the deoxygenated air is exhaled with carbon dioxide in its place.

The oxygen–carbon dioxide swap is made in the *parenchyma* (functional tissue) of the *lung*. There are two lungs, a right and left, separated into lobes. The right lung has three lobes: upper, middle, and lower. The left lung has two lobes: upper and lower. They are covered by a *pleural* sac, a protective membrane. This is a continuous membrane, which also lines the thoracic cavity.

The word *diaphragm* means a separating membrane. The word element *phrenic* pertains to the diaphragm. The diaphragmatic muscle is the major inspiratory muscle that separates the abdominal and thoracic cavities. It creates the negative pressure that draws air in on inspiration. Other inspiratory muscles are of the chest wall.

Respiratory infections may present themselves in a variety of ways (nasal congestion, postnasal drip, coughing, sore throat, hoarseness, shortness of breath, wheezing, etc.). The infections may be due to a number of organisms, which have differing propensities for where they take up residence in the respiratory tract. They may manifest themselves in the sinuses, the ear, the larynx, the bronchi, or elsewhere. Ear infections are especially common in young children because of the anatomy of the juvenile ear. *Otitis media*, or infection of the middle ear, is most often the site of infection. *Pneumonias* choose particular lobes of the lung, which aids in their diagnoses. They will be described by their residences as well, such as *left upper lobe pneumonia.*

It is important to note that viruses are far more likely to raid the respiratory tract. Viruses are usually short-lived, show varying degrees of acute symptomatology, and resolve on their own. Bacterial infections may become more severe and require the use of antibiotics. Antibiotics are chosen for the bacterial organisms susceptible to them. This is determined through past experience and knowledge and by taking cultures. *Antibiotics do not work on viruses.*

*Aspiration* of foreign objects is commonly seen in emergency rooms. Foreign objects are inhaled into the respiratory tract, thereby blocking the airway. This is most common in children, who will present with cough, chest pain, difficulty breathing, or frank respiratory arrest. The most common intruders—small pieces of food like peanuts or hot dogs—often lodge themselves in the right bronchus, which because of its vertical orientation is more susceptible to their entry.

Respiratory complaints are often associated with cases of chemical exposure where toxic fumes are inhaled. Types of abnormal breath sounds will be described during the auscultative examination. These are important to document. They are:

*rales or crackles*—fine, medium, or coarse sounds heard on inspiration

*rhonchi*—low, loud sounds resembling snoring heard on inspiration or expiration

*wheeze*—a whistling sound; usually louder on expiration than inspiration

*stridor*—a harsh, high-pitched respiratory sound

*pleural friction rub*—a dry, grating sound caused by inflammation of the pleural surfaces, causing them to rub together

## RESPIRATORY DRUGS

### Treatment of Asthma

The American Thoracic Society defines asthma as a disease characterized by increased responsiveness of the trachea and bronchi to various stimuli and manifested by widespread narrowing of the airways; the disease changes in severity either spontaneously or as a result of treatment. There is also a resulting increased production of mucus. The clinical symptoms consist of coughing, shortness of breath, tightness in the chest, and wheezing. Treatment is directed at reversing the bronchostriction and/or decreasing mucus production. Asthma may be induced by allergic reactions, upper respiratory tract infections, exercise, irritants, stressors, or climate.

Beta-adrenergic agonists, anticholinergics, corticosteroids, theophylline, and cromolyn sodium are useful agents in the management of asthma. Aerosolized therapy is often administered as well.

*Bronchodilator agents* act primarily by relaxing the contracted airway smooth muscle.

**Methylxanthines**

Theophylline (Marax, Quibron, Theo-Dur, Aerolate, Constant-T, Primatene, Respbid, Slo-bid, T-PHYL, Tedral, Uniphyl, Theo-Dur, Theo-24)

Caffeine (Esgic)

**Other Xanthine Derivatives (and combinations)**

Asbron

Choledyl

Dilor

Lufyllin

Quandrinal

Quibron

Theolair

Theo-X

Theophylline-ethylenediamine (Aminophylline)

*Beta-adrenergic agonists* act primarily by reversing the contraction of airway smooth muscle and stabilizing mast cells, thereby inhibiting their chemical mediators of inflammation. They provide rapid onset and are the treatment of choice for acute exacerbations. Side effects are dose related and include tremor, tachycardia, and palpitation.

**Nonselective**

Epinephrine (Primatene Mist)

Isoproterenol (Isuprel)

Ephedrine hydrochloride (Primatene, Quadrinal, Tedral)

Ephedrine sulfate (Marax)

Ephedrine tannate (Rynatuss)

**Selective**

Albuterol (Airet, Proventil, Ventolin)

Metaproterenol sulfate (Alupent, Metaprel)

Terbutaline sulfate (Brethaire, Brethine, Bricanyl)

Bitolterol mesylate (Tornalate)

Pirbuterol acetate (Maxair Inhaler)

**Miscellaneous (for maintenance treatment of bronchospasm)**

Ipratropium bromide (Atrovent)

Chapter 17

# The Digestive System

**Disciplines**

Gastroenterology

Internal medicine

Organs of the digestive system function to ingest food, break it down into absorbable nutrients, absorb those nutrients, and eliminate the waste products. The *alimentary canal* is the route the food follows from ingestion to elimination (see Figure 17.1).

## ANATOMY OF THE DIGESTIVE SYSTEM

The *mouth* (stoma) takes in food, and with the aid of the tongue, teeth, and salivary glands, digestion begins. Salivary glands produce an enzyme called *amylase*, which catalyzes the hydrolysis of starch into simpler compounds. The teeth grind the food, and the tongue pushes it back to the *oropharynx* (the part of the pharynx behind the oral cavity) where *deglutition* (swallowing) occurs, pushing the food down into the *esophagus*.

*bucc-*—cheek

*lingu-*—pertains to the tongue (*Sublingual* means "beneath the tongue")

*stoma*—mouth

*-itis*—inflammation

*stomatitis*—inflammation of the mouth

**Figure 17.1**
**The Digestive System**

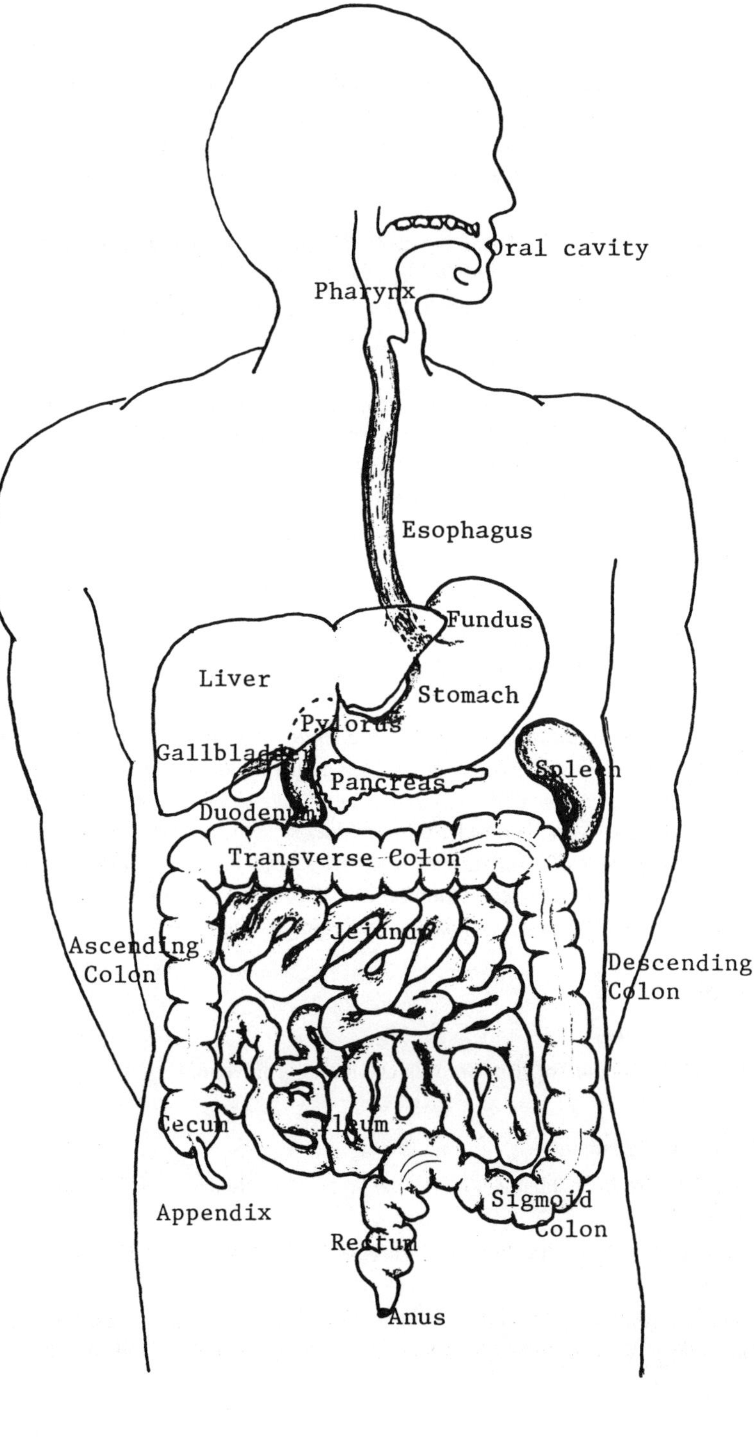

*aden-*—refers to gland

*adenoma*—glandular tumor

The esophagus is a hollow, muscular tube that extends from the pharynx to the *stomach.* It is typically separated anatomically into upper, middle, and lower esophageal sections because the makeup of the muscular fibers differs. *Paristalsis* is the wavelike movement by which the muscles push the food into the stomach.

The entrance to the stomach is called the *cardiac orifice* (opening closest to the heart) guarded by the *cardiac sphincter,* which keeps the acidic stomach contents from reflux into the esophagus. The stomach itself is separated into the fundus, the corpus, the antrum, and the entrance to the duodenum, which is called the *pylorus.* The injested food arrives in the stomach, where it is soaked in more enzymes and hydrochloric acid. It is then spasmodically released into the duodenum by *gastric* (gaster = stomach) peristalsis. The *pyloric sphincter* is a muscular closure between the stomach and the duodenum. *Peritoneum* is the name for the fibrous covering around the stomach and the abdominal cavity.

*gastric*—stomach (*gastro*enterology)

*-itis*—inflammation

*gastritis*—inflammation of the stomach. Severe inflammation can produce *ulcers* (erosion, sometimes resulting in bleeding).

The *duodenum* is the first section of the *small intestine.* It passes just beneath and in front of the *liver,* which is just beneath the *diaphragm* in the right abdominal cavity. The word root *hepar-* means "liver." The liver is a large organ, usually weighing over 3 pounds, which functions to store and filter blood, secrete bile, detoxify toxic substances, convert carbohydrates into sugar and sugar into glycogen, and many other metabolic activities. Any medical word containing the element *hepato-,* like *hepatitis,* pertains to the liver.

*hepat-*—liver

*-itis*—inflammation

*hepatitis*—inflammation of the liver (via chemicals or infection)

*-oma*—tumor

*hepatoma*—a liver tumor

*cirrhosis*—severe liver inflammation to the point of malfunction, often associated with alcohol abuse

*jaundice*—yellowing of the skin often associated with a malfunctioning liver

In the duodenum the contents of the *gallbladder* (cholecyst), *bile* (chole), are released into the uppermost portion of the small intestine. This is also where the contents of the *pancreas*—pancreatic enzymes—are released. The pancreas is a glandular organ responsible for insulin production, which goes awry in *diabetes* mellitus. Diabetes is typically broken down into two types, depending on severity. Type I (more severe) is known as insulin-dependent diabetes mellitus (or *IDDM*). Type II is non-insulin-dependent diabetes mellitus (*NIDDM*). Insulin is the substance that allows the cells to utilize sugars in the body. The pancreas produces glucagon and other digestive enzymes as well. Pancreatic secretion produces 1–2 liters of pancreatic fluid, a clear, watery substance containing electrolytes and proteins with a normal pH between 7.6 and 8.3.

*cholecystitis*—inflammation of the gallbladder

*duodenitis*—inflammation of the duodenum

*pancreatitis*—inflammation of the pancreas

*-lysis*—destruction

*pancreatolysis*—destruction of pancreatic tissue

*-ectomy*—to excise

*pancreatoduodenectomy*—excision of the head of the pancreas with the accompanying portion of the duodenum

The small intestine consists of the duodenum, the *jejunum*, and the *ileum.* The small intestine is approximately 20 feet in length in the normal adult. The word element *entero* pertains to the intestine (gastro*entero*logy). *Parenteral* means "outside the intestine."

*-ostomy*—an operation to form an artificial opening

*jejunostomy*—creation of an opening between the jejunum and the abdominal surface

*ileostomy*—to connect two portions of the ileum surgically

The small intestine is connected to the large intestine (*colon*) at the *ileocecal junction.* This is where you will find an outpouching called the *appendix.* The appendix is a vestigial organ, the function of which has disappeared. When it becomes inflamed (most common between the ages of 5 and 20), *appendicitis* is commonly treated by surgical removal, *appendectomy.* The most common symptomatic presentation of acute appendicitis includes gripping colicky pain generalized to the navel and epigastrum, followed by nausea, vomiting, and anorexia; localized pain at McBurney's Point, in the lower right quadrant; and fever and leukocytosis.

The large intestine consists of the *cecum,* the pouch at the lower right portion of the abdomen where the small intestine ends, the *ascending* (upward) colon, *transverse* (across) colon, and *descending* (downward) colon. The large intestine's major function is to absorb water from the bowel. Bacteria present within the bowel serve various functions, such as assisting in the absorption of vitamin

$B_{12}$ and keeping harmful organisms in check. The *spleen* lies in the area called the *splenic flexure*, where the transverse and descending colon meet. The spleen, not the digestive system, produces elements of the blood. The terminal portion of the colon, the *sigmoid* (S-shaped) colon, empties into the *rectum*, and to the outlet, the *anus*. A *sphincter* is a ringlike muscle that closes off an *orifice* (entrance or outlet).

*entero*—referring to intestine

*enteropathogenesis*—the production of disease of the intestine

Common conditions of the colon are *diverticula* (saclike outpouchings) and polyps (inward growths). These can usually be seen with a *colonoscope*. The term *oscopy* means "to view through a scope." So a *colonoscopy* is a procedure by which the physician views the colon through a scope, often to look for cancerous lesions. A cancerous-looking lesion is often *biopsied*, or snipped off for review by a pathologist through a microscope to confirm diagnosis.

## GASTROINTESTINAL DISORDERS

Diagnostic evaluation of the GI tract includes a complete history and physical examination, barium enemas, gastric analysis, laboratory tests, cytological brushing, endoscopy, radionucleotide scanning, angiography, CT scan, laparoscopy, paracentesis, biopsy, stool samples, and others, the method being determined by the symptoms with which the patient presents. More than half of the disorders of the GI tract have no structural cause that can be found and are therefore referred to as functional.

Disorders of the GI tract can be broken down by anatomical section.

*Esophageal disorders* manifest themselves by difficulty swallowing (*dysphagia*), heartburn (*dyspepsia*), pain during swallowing (*odynophagia*), or chest or back pain. Problems with *deglutition* (swallowing) may be due to many possibilities involving the tongue muscles, the mouth, the soft palate, the pharynx, or the esophagus, or they may be psychological in origin. This may be evaluated by seeing if the patient has more difficulty swallowing water than solids. If so, it may be psychogenic. If not, further studies such as a barium swallow should be performed to rule out the possibility of cancer. Evaluation includes x-ray studies, esophagoscopy, manometry (determines pressure of sphincters, propulsive movements, and contractions), pH monitoring, and acid perfusion tests. Its disorders can be broken down into preesophageal dysphagia, esophageal dysphagia of obstructive or motor origin, gastroesophageal reflux, corrosive esophagitis and structure, diverticula, hiatus hernia (protrusion of the stomach above the diaphragm), laceration, rupture, tumor, carcinoma, and infections.

*Stomach disorders* include gastritis, GI bleeding, ulcer (which may cause perforation, hemorrhage, or obstruction), infections, gas, viruses or food poisoning, neoplasms, and abdominal pain, which may be *visceral* (from another organ), *parietal* (from the wall of the abdominal cavity), superficial, or *referred* (the pain manifests at a site other than the dysfunction). A complete history and physical will help the clinician distinguish possible causes. This list is called a *differential diagnosis*. The clinician should question the patient with details about the pain: its onset, duration, location, radiation, character, and factors that aggravate or relieve it. The clinician will also note the position the patient assumes, palpate the stomach with special diagnostic techniques, and note distension, bowel sounds, or discoloration. These answers will determine which diagnostic tests should be ordered.

*Bowel disorders* may be due to duodenal ulcers, obstruction, cancer, infections, foreign bodies, diverticula, polyps, ulceration, malabsorptive syndromes, inflammatory diseases, functional disorders, abscesses, fistula, diarrhea, constipation, or hemorrhoids. Again, the physician's history and physical will determine which diagnostic procedures to perform and which treatment to render. Adhesions are the most common cause of bowel obstruction.

*Related structures* in the abdominal cavity that may produce abdominal symptoms are the abdominal wall, appendix, pancreas, spleen, liver, kidneys, adrenal glands, and the reproductive organs.

## GASTROINTESTINAL DRUGS

Treatment of gastrointestinal disorders depends on the diagnosis, any complicating factors, the individual patient, and any allergies or contraindications to treatment. Many upper GI complaints are due to the overproduction of stomach acid; therefore, treatment is based on reducing the production of stomach acid, reducing stress, or protecting the organs from the effects of the acid.

*Antacids* functions as a chemical buffer, neutralizing hydrogen ions and binding bile acids. They may also enhance the production of prostaglandins and alkaline, stimulate the growth of epithelium, increase the pressure of the lower esophageal sphincter, and decrease pepsin activity. Adverse reactions include delays in gastric emptying (aluminum compounds); aluminum and calcium salts tend to cause constipation. Phosphate depletion and osteomalacia may result from long-term use of aluminum preparations, which can cause phosphate precipitation in the bowel, and magnesium preparations may cause diarrhea. A "milk-alkali" syndrome may result from prolonged exposure to absorbable antacids, causing hypercalcemia and renal insufficiency. Acid rebound may occur when the increased pH causes the release of gastrin. Calcium also may stimulate gastrin release. Antacids can alter the intestinal bacteria and may decrease the absorption of other drugs, such as digoxin, tetracyclines, aspirin, cimetidine, and iron. Increased sodium levels (hypernatremia) may result, causing water retention and hypertension. Magnesium toxicity may cause muscle weakness.

The constituents of common antacid and antiflatuant preparations are as follows:

Aluminum hydroxide (AlternaGEL)
Aluminum and magnesium hydroxides (Aludrox)
Aluminum hydroxide (Amphojel)
Aluminum carbonate (Basaljel)
Sodium citrate and citric acid (Bicitra)
Aluminum and magnesium hydroxides, calcium carbonate (Calmalox)
Aluminum and magnesium hydroxides (Delcid)
Acetaminophen with calcium carbonate (Extra Strength Tylenol with antacid)
Aluminum and magnesium hydroxides, simethacone (Gelusil)
Aluminum and magnesium hydroxides (Maalox TC)
Aluminum and magnesium hydroxides, simethacone (Maalox Plus)
Magnesium oxide (Mag-Ox)
Calcium carbonate and magnesium hydroxide (Mylanta)
Calcium carbonate and magnesium hydroxide (Mylanta Double Strength)
Aluminum and magnesium hydroxides, simethacone (Mylanta II)
Simethacone (Mylanta Gas Relief)
Simethacone (Mylicon Infant Drops)
Aluminum hydroxide (Phosphaljel)
Aluminum and magnesium hydroxides (Riopan)
Aluminum and magnesium hydroxides (Riopan Plus)
Aluminum carbonate (Rolaids)
Calcium carbonate and glycine (Titralac)
Calcium carbonate (Tums)
Magnesium oxide (Uro-Mag)

*$H_2$-receptor antagonists* competitively antagonize histamine at $H_2$ receptors in the stomach, thereby selectively reducing basal, food-stimulated, and nocturnal acid secretion. These drugs are metabolized by the hepatic cytochrome P-450 oxidase system and thus may alter the bioavailability of other drugs metabolized by the same system. Patients with renal damage should be monitored closely. These drugs are used for gastric and duodenal ulcers and for Zollinger-Ellison syndrome (gastrin-producing tumors). Adverse reactions include fatigue, muscle pain, fever, rash, alopecia, headache, restlessness, anxiety, and confusion (in elderly patients or those with reduced renal function). Seizures are possible. Cimetadine can cause an antiandrogenic effect in males: loss of libido, impotence, reduction of sperm count, and breast growth. Bone marrow changes can result in lower production of certain blood cells. The car-

diovascular and renal effects include hypotension, sinus bradycardia, interstitial nephritis, increased creatinine, and uric acid levels. GI effects include abdominal pain, nausea, vomiting, diarrhea, dry mouth, $B_{12}$ anemia, pancreatitis, toxic hepatitis, insulin and glucose interference.

Cimetidine (Tagamet)

Ranitidine (Zantac)

Famotidine (Pepcid)

Nizatidine (Axid)

*Proton pump inhibitors* inhibit gastric acid secretion by binding to the H+, K+-ATP-ase enzyme, thereby permanently inactivating the enzyme pump. Gastric secretions and mobility are altered only slightly. Omeprazole is used for peptic ulcer patients who do not respond to $H_2$ antagonists and in Zollinger-Ellison syndrome (gastrinomas). Lansoprazole is indicated for short-term treatment of active duodenal ulcers and erosive esophagitis and in Zollinger-Ellison syndrome. These drugs also may interfere with the cytochrome P-450 metabolism of drugs and also decrease clearance of diazepam by about 50 percent. Adverse effects include nausea, diarrhea, headache, dizziness, somnolence (unnatural drowsiness), rare skin rashes, decrease in white blood cells and increase in hepatic enzymes.

Omeprazole (Losec, Prilosec)

Lansoprazole (Prevacid)

*Cytoprotective agents. Sucralfate* (Carafate) has no buffering capability but inhibits a back diffusion of acid by forming a complex of sulfated sucrose and aluminum hydroxide, which binds to the ulcerated site, protecting it from further acid deterioration. It is not to be used prophylactically. Antacids and $H_2$ antagonists interfere with its activity. It also interferes with the bioavailability of certain other drugs like tetracycline and phenytoin. Gastrointestinal complications include constipation, diarrhea, indigestion, and gastric discomfort. This drug is not intended to be absorbed from the GI tract; yet if it occurs, certain central nervous system effects are possible, including dizziness and sleepiness. Rashes, dry mouth, and back pain are also possible.

*Misoprostol* (Cytotec), a *prostaglandin derivative*, suppresses acid secretion, and protects the gastric mucosa. Abdominal cramps, diarrhea, and uterine contractions are its main adverse effects. It is contraindicated for use in pregnancy.

*Prokinetic agents* stimulate the motility in the upper GI tract, sensitize tissue to increased release of acetylcholine, and have an antidopamine activity. Used in diabetic gastroparesis, gastric ulcers, gastroesophageal reflux, and as a chemotherapy/surgery/delivery-associated antiemetic, it may cause drowsiness, depression, restlessness, headache, nausea and bowel disturbances, increased prolactin release and menstrual disorders.

Metoclopramide (Reglan)

Metoclopramide hydrochloride

*Anticholinergic agents* reduce basal and stimulated acid secretion by competition at muscarinic receptor sites in parietal cells. These drugs have side effects related to decreased functioning of the gastrointestinal and genitourinary systems. Atropine is not very selective, and therefore high doses must be used to reach the insensitive parietal cells. Dry mouth, eye problems, and tachycardia may result. Anticholinergics are contraindicated in patients with reflux esophagitis, pyloric stenosis, narrow-angle glaucoma, and prostatic hypertrophy. Atropine drugs may be used to treat nonspecific diarrhea as well.

Atropine

Propantheline (Probanthine)

Some tricyclic antidepressants with significant anticholinergic activity do not readily cross the blood-brain barrier and are reasonably selective for gastric glands.

**Laxatives**

Laxatives and cathartic agents are drugs that promote defecation. Effects are dose related. Most are self-medicated and used for constipation. Medical use may be for radiological or endoscopic visualization, for stroke and cardiac patients, to obtain stool samples, or to expel parasites. Their main danger is misuse, abuse, and dependency. Other adverse effects include flatulence and wrongful use when the main problem may be obstruction or fecal impaction.

Laxatives may be broken down into several categories.

Bulk-forming laxatives like *bran, psyllium* (Metamucil), and *methylcellulose* (Cologel) increase the mass of the stool and decrease colonic transit time.

*Docusates* (Colase, Surfak, Kasof) are anionic detergents that act as emulsifying agents. They act on colonic mucosa. These drugs may enhance the absorption of concurrently administered drugs.

Fecal softeners like *mineral oil* may cause rectal leakage and cause lipid pneumonitis in the elderly. They may also prevent the absorption of fat-soluble vitamins.

Diphenylmetanes like *phenolphthalein* (Ex-lax, etc.) and *bisacodyl* (Dulcolax) have a potential for fluid and electrolyte depletion with excessive catharsis.

Anthroquinones increase the secretion of fluid into the large intestine. They may cause cramping, diarrhea, or a harmless pigmentation of the colonic mucosa; abuse may cause nephritis. *Senna* (Senokot), *danthron* (Dorbane), and *cascara sagrada* are examples of these drugs.

*Castor oil* is used as a stimulant cathartic to cause complete evacuation within a few hours. It is too harsh to be used routinely; it may cause dehydration or mucosal damage; and it can promote uterine contractions.

Saline cathartics like *magnesium salts* (milk of magnesia) or phosphate salts may be taken orally or rectally (enemas). *Lactulose* (Chronulac) stimulates motility osmotically. Systemic effects from magnesium salts can produce renal toxicity. Sodium salts may produce volume problems for cardiac patients, and phosphate salts may produce hypocalcemia.

### Antidiarrheals

Persistent or chronic diarrhea should be investigated to understand the cause. Attention should be given to fluid and electrolyte replacement. Nonspecific pharmacological treatment of diarrhea is confined to opiates and adsorbents.

Opiates have a constipating action by decreasing the propulsive motility, especially in the jejunum. These should not be used in patients with infectious diarrhea when fever or dysentery is present. *Diphenoxylate with atropine* (Lomotil) may cause euphoria and dependency. *Loperamide* (Imodium) decreases propulsive motility. This is recommended only for symptomatic relief of diarrhea that is not secondary to bacterial infection. It can cause abdominal pain, distension, constipation, dry mouth, and vomiting.

Adsorbents are supposed to bind the toxin or offending agent, and/or protect the mucosa from irritation. *Kaolin plus pectin* (Kaopectate), *hydrophilic cholestyramine resin* (Questran), and *bismuth subsalicylate* (Pepto-Bismol) are examples of these drugs.

### Emetics

Emetics chemically induce vomiting after acute poisoning by oral ingestion of certain toxic substances. *Ipecac syrup* has a local irritant effect of the duodenum, which initiates a reflex mediated via the vomiting center and the chemoreceptor trigger zone. It should not be used with activated charcoal, which will bind to the ipecac. It is potentially toxic to the myocardium. If emesis does not occur, it should be removed from the stomach by gastric lavage.

*Apomorphine*, a morphine derivative, is a very strong stimulant of the chemotactic trigger zone to induce vomiting, but it can also potentiate respiratory depression in patients poisoned by central nervous system depressants. Respiratory depression caused by apomorphine should be reversed with a narcotic antagonist.

**Antiemetics**

Antiemetics are used to stop nausea and vomiting, but the choice of agent depends on the reason for the upset.

*Emetrol* quiets the gastrointestinal tract and can be used for motion sickness, pregnancy, or drug-induced nausea and vomiting. As an oral suspension of fructose, glucose, and phosphate, it should not be used by diabetic patients.

Antihistamines like *dimenhydrinate* (Dramamine), *cyclizine* (Marezine), and *meclizine* (Antivert) are used primarily for motion sickness and vertigo (dizziness). These drugs also have a central nervous system depressive effect and anticholinergic effects.

*Phenothiazines* are extremely effective by inhibiting dopamine transmission at the chemotactic trigger zone. Their toxicities include masking of other symptoms and dystonia (impairment of muscular tone). Given orally, rectally, or intramuscularly, these drugs include *Promethazine* (Phenergan), *prochloroperazine* (Compazine), and *chlorpromazine* (Thorazine).

*Scopolamine* is an antimuscarinic belladonna alkaloid, used orally, parenterally, or transdermally. It is extremely effective for motion sickness and vertigo. It also has an anticholinergic effect.

Dopamine antagonists such as *trimethobenzamide* (Tigan) and *metoclopramide* (Reglan) block nausea and vomiting by delaying gastric emptying. They may cause drowsiness and diarrhea.

Chapter 18

# The Urogenital System

**Disciplines**

Urology

Gynecology

Nephrology

Internal medicine

Medical examinations often contain reference to the KUB—an acronym for kidneys, ureters, and bladder, which are the components of the urogenital system (Figure 18.1). This system is responsible for filtration and excretion of wastes not handled by the gastrointestinal system, reabsorption and electrolyte balance, and the production and excretion of urine.

*renal*—pertains to the kidney

*nephron*—the functional unit of the kidney; hence, nephrology is the study of the kidney

*glomerulus*—a conglomeration of renal capillaries, which function as the smallest filter level

*glomerulonephritis*—inflammation of the renal glomerulus. The patient is usually tired (malaise), nauseous, and aching (arthrialgias).

*ATN*—acute tubular necrosis, indicating damage to the nephron

*nephritis*—kidney infection

*nephrosis*—degeneration of the renal tubules

*renal failure*—described as *acute* (sudden impairment) or *chronic* (slow, insidious, and irreversible)

**Figure 18.1**
**The Urogenital System**

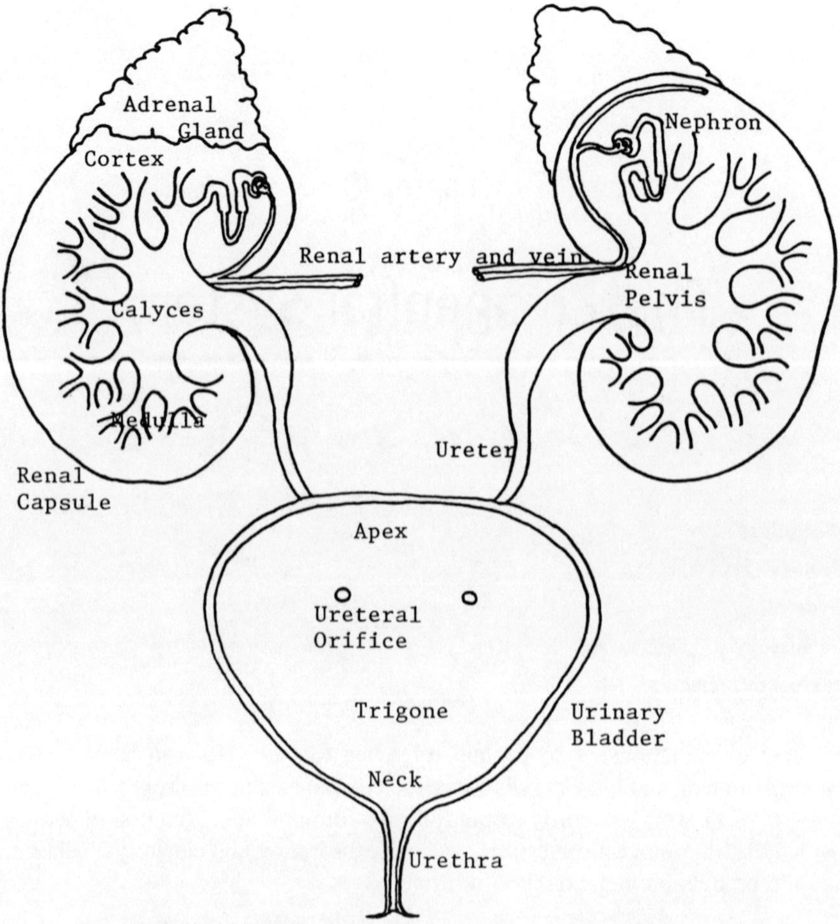


## ANATOMY OF THE KIDNEYS, URETERS, AND URINARY BLADDER

On top of each kidney lies an *adrenal* or *suprarenal* gland, responsible for activating the ''fight-or-flight'' response, in sending out *adrenalin* (epinephrine) to *adrenergic* receptors in response to stress.

The anatomical structure of the kidney consists of the superficial fibrous capsule, the *cortex* (outer layer), the *medulla* (the innermost part), whose *papillae* (projections) jut into minor *calyces*, then *major* calyces, into the renal pelvis, which narrows into a *ureter*.

The balance of solutes and water takes place in the *renal tubule*. Acid-base balance is maintained as well. Water conservation and elimination are controlled by the collecting ducts of the kidney as needed. This is modified by production of a hormone referred to as *ADH* (*antidiuretic hormone*), which functions as its name implies: to inhibit the excretion of urine. This hormone is produced *endogenously*—meaning that the body makes it. The term *diuresis* means "to promote urine excretion." The ADH hormone inhibits reabsorption of water in the renal loop of Henle by modifying sodium reabsorption. The diuretics most people are familiar with are *exogenous* (introduced by an outside source) administrations of drugs that have the effect of increasing urine production and therefore eliminating water from the body.

When the kidney is damaged—by any number of disease processes, poisoning, or congenital defects, for example—urine and blood tests easily performed in a laboratory will detect abnormalities. Abnormalities in renal function will be described as being prerenal, renal, or postrenal.

*azotemia*—excess or urea or nitrogenous substances in the blood

*bacteruria*—the presence of bacteria in the urine

*glucosuria*—sugar in the urine

*hematuria*—blood in the urine

*olig*—scanty

*oliguria*—diminished urinary excretion, relative to fluid intake

*proteinuria*—protein in the urine

The main tests referenced for renal function are:

Glomerular filtration rate (GFR)

Creatinine clearance

Blood urea nitrogen (BUN)

BUN/creatinine ratio

Urinalyses are performed by analyzing a fresh, clean-catch urine sample. The normal appearance should be straw colored—between clear and yellow. The specific gravity should be between 1.001 and 1.035 in the adult. The pH should be above 4.6 and below 8. There should be no blood, bilirubin, glucose, protein, nitrite, reducing substances, crystals, bacteria, or leukocyte esterase. There should be few white or red blood cells, few epithelial cells, or hyaline casts.

Kidney stones, or *renal calculi*, are most commonly composed of calcium, struvite, uric acid or cystine, and combinations or variations of these. They may be singular or multiple. Symptoms are often very painful. (A small stone, however, may pass unnoticed—*asymptomatic*.) The stones are usually formed in the renal pelvis but may lodge in the ureters as well and are characterized by hematuria, crystalluria, fever, and flank pain, which may radiate to the groin.

Blood is steered to the kidneys by way of the renal arteries. The kidneys perform their filtration function and direct the products through the renal pelvis to the *ureters*, two hollow tubes that empty into the *bladder*, through openings on both sides called *ureteral orifices*. The urinary bladder is a holding tank, which stores urine to be excreted. When the walls of the urinary bladder stretch to capacity, an urge to urinate results. This process is allowed by relaxing the muscle of the *urethral sphincter*, and the urine is released to the exterior via the (single) *urethra* in both males and females.

*Urinary incontinence* is an involuntary release of urine, which may be caused by a number of factors—mechanical, psychological, or physical. This problem can be repaired (or caused) by surgery. Childbirth may cause temporary incontinence in women. Women with a history of multiple births (*multiparous*) may have an increased likelihood of developing chronic urinary incontinence as they age. Chronic urinary incontinence is often *neurogenic* in nature (arising from a condition originating in the nervous system).

## DIURETICS

Kidneys excrete the end products of metabolism and regulate the internal osmotic environment. Diuretics are drugs that act primarily in the kidney to facilitate the elimination of excess salt and fluid. They are categorized by the region of the kidney on which they act or their overall mechanism. They are used therapeutically in the treatment of various cardiovascular diseases, as the heart is overburdened by increased pressure and volume.

*Osmotic diuretics* increase the osmolarity of the filtrate, hindering reabsorption. This increases urine volume. They are not absorbed orally and are only given parenterally (IV infusion). They are used prophylactically for the treatment of acute renal failure in performing some cardiovascular operations and infusions; for severe traumatic injuries; to treat glaucoma; to reduce cerebrospinal fluid pressure; and to treat low urine formation.

Mannitol (Osmitrol)

*Carbonic anhydrase inhibitors* increase the secretion of sodium, potassium, and bicarbonate, thereby increasing urine pH and volume.

Acetazolamide (Diamox)

Dichlorphenamide (Daranide)

Methazolamide (Neptazane)

*Thiazide diuretics* inhibit the reabsorption of sodium and chloride, facilitating their excretion, along with accompanying water. They are used to treat congestive heart failure, nephrotic syndrome, and edematous states as well as hypertension and diabetes insipidus.

Chlorothiazide (Diuril, Aldoclor)

Hydrochlorothiazide (HydroDIURIL, Aldoril, Apresazide, Capozide, Esidrix, Esimil, Hydropres, Inderide, Lopressor, Oretic, Oreticyl, Prinzide, Ser-Ap-Es, Timolide, Vaseretic, Zestoretic)

Polythiazide (Minizide)

Chlorthalidone (Combipres, Tenoretic)

Metolazone (Mykrox, Zaroxylin)

Indapamide (Lozol)

*Loop diuretics* act in the kidney's loop of Henle, increasing excretion of sodium chloride, as well as magnesium and calcium. These drugs are bound to plasma proteins and rapidly absorbed. They are used to treat edema, congestive heart failure, cirrhotic ascites, hypertension, nephrotic syndrome, and early stages of acute renal failure. They have numerous side effects because of their action.

Furosemide (Lasix)

Bumetanide (Bumex)

Ethacrynic acid (Edecrin)

*Aldosterone antagonists* and *potassium-sparing diuretics* decrease the excretion of potassium and hydrogen. They also inhibit the potassium excretion of other diuretics. They treat primary aldosteronism (spirinolactone), and other edematous conditions to prevent the development of hypokalemia (not enough potassium.)

**Aldosterone blocker**

Spironolactone (Aldactone)

**K+ Sparing**

Triamterene (Dyrenium)

Amiloride (Midamor)

*Indolines*, a new class of diuretics, decrease peripheral resistance without affecting cardiac output. They are used for congestive heart failure and hypertension.

Indapamide (Lozol)

**Combinations**

Amiloride + hydrochlorothiazide (Moduretic)

Spironolactone + hydrochlorothiazide (Aldactizide)

Triamterene + hydrochlorothiazide (Maxzide, Dyazide)

## Chapter 19

# The Endocrine System

The endocrine system consists of glandular organs. Glands secrete substances into bodily fluid. Exocrine glands release them via a duct, and endocrine glands release hormones directly into the bloodstream.

*pituitary gland*—various hormones are released from the anterior and posterior lobes. Pituitary hormones such as FSH (follicle-stimulating hormone) and TSH (thyroid-stimulating hormone) cause other glands to respond.

*thyroid gland*—produces thyroid hormones, which primarily influence the body's metabolism

*parathyroid glands*—regulate the body's calcium and phosphorus metabolism

*thymus gland*—produces T lymphocytes (this gland involutes after puberty)

*pancreas*—secretes digestive enzymes, insulin, and glucagon

*adrenal glands*—situated above each kidney; the cortex elaborates steroid hormones, and the medulla produces epinephrine and norepinephrine.

*gonads*—elaborate the body's sex hormones

A *hormone* is a substance secreted by a specific tissue and transported to a distant site, where it exerts its effect on other specific tissues. When the body cannot produce sufficient quantities of these chemical messagers, they must be introduced in a natural or synthetic form.

Hormones will be distinguished into several classifications:

*Peptide hormones* are composed of amino acids.

*Growth hormone* is responsible for initiating growth in almost every organ and tissue (except the brain and the eye), increasing the number of cells. It builds protein, increases glucose output from the liver, and increases levels of circulating free fatty acids. Some growth hormone analogs are:

**Endocrine drugs**

Somatropin (Humatrope)

Somatrem (Protropin)

**Stimulators**

Levodopa (Dopar, Larodopa, Sinemet)

Bromocryptine mesylate (Parlodel)

Alpha agonists

**Inhibitors**

Somatostatin

Octreotide acetate (Sandostatin)

Beta agonists

Glucocorticoids

*Thyroid hormones* T3 and T4 are synthesized by the thyroid gland, and regulated by TSH. TSH release is regulated by TRH, which comes from the hypothalamus.

**T3**

Liothyronine sodium (Cytomel, Triostat)

**T4**

Levothyroxine sodium (Levothyroid, Levoxine, Synthroid)

**Natural T3 and T4**

Pork thyroid capsules (S-P-T)

**Synthetic T3 and T4**

Liotrox (Euthroid)

**Thyroid suppressants**

Methimazole (Tapazole)

**Other**

Thyroglobulin (Proloid)

Thiocyanate

Potassium Iodide

Sodium Iodide (Iodotope)

Propylthiouracil

Cholesterol is the common precursor for synthesizing adrenal and gonadal *steroid hormones*. The cortex of the adrenal gland produces hormones called *adrenocorticoids*. These steroids, grouped into five classes, are regulated by ACTH (adrenocorticotropic hormone), which comes from the anterior pituitary gland. (Aldosterone is regulated by blood volume.)

*Glucocorticoids* that the body possesses endogenously are cortisol and cortisone. They are involved in carbohydrate, fat, and protein metabolism, and they alter connective tissue response to injury. Their main medicinal function is to inhibit inflammatory and allergic reactions. Glucocorticoids may be given as an adjunct in stressful situations such as surgery and may be indicated for endocrine disorders.

Tramcinolone acetonide (Aristocort, Kenacort, Kenalog, Azmacort, Mycalog, Mytrex, Nasacort)

Tramcinolone diacetate (Aristocort)

Tramcinolone hexacetonide (Aristospan)

Betamethasone sodium (Celestone)

Beclomethasone dipropionate (Vanceril)

Hydrocortizone acetate (Cortifoam [rectal], Analapram-HC, Anusol, Carmol HC, Chloromycetin, Coly-Mycin, Cortisporin, Epifoam, Hydrocortone, Mantadil, Orabase, Pramosone, Proctocream, Proctofoam, Terra-Cortil)

Hydrocortisone (Bactine, Cortef, Carmol, Cortenema, Cortisporin, Eldecort, Fungoid, Hydrocortone, Hytone, LazerSporin, Nutracort, PediOtic, Preparation H, Synacort, Vioform, VoSol)

Cortisone (Cortone)

Hydrocortisone butyrate (Locoid)

Hydrocortisone sodium phosphate (Hydrocortone Phos)

Hydrocortisone sodium succinate (Solu-Cortef)

Hydrocortisone valerate (Westcort)

Dexamethasone (Decadron, Tobradex)

Dexamethasone acetate (Dalalone)

Dexamethasone sodium phosphate (Decadron, Neo-Decadron)

Methylprednisolone acetate (Depo-Medrol)

Methylprednisolone (Medrol)

Prednisolone sodium phosphate (Hydeltrasol, Pediaped)

Prednisolone tebutate (Hydeltra-TBA)

Cortisone acetate (Cortone)

Desoximetasone (Topicort)

*Inhibitors of steroid biosynthesis* decrease the amount of active steroid.

Metyrapone (Metopirone)
Aminoglutethimide (Cytadren)
Ketoconazol (Nizoral)
Trilostane (Modrastane)

*Androgens* stimulate characteristics that are typically thought of as male (virilization): musculature development, facial and body hair, gonadal development, larynx enlargement, acne, and hair recession.

Testosterone proprionate (Oreton)
Testosterone ethanate (Delatestryl)
Testosterone cypionate (Depo-testosterone)
Methyltestosterone (Android, Testred, Metandren)
Fluoxymesterone (Halotestin)
Danazol (Danocrine)

*Anabolic steroids* build up or increase the steroid response.

Testolactone (Teslac)
Stanozolol (Winstrol)
Nandrolone (Durabolin)
Nandralone decanoate (Deca-durabolin)
Ethylestrenol (Mamxibolin)
Oxandrolone (Anavar)
Oxymethalone (Anadrol 50)

*Mineralcorticoids* are corticosteroids which are predominantly involved in regulating water and electrolyte balance.

Aldosterone (the prototype)
Deoxycorticosterone (DOC)
11–desoxycorticosterone
Fludrocortisone (Florinef)

*Mineralcorticoid antagonists*

Spironolactone (Aldactone)

*Progesteroids* mimic the function of progesterone.

**Progesterone/Progestogen**
Medroxyprogesterone acetate (Cycrin, Amen, Depo-Provera)

Norethindrone acetate (Aygestin, Micronor Norlutate, Norlutin)

Norethindrone (Nor-Q-D, Ovrette, Provera)

Norethindrone and mestranol (Norinyl)

*Estrogen* preparations

Diethylstilbestrol

Polyestradiol phosphate (Estradurin)

Estrogen esterified (Estratab)

Estrogen with androgen (Estratest, Menrium)

Estrogen conjugated (PMB, Premarin)

Estrogen with androgen (Premarin +, Methyltestosterone)

Chlorotrianisene (TACE)

Estradiol (Emcyt, Estrace, Estraderm)

Estrone (Ogen)

Estropipate (Ogen)

*Combinations* are estrogen and progesterone combinations.

Ethinyl estradiol with norethindrone (Brevicon, Demulen, Levlen, Loestrin, Modicon, Nordette, Norethin, Norinyl, Norlestrin, Ortho Novum, Ovcon, Tri-Levlen, Tri-Norinyl, Triphasil)

Ethinyl estradiol with norgestryl (Lo/Ovral, Ovral)

**Other**

Urofollitropin (Metrodin)

Menotropin (Pergonal)

*Gonadotropins* from the anterior pituitary gland stimulate the gonads to secrete their respective hormones.

Chorionic gonadotropin (APL)

Pancuronium bromide (Pregnyl, Profasi)

**Gonadotropin-Releasing Hormone**

Gonadorelin acetate (Lutrepulse)

Histrelin acetate (Supprelin)

**Luteinizing Hormone–Releasing Hormone**

Nafarelin acetate (Synarel)

Leluprolide acetate (Lupron)

*ACTH* is released from the anterior pituitary gland and stimulates the adrenal gland to synthesize and secrete cortisol, corticosterone, aldosterone, and several weak androgens. It is used to diagnose adrenal insufficiency and to treat adrenocortical insufficiency and nonendocrine disorders that respond to glucocorticoids.

Corticotropin (natural, purified)

Cosyntropin

**Adrenocortical Steroid Inhibitor**

Aminoglutethimide (Cytadren)

*Hormones from the posterior pituitary gland* include oxytocin, which induces labor, and vasopressin, an antidiuretic.

Oxytocin (Pitocin, Syntocinon)

Vasopressin (Pitressin)

Desmopressin acetate (DDAVP)

Lypressin (nasal solution) (Diapid)

*Somatostatin* is a polypeptide released from the hypothalamus to inhibit the release of various hormonal substances

Octeotide acetate (Sandostatin)

*Hypocalcemic*: These polypeptide hormones normally released by the thyroid and parathyroid glands lowers plasma calcium and phosphate concentrations, and inhibit bone resorption.

Calcitonin salmon (Calcimar, Miacalcin)

Calcitonin (human) (Cibicalcin)

Calcitonin (synthetic) (Cibacalcin)

Sodium etidronate

Calcitriol (Calcijex, Rocaltrol)

**Erythropoietin**

Epoetin (Epogen)

**Hormone Suppression**

Danazol (Danocrine)

Nafarelin (Synarel)

Goserelin acetate (Zoladex)

Tamoxifen citrate (Nolvadex)

## Pancreatic Enzymes

The pancreas is an abdominal organ that produces a number of enzymes, including *insulin*, a fuel-regulating hormone secreted into the blood in response to increased levels of blood sugar, and *glucagon*, secreted in response to low blood sugar.

Diabetes is a condition where the insulin response goes awry and therefore must be supplemented. Diabetes is broken down into two types: Type I, insulin-dependent diabetes mellitus, wherein insulin supplements are required; and Type II, non–insulin-dependent diabetes mellitus, where sometimes treatment consists of only dietary control.

Many agents interact with hypoglycemic agents: diuretics, corticosteroids, oral contraceptives, tricyclic antidepressants, and calcium channel blockers, among others.

*Hyperglycemic agents* stimulate glycogenolysis to interrupt hypoglycemia.

Glucagon

Diazoxide (Proglycem)

**Glucose-lowering agents**

Glyburide (Diabeta, Glynase, Micronase)

Glipizide (Glucatrol)

**Somatostatin inhibits both glucagon and insulin.**

Somatropin (Humatrope)

*Insulin*: A major fuel regulating hormone released by the pancreas, needs to be supplemented in certain types of diabetes.

Human isophane (Novolin N)

Human NPH (Humulin N, Isulatard NPH, Novolin N)

Human regular (Humulin-R, Humulin-BR, Novolin R, Velosulin)

Mixture of human NPH and regular (Humulin 50/50, Humulin 70/30, Mixtard Human 70/30, Novolin 70/30)

Human (zinc suspension) (Humulin-L, Humulin-U, Novolin L)

NPH (NPH Iletin I)

NPH (beef) (NPH Iletin II)

NPH (pork) (NPH Iletin II, Insulatard NPH, NPH insulin, NPH purified pork, Isophane)

Regular (Iletin I)

Regular (beef) (Iletin II)

Regular (pork) (Iletin II, regular purified pork, Velosulin)

Regular and NPH mixture (Mistard 70/30)

Regular and NPH mixture (zinc crystals) (NPH Iletin I)

Regular and NPH mixture (zinc suspension) (Lente Iletin I, Semilente Iletin I, Ultralente Iletin I, Iletin I, Iletin II)

Regular and NPH mixture (beef) (Lente Iletin II)

Regular and NPH mixture (pork) (Lente Iletin II, Lente Insulin, Lente purified pork, Semilente Insulin, Ultralente Insulin)

Chapter 20

# The Nervous System

**Disciplines**

Neurology

Psychiatry

The nervous system is probably the most complex and least understood structure of the human body. For our purposes, we will make it as simple as possible. The nervous system can be broken down into the central nervous system (CNS) (brain and spinal cord), and peripheral nervous system (nerves outside the CNS).

## NEUROANATOMY

The brain, also referred to as the *cerebrum*, is separated into halves, called *cerebral hemispheres*, connected by the *corpus callosum* fibers, and further divided into lobes:

*frontal lobe*—voluntary motor control and speech formation, emotions, personality, drive, and self-awareness

*parietal lobe*—processes and interprets sensory data, comprehension

*occipital lobe*—vision and visual interpretation

*temporal lobe*—perception and interpretation of sound and written matter, integration of sensory data, and some behavior

The *cerebellum* is tucked beneath the occipital lobe and behind the brainstem, and is responsible for balance, coordination, and equilibrium. It aids the cerebrum in integrating voluntary movement. The brain is covered by the skull or *cranium.* Openings in the cranium are typically referred to as *foramen* (apertures through bones).

Primitive functions such as breathing and other involuntary functions are generated in the *brainstem.* Therefore, damage to the brainstem usually causes death. The *cranial nerves* also originate from the brainstem area. These nerves (CN I–XII) are examined in the typical neurological exam by evaluating taste and tongue control, smell, hearing, eye movement and visual fields, facial tone, gag, swallowing, and neck tone.

The *spinal cord* leaves the cranium through the *foramen magnum* (large hole). The spinal cord lies in the vertebral canal, formed by foramen in each vertebra. The column is a tubelike structure consisting of the spinal cord and nerve roots. The nerves are identified by the vertebrae from which they originate. They exit the spinal cord at intervertebral foramen (see Figure 20.1).

C = cervical vertebrae 1–8

T = thoracic vertebrae 1–12

L = lumbar vertebrae 1–5

S = sacral vertebrae 1–5

Thirty-one pairs of peripheral nerves are distributed over the entire body. A nerve is described as "innervating" a particular structure or area. A *dermatome* is the area of skin supplied by fibers from a single nerve root (i.e., the C6 dermatome is the cutaneous innervation of the lateral arm and thumb provided by the nerve root originating from the sixth cervical vertebra.)

You will commonly find reference made to the *brachial plexus,* a group of nerves whose origin comes primarily from the roots of cervical nerves 5–8 plus the first thoracic nerve. These nerves supply the upper limb and often become impinged from traumatic injury.

Similarly, the *sciatic nerve* is composed of nerve roots emanating from L4–S4 and supplying the lower limb. *Sciatica* is a type of *neuralgia,* a condition in which the patient experiences pain extending along the course of the nerve. The sciatic nerve has an immense area to supply, and therefore the pain associated with sciatica will often extend from the buttock down the lower leg. The most common cause of sciatica is a herniated lumbar disk.

The brain and spinal cord are bathed in *CSF* (cerebrospinal fluid), which originates from the cerebral ventricles. (You will often find reference to CSF in medical records. This is the fluid evaluated during a spinal tap.) The CSF is covered by a tough, protective membrane called *dura mater* (literally, "tough mother"). (You will find the word element *dura* in many forms in medical records.) An *epidural catheter* is an instrument that delivers injections just outside the dura, most often to deliver anesthesia to the spinal nerves. There are two other membranous layers deep to the dura mater: the *pia mater* and *arachnoid* layers.

**Figure 20.1**
**The Nervous System**

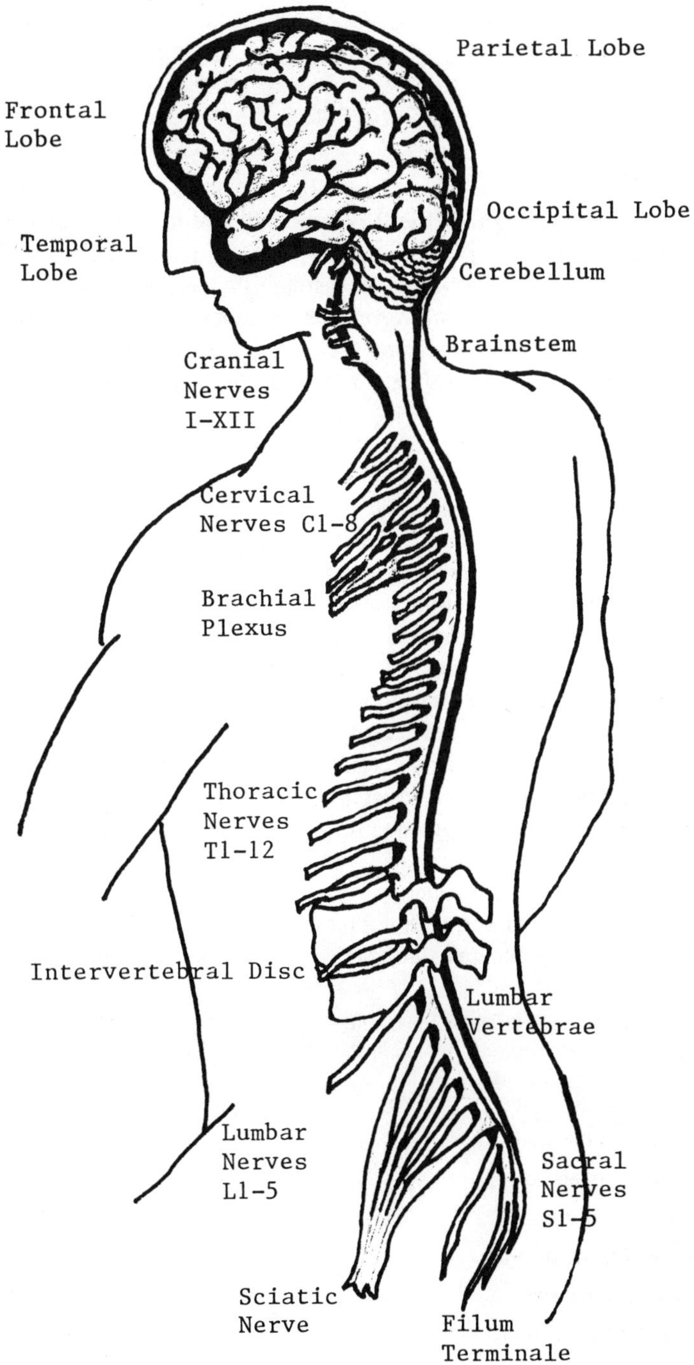

The word element *cephalo* refers to the head. Often medical terms associated with the brain contain *cephalo*, such as *encephalitis* (inflammation of the brain). *Anencephaly* means failure of the brain to develop. *Hydrocephalus*—literally "water on the brain"—means an overproduction of CSF, which collects in the ventricles.

## NEUROLOGY

An *electroencephalogram* (EEG) is a recording of the electrical activity generated by the brain. Other brain scans are the *CT scan (computerized tomography)*, a precise form of x-ray that distinguishes different densities of brain matter; and the *MRI (magnetic resonance imaging)*, which demonstrates slices of the brain through aligning protons of the tissues in a magnetic field. Radio frequencies then are absorbed, emitted, and analyzed by a computer, which constructs an image.

Lesions of the brain are typically identified and diagnosed by loss of function to the area of the body that is governed by that particular section of the brain and affected by its loss. Consider a stroke, a sudden and severe attack. Usually it refers to a cerebrovascular accident (CVA): the blood supply to a certain section of the brain has been interrupted, thereby causing its demise. The blood supply to the brain comes from two internal carotid arteries, two vertebral arteries, and the basilar arteries. This may be due to an embolic event, a hemorrhagic event, or unknown causes. *Transient ischemic attacks* are small strokes. Body functions that are regulated by the portion of the brain supplied by the blocked artery or its branches therefore cease to function properly. If motor function is interrupted, a paralysis results. The terms *paralysis, plegia*, and *palsy* are used interchangeably. A *hemiplegia* is paralysis of half the body. Interruption of the blood supply to the right side of the brain produces symptoms on the left side of the body.

A patient's neurological state is assessed by evaluating many factors, including gait, balance, posture, mood, expression, speech, and hearing.

Defining neurological states utilizes words with several common elements:

*esthe*—refering to perception or sensation

*gno*—to discern

*nomia*—the ability to name something

*opia*—describes the visual fields

*phasia*—to comprehend

*phonia*—to vocalize

*taxic*—coordination or order

*tonic*—refers to tension

*ataxia*—failure of coordination

*hemihypotonia*—diminished muscle tone on one side of the body

*hypophonia*—weak voice

*bitemporal hemianopia*—the visual fields on both temporal halves are not operating

*anomic aphasia*—does not have the ability to name something

*astereognosis*—inability to perceive an object using the sense of touch

## NEUROLOGICAL TESTS

A neurologist can discern what section of the brain is malfunctioning based on which function cannot be performed.

Head injuries are a significant cause of death and disability. Causes of head trauma include automobile and road accidents, assaults, slip and fall injuries, industrial accidents, diving, and other sports injuries. Contributors include faulty vehicles, unsafe workplaces, alcohol intoxication, and failure to use safety devices.

An accident that damages the CNS may produce numerous abnormalities, including paralysis, intercerebral hemorrhage (bleeding into the brain), subdural hematoma (bleeding beneath the dura) seizure, neurological deficit, coma, and death. When an accident induces unconsciousness, a number of diagnostic tests will aid the physician in determining the type and extent of damage.

Skull fractures are a common cause of subdural hematomas, vehicle accidents being the most common cause of skull fractures. These usually develop within hours of injury, yet some may develop up to weeks following. Subdural hematomas produce increased pressure from bleeding, displacing the brain. Common symptoms include loss or decrease in the level of consciousness, *ipsilateral* (one-sided) pupillary dilation and *contralateral* (the other side) *hemiparesis* (one-sided paralysis).

Head examination may reveal diagnostic signs such as "raccoon's eyes" (blood leaking into periorbital tissue), suggesting an orbital fracture; "Battle's sign" (postauricular hematoma) indicates a mastoid fracture. Nasal or *aural* (pertaining to the ear) bleeding may indicate a basilar skull fracture. Neck stiffness may be due to a subarachnoid hemorrhage (bleeding beneath the arachnoid layer). A Babinski sign is elicited when the foot is stroked (toes flare and big toe flexes) in trauma involving the corticospinal tract.

In coma victims, spontaneous posturing assists in discerning the cause. Flexion and adduction of the arms accompanied by leg extension (*decorticate posturing*) indicate a deep hemispheric process. When the arms are extended, adducted, and internally rotated and there is leg extension (*decerebrate posturing*), there is upper brainstem involvement.

The type of breathing pattern may help in localizing lesions as well. Hyperventilation tapering to apnea (fast to slow to no breathing), called *Cheyne-Stokes* respirations, suggests dysfunction originating in the basal ganglia or deep hemisphere. *Apneustic* breathing (a long inspiration followed by apneic expiration) implies lower pontine damage.

Eye positioning and displacement are also important, as is the reactivity of the pupils. Pupils that react to light indicate that the midbrain is intact. Pupils approximately 4 mm in diameter that do not react to light indicate damage to the midbrain. A unilaterally (one-sided) dilated, unreactive pupil indicates temporal lobe herniation with third nerve compression (*Hutchinson's pupil*). A *Marcus Gunn* defect is one in which the pupillary response is stronger in the consensual pupil than the damaged one, indicating damage to the retina or optic nerve. *Bilateral* (both-sided) small pupils indicate either a drug effect or pontine injury. You will find the gaze described as well. A "doll's head maneuver" allows the physician to observe eye movement when the head is turned. If the eyes do not move opposite the head direction, destruction to the pons or midbrain is suggested, a bad diagnostic sign. This test should never be elicited with cervical damage. Papilledema is indicative of increased intracranial pressure.

A test where ice water is introduced into the ear canal will produce a *nystagmus* (involuntary, rapid eye movement) in the conscious patient toward the other side. In a comatose patient, the eyes deviate toward the cold side.

Seizures are classified as primary, generalized, or partial. They are further described as tonic-clonic or grand mal, absence or petit mal, simple or focal, and temporal or complex. Lip smacking indicates a focus in the temporal lobe.

The *Glasgow Coma Scale* evaluates groups of three criteria and provides a total score from 3 (lowest) to 15 (highest):

| **E—Eye opening** | |
|---|---|
| Spontaneous | 4 |
| To speech | 3 |
| To pain | 2 |
| No response | 1 |
| **M—Motor response** | |
| Obeys | 6 |
| Localizes | 5 |
| Withdraws | 4 |
| Abnormal flexion | 3 |
| Extensor response | 2 |
| No response | 1 |
| **V—Verbal response** | |
| Oriented | 5 |
| Confused | 4 |
| Inappropriate words | 3 |

| | |
|---|---|
| Incomprehensible sounds | 2 |
| No response | 1 |

The resulting score allows the physician to rate the extent of damage and to categorize the results of treatment. Outcome levels are:

Death
Persistent vegetative state
Severe disability (dependent on others for activities of daily living)
Moderate disability (independent in activities of daily living)
Good recovery

Other tests for CNS damage include various laboratory examinations, including evaluation of the cerebrospinal fluid. EEGs, MRIs, and CT scans are often employed as well.

The Mini-Mental Status Exam is a quick screening tool for mental status. The following questions aid the examiner in assessing the patient numerically. The maximum score possible is 30. A score below 20 indicates a patient with altered mental status.

*ORIENTATION*

What is today's (date) (year) (season) (month) (day)? (5)
Where are we now (state) (county) (town) (hospital)? (5)

*REGISTRATION*

Slowly name three objects. Ask the patient to repeat them. (3)

*ATTENTION AND CALCULATION*

"Serial sevens." Ask the patient to start at 100 and count backwards by seven. Stop after five subtractions. (100, 93, 86, 79, 72, 65) (5)

*RECALL*

Ask the patient what the three objects mentioned above were. (3)

*LANGUAGE*

Ask the patient to provide the names of two objects.
Show him a pencil and a watch. (2)
Ask the patient to repeat a short sentence after you. (1)
Follow a three-stage command: "Take this paper in your left hand.
Fold it in half. Put it on the floor." (3)
Read and obey the following command. Write, "Close your eyes." (1)
Ask the patient to write a sentence. (1)
Ask the patient to copy a design. (1)
TOTAL (30)

## PSYCHIATRY

Psychiatric cases require some delicacy. Because of the confidential nature of psychiatric records, special releases of medical information and authorizations must be signed in order for the institution to release them. The physician-patient relationship is especially important to honor in this discipline of medicine, and consequences are severe for breaching confidentiality.

Psychiatrists are certified by the American Board of Psychiatry and Neurology.

Psychiatric illnesses, organic brain syndromes, and other psychiatric disorders have a unique system of classification, established by the American Psychiatric Association. This nosology (disease classification) is set forth in the *Diagnostic and Statistical Manual of Mental Disorders* (DSM).

The diagnostic criteria are very specific for each mental disorder. There is a systematic description for each disorder, describing its essential and associated features. The evaluation is based on five axes:

*Axis I*—Clinical syndromes, not attributable to a mental disorder.

*Axis II*—Developmental disorders and personality disorders.

*Axis III*—Physical conditions in addition to a mental disorder.

*Axis IV*—Provides a six-point rating scale for psychosocial stressors that may exacerbate the current disorder.

*Axis V*—Global Assessment Scale, which judges the patient's highest level of functioning during the past year as it relates to social relations, occupational functioning, and psychological functioning.

Disorders are grouped as follows:

1. Developmental Disorders
2. Organic Mental Syndromes and Disorders
3. Psychoactive Substance Abuse Disorders
4. Schizophrenia
5. Delusional Paranoid Disorders
6. Psychotic Disorder Not Elsewhere Classified
7. Mood Disorders
8. Anxiety Disorders
9. Somatoform Disorders
10. Dissociative Disorders
11. Sexual Disorders
12. Sleep Disorders
13. Factitious Disorders
14. Impulse Control Disorders Not Elsewhere Classified
15. Adjustment Disorders
16. Psychological Factors Affecting Physical Condition
17. Personality Disorders

18. Conditions Not Attributable to a Mental Disorder That Are a Focus of Attention or Treatment

Psychosocial stressors are scaled as follows

0 Inadequate information

1 None (no relevant stressors revealed)

2 Mild (arguments, dissatisfaction, child left home)

3 Moderate (major change like retirement, miscarriage, financial trouble, marital separation)

4 Severe (divorce, poverty)

5 Extreme (serious illness diagnosed, death of a spouse, severe abuse)

6 Catastrophic (death of a child, concentration camp victim)

The Global Assessment of Functioning Scale (GAF Scale) is a continuum, from 1 (in persistent danger of hurting self or others) to 90 (absent or minimal symptoms.)

An example of a multiaxial diagnosis is as follows:

Axis I Psychoactive Substance Abuse Disorder

Axis II Paranoid personality

Axis III Corrosive Esophagitis

Axis IV Moderate (marital separation and loss of job)

Axis V 60 (occasional panic attacks and fights with friends, but no serious impairment in judgment)

## PSYCHOLOGICAL TESTS

The standard intelligence tests utilized are the Stanford-Binet and the Wechsler tests. The Minnesota Multiphasic Personality Inventory (MMPI) is a commonly used tool to assess an individual's psychological capacity in various areas. Tests designed to evaluate competency include the Rorschach ink blot tests, projection tests (the individual draws pictures), and the Szondi tests (individuals separate photographs they "like" from those they "dislike").

## PHARMACOLOGY OF THE CENTRAL NERVOUS SYSTEM

Most drugs that alter the functioning of the CNS act by modifying neurotransmitter activity within the brain. *Neurotransmitters* are chemicals released by nerve cells within the brain to communicate with one another at their synapses. The classic neurotransmitters include epinephrine, norepinephrine, dopamine, serotonin (5–HT), and acetylcholine. For instance, opioid agonists like morphine and its derivatives act at opioid receptors (mu, kappa, and delta). They activate serotonin pathways to inhibit pain input and perform other physiological regulations. Stimulants like amphetamine, cocaine, and apomorphine increase the release of dopamine and norepinephrine and decrease their uptake. Some hallucinogens act as serotonin and sigma receptor agonists, blocking the uptake of dopamine and serotonin. Antiparkinson drugs increase the synthesis and release of dopamine and act as dopamine agonists. Antipsychotic drugs like the phenothiazines and butyrophenones act as dopamine antagonists. Lithium, a common antimanic drug, decreases the release of norepinephrine and dopamine. Since many psychiatric conditions are caused at least partly by chemical imbalances, the effect of most of these drugs is to restore the brain's chemistry to a more balanced state. Others act to manipulate certain physiological pathways for an intended purpose, such as pain relief.

### Opioids

*Opiate* is a generic term applied to substances that bind to the brain's opioid receptors to produce an agonist action. Opioid analgesics affect the reaction to pain. They decrease the subjective response to pain, raise the threshold for pain, and dissociate the emotional response to the pain from the pain itself. They may also produce a state of mental clouding, dysphoria, and/or euphoria. Opioid antagonists bind to opioid receptors but do not stimulate them. *Narcotics* are drugs derived from opium or opium-like substances. They relieve pain by interfering with chemical pathways associated with pain perception. Their propensity to alter mood and behavior creates the potential for dependence and tolerance.

Opioids can be broken down into natural, semisynthetic, and synthetic narcotic analgesics. Natural narcotic analgesics are obtained from the opium poppy (*Papaver somniferum*), the natural source of morphine and codeine. Semisynthetic narcotic analgesics are derived by chemical modification from the naturally occurring substances. These include:

Diacetylmorphine (heroin)

Dihydrocodeine (DHCplus, Drocode)

Ethylmorphine (Diomin)

Hydromorphone (Dilaudid)

Hydrocodone plus acetaminophen (Hycodan, Anexsia, Lorcet, Lortab, Vicodin)

Oxymorphone (Numorphon)

Oxycodone (Procodone)

Oxycodone plus aspirin (Percodan)

Buprenorphine (Buprenex, Temgesic)
Methyldihydromorphone (Pretogon)

Synthetic narcotic analgesics are man-made:

**Piperidines**
Meperidine (Demerol)
Alphaprodine (Nisentil)
Fentanyl (Sublimaze)
Sufentanil (Sufenta)
Alfentanil (Alfenta)

**Morphinan**
Levorphanol (l-Dromoran)
Butorphanol (Stadol)

**Alipathic**
Methadone (Amidone, Dolophine)
Propoxyphene (Darvon)

**Benzomorphan**
Pentazocine (Talwin)
Phenazocine (Prinadol)

Opioid agonist-antagonists have agonist activity at certain receptors and antagonist activity at others:

Dezocine (Dalgan)
N-allylnormorphine (Nalorphine)
Nalbuphine (Nubain)
Butorphanol (Stadol)
Buprenorphine (Buprenex)

Opioids may induce nausea and vomiting. The most serious untoward effect of narcotic analgesics is respiratory depression, the major cause of death with opioid overdose. The classic symptoms of opioid overdosage are pinpoint pupils, unconsciousness, and depressed respiration. Additional effects include an antitussive effect (suppresses the cough reflex), release of antidiuretic hormone (causing urinary retention), and reduced release of gonadotropin and adrenocorticotropic hormone (ACTH). Meperidine and propoxyphene may cause excitatory states, and codeine is often excitatory in children. These drugs should be used with caution in people with epilepsy. Hypothermia and hyperglycemia may result. The cardiovascular system may be affected by reducing anxiety, sympathetic tone, venous and arterial tone, myocardial oxygen consumption, and cardiac muscle contractility. Opioids increase $pCO_2$, which causes cerebral vasodilation, increasing cerebrospinal fluid pressure. When respiration is maintained, intracranial pressure does not increase; however, this effect can become markedly exaggerated in head injury. Therefore, morphine is relatively contraindicated in patients with head injuries. The entire gastrointestinal tract functioning is delayed with opioid usage, causing constipation. The biliary tract may be altered as well. A histamine "flush" is often noted.

*Narcotic antagonists* seek to occupy opioid receptors, competing with narcotic substances. They are used to reverse narcotic depression induced by opioids, to diagnose addiction, and to treat compulsive opioid abuse. They may also produce withdrawal symptoms.

Naloxone (Narcan)

Naltrexone (ReVia)

Nalmafene (Revex)

### Antipsychotic Drugs

The management of patients with psychoses has improved dramatically with the use of psychoactive drugs, enabling many previously hospitalized patients to function well in society. Antipsychotics and antidepressant drugs have had a revolutionary impact on the field of psychiatry. Despite striking improvements in these drugs, their efficacy is still limited, and their use presents the risk of causing potentially irreversible neurological toxicities. One such disorder is tardive dyskinesia, manifested by repetitive involuntary movements of the mouth, lips, and tongue, caused by high doses of phenothiazines given over a long time to schizophrenics. This condition is treated with reduction or withdrawal of the medication, and the employment of a dopamine-depleting drug or an antianxiety agent. This condition may be irreversible.

The primary therapeutic use of antipsychotics is for the treatment of schizophrenia and acute psychosis. Schizophrenia is a clinical syndrome with diverse etiology, symptom manifestation, course, and outcome. Theories on etiology support an overactivity of dopamine in the frontal cortex. The nature of the illness shifts over time within individuals; optimal treatment for one phase of the illness may be inappropriate in another. The desired outcome in treating schizophrenic patients is to allow the patient to become less withdrawn, agitated, hostile, irritable, anxious, and suspicious. Continued use may diminish delusions, hallucinations, paranoia, and disordered thought processes.

Other adverse manifestations of antipsychotic drugs include loss of accommodation of the pupil, dry mouth, difficulty urinating, constipation, hypotension, impotence and failure to ejaculate, Parkinson's syndrome, akathisia (a disorder manifested by extreme motor restlessness), dystonia (spasms involving the head, neck, trunk, and extremities), a toxic confusional state, loss of menstruation and persistent milk secretion from the breasts, and infertility. The mechanisms of these effects are due to the receptor blockades caused by their intended actions.

*Phenothiazines* function to reduce hallucinations and delusions and to help quiet agitated patients:

Chlorpromazine (Thorazine)

Thioridazine (Mellaril)

Trifluoperazine (Stelazine)

Perphenazine (Etrafon)

Fluphenazine (Compazine)

Mesoridazine (Serentil)

In addition, phenothiazines possess antihistaminic and antiserotonergic activity. They may cause weight gain and toxic retinopathy. Temperature regulation may be depressed by phenothiazines, causing the patient to assume the temperature of the environment, like poikilotherms. These drugs are sometimes used as premedication for certain surgeries to facilitate hypothermia. Neuroleptic malignant syndrome may occur in approximately 1 percent of patients receiving high-potency neuroleptics, resulting in fever, muscular rigidity, stupor, leukocytosis, respiratory and autonomic dysfunction, and potential death from respiratory or renal failure, cardiovascular collapse, or arrythmias. The drug must be stopped in this situation. Bromocriptine and dantrolene are effective drugs employed to treat this condition. This class of drugs potentiates the effects of CNS depressants, opioids, and alcohol. Among these drugs are the following:

*Risperidone* (Risperdal)—also used to manage manifestations of psychotic disorders; has a lower incidence of extrapyramidal side effects and tardive dyskinesia.

*Perphenazine* (Trilafon)—acts at all levels of the central nervous system to manage psychotic manifestations and severe nausea and vomiting.

*Prochlorperazine* (Compazine)—useful as well for short-term treatment of generalized nonpsychotic anxiety but should not be used indiscriminantly because of its side effects.

*Trifluoperazine* (Stelazine)—an antipsychotic/antianxiety medication.

*Haloperidol* (Haldol)—often employed for acute mania, with therapeutic effects similar to phenothiazines. Parkinsonism may result from its use. It causes fewer side effects and lacks anticholinergic effects.

*Thiothixene* (Navane)—similar to chlorpromazine and offers an alternative.

*Loxapine* (Loxitane)—an alternative for patients refractory to other antipsychotics; side effects include hypertension, oxylogyric crisis, and seizures.

*Molindone* (Moban)—an effective antipsychotic drug that is unlikely to cause weight gain.

*Clozapine* (Clorazil)—has fewer extrapyramidal side effects but may cause sedation, tachycardia, seizures, and agranulocytosis.

### Antidepressant Drugs

*Depression* is an imprecise term used to designate normal variants of mood, character traits, medical symptoms, or a collection of psychiatric syndromes. Depression as an illness can be present with many symptoms, such as sadness, pessimism, loss of interest in usual activities, feelings of worthlessness, guilt, and the loss of ability to feel pleasure. Physical symptoms can be part of the syndrome as well, with sleep disturbances, weight loss, GI distress, backaches, and hypochondriasis. The most immediately dangerous symptom of depression is suicidal ideation.

There is no universally accepted classification for depressive subtypes. The *DSM* identifies several subgroups of depression:

- Depressive episodes
- Manic episodes
- Affective or mood disorders, including bipolar disorder (alternating manic and depressive episodes), major (unipolar) depression, dysthymic depression, and other classifications (cyclothymic disorder, reactive depression, and uncomplicated bereavement).

Antidepressant agents can be broadly classified into groups based on their chemistry. Their therapeutic uses include treating depression, panic disorder, narcolepsy symptomatology, and occasional use for bedwetting in childhood and attention deficit disorder. Antidepressants are believed to cause downregulation of norepinephrine receptors and increased synaptic concentrations of serotonin, responsible for their effectiveness. They may also produce sedation, weakness, fatigue, headaches, anticholinergic effects like dry mouth, constipation, sexual dysfunction, and others. Cardiovascular effects may include an increase in heart rate, ECG charges, and lengthening cardiac conduction time (a serious effect in patients with preexisting conduction disease). They may also cause orthostatic hypotension. They should also be used with caution with patients who have glaucoma or prostatic hypertrophy. These drugs may lower the seizure threshold, resulting in seizure activity. Toxic levels may produce cardiac arrythmias, hypotension, bowel and bladder paralysis, respiratory depression, convulsions, and coma.

*Tricyclic compounds* are not intended to produce elevations of mood; they simply remove the symptomatology of depression:

Imipramine (Tofranil)
Desipramine (Norpramin)
Nortriptyline (Aventyl, Pamelor)

Doxepin (Sinequan, Adapin)
Protriptyline (Vivactil)
Trimipramine (Surmontil)
Amitryptiline (Endep, Elavil)
Amitryptiline plus perphenazine (Entrafon, Triavil)
Amitriptyline plus chlordiazepoxide (Limbitrol)

*Second-generation compounds* provide alternatives to the older drugs, with less anticholinergic activity:

Amoxapine (Asendin)
Maprotiline (Ludiomil)
Trazodone (Desyrel)
Fluxetine (Prozac)
Sertraline (Zoloft)
Nefazodone (Serzone)
Paroxetine (Paxil)
Venlafaxine (Effexor)

*Monoamine oxidase inhibitors* produce mood elevations. Autonomic effects are similar to tricyclic compounds; their serious toxicities involve the liver, brain, and cardiovascular system. Interactions with other drugs are common, and even over-the-counter cold medications may produce a hypertensive crisis when taken with MAOI. Foods containing tyramine should be avoided. These drugs inhibit the metabolism of other drugs as well.

Phenelzine (Nardil)
Tranylcypromine (Parnate)

### Antimanic Agents

*Lithium* (Eskalith, Lithonate, Lithotabs, Lithobid) is a specific antimanic agent for the treatment of bipolar disorder. Adverse reactions include thirst, increased urination, fine tremor, GI irritation, mild diarrhea, weight gain, edema, and acne. Lithium toxicity may result from low sodium levels. At higher levels, confusion, vomiting, slurred speech, lethargy, blurred vision and speech, weakness, delirium, stupor, coma, and convulsions may result. This drug is contraindicated in pregnancy. Lithium levels should be monitored to avoid toxicity.

*Carbamazepine* (Tegretol) is an alternative to lithium in the treatment of bipolar disorder.

*Divalproex* (Depakote) is used to treat manic episodes associated with bipolar disorder and also used for the treatment of epilepsy.

### Antianxiety Medication

Anxiety may accompany almost any physical or psychological disorder. Psychological anxiety states include tension, nervousness, irrational fear, apprehension, and others. Psychiatric disorders classified as anxiety states include panic disorder, anxiety disorder, obsessive-compulsive disorder, and posttraumatic stress disorder.

*Benzodiazepines* are widely prescribed for patients with a generalized anxiety disorder. Their dosage should be limited to the lowest possible level for the shortest time possible. Panic disorder, for which Xanax is appropriately prescribed, may require prolonged treatment. These drugs are often overprescribed for stress-related symptoms. They should not be used to treat depression. Dependence on these drugs may occur with prolonged usage and in those with a history of substance abuse. Insomnia is often treated by benzodiazepines, but tolerance may develop, and withdrawal symptoms may occur after only 4 to 6 weeks of treatment. Seizure disorders are sometimes treated with diazepam. Diazepam is also utilized as premedication for surgery. These drugs may also be employed to lessen the symptoms of alcohol withdrawal syndrome. Benzodiazepines cause drowsiness, sleep disturbances, dizziness, lightheadedness, difficulty with coordination, and sometimes amnesia. These drugs should not be used in early pregnancy and should not be used with other CNS depressants or alcohol.

Lorazepam (Ativan)
Diazepam (Valium)
Chlordiazepoxide (Librium)
Chlorazepate (Tranxene)
Oxazepam (Serax)
Alprazolam (Xanax)
Flurazepam (Dalmane)
Halazepam (Paxipam)
Temazepam (Ristoril)
Triazolam (Halcion)
Quazepam (Doral)
Estazolam (Prosom)

Among other anxiolytic drugs are:

*Buspirone* (Buspar)—used to treat chronic anxiety states, with less sedation and psychomotor impairment than benzodiazepines.

*Hydroxyzine* (Atarax, Vistaril)—used to relieve symptoms of anxiety and tension.

*Beta blockers* (e.g., propranolol, nadolol, and atenolol)—to alleviate the somatic symptoms of anxiety like palpitations and tremulousness; may be effective for some of the psychic components as well.

*Barbiturates*—have a long history of extensive use as sedative-hypnotic agents but have more recently been replaced by the benzodiazepines. They depress the activity of all exitable tissues. The clinical uses are for anxiety and sedation, hypnosis, anesthesia, and seizure disorders. The most serious adverse effect from their use is respiratory depression. Their abuse potential is high.

Phenobarbital (Luminal)

Amobarbital (Amytal)

Pentobarbital (Nembutal)

Secobarbital (Seconal)

Thiopental (Pentothal)

Thiamylal (Surital)

Methohexital (Brevital)

Other sedative-hypnotic agents:

Meprobomate (Miltown, Equanil, Equagesic)

Chloral hydrate (Noctec)

Zolpidem (Ambien)

Ethchlorvynol (Placidyl)

## TREATMENT OF EPILEPSY

Epilepsy is a spontaneous, chronic, and recurrent disturbance of the functioning in the CNS, characterized by an abnormal and excessive neuronal discharge in the brain, which can be recorded on an EEG. The specific symptoms depend on the anatomical location and the portion of the CNS involved.

Accurate diagnosis is essential, since drug therapy is selective for a particular type. Convulsions are involuntary skeletal muscle contractions and are often a feature of an epileptic seizure; however, seizures may have other causes as well. The classification of epileptic seizures is based on *ictal* (seizure associated) and *interictal* (between seizures) EEG patterns. Epileptic seizures are classified as partial (originating in a localized area of the brain) or generalized, and further broken down by their EEG and clinical manifestations:

**Partial**

Simple partial (no alteration in consciousness)

Complex partial (consciousness is lost)

Partial evolving to secondary generalized seizures

**Generalized**

Absence seizures (petit mal)

Myoclonic (jerklike contractions)

Clonic (repetitive muscle jerks)

Tonic (rigid, violent muscular contractions)

Tonic-clonic (grand mal-loss of consciousness with convulsions)

Atonic (loss or diminution of muscle tone)

Antiepileptic drugs elevate the discharge threshold of neurons that have lost their inhibitory potential and prevent the spread of seizure activity to normal neurons. The ultimate objective in treatment is to prevent the occurrence of seizures or to decrease their frequency. This is achieved through maintaining an effective plasma concentration of the drug. Correct diagnosis, made by EEG and seizure pattern, should lead to the proper antiepileptic agent. Other factors may contribute to lowering the seizure threshold (e.g., fever, hyponatremia, hypoglycemia, hypocalcemia, physical and mental stress) and should be corrected when possible. The selected agent should be started with a small dosage until the seizures are controlled. When the patient approaches toxic levels, another drug should be substituted or a second may be cautiously added, if required. The patient should be warned about the dangers inherent in their use. When the patient has been seizure free for a period of time (usually two to three years), and the clinical picture justifies discontinuance, the medication should be withdrawn gradually.

*Hydantoin derivatives* are useful in generalized tonic clonic, simple and complex partial seizures, and status epilepticus, by limiting high-frequency repetitive firing of neurons. These drugs may exacerbate absence seizures and possess potential cardiac toxicity. Other toxicities are related to serum concentration. Central nervous system changes are possible; gum overgrowth, excessive growth of body hair, and blood disorders; congenital malformations may occur; there may be interference with vitamin D metabolism; and hypersensitivity may result. There are also many potential drug interactions with phenytoin (some anticoagulants compete for plasma protein binding; cimetidine and isoniazid inhibit phenytoin metabolism; phenobarbital and carbamazepine stimulate phenytoin metabolism; and phenytoin stimulates the metabolism of theophylline and corticosteroids).

Diphenylhydantoin

Phenytoin (Dilantin)

Mephentytoin (Mesantoin)

Ethatoin (Peganoke)

*Carbamazepine* (Tegretol), an anticonvulsant that resembles phenytoin, is effective in the treatment of complex partial seizures. It may worsen absence seizures. Toxicities include dizziness, drowsiness, double vision, anorexia, nausea, rash, edema, blood disorders, and congestive heart failure. Renal, hepatic, and bone marrow function should be monitored.

*Barbiturates* are used to treat generalized tonic-clonic, complex partial, and simple partial seizures in infants and preschoolers and for status epilepticus. They are also used in the treatment of febrile seizures in infants and children. They limit the spread of seizure activity but are less selective than the hydantoin derivatives and therefore produce more sedation. These drugs should always be withdrawn gradually to avoid seizures or status epilepticus. Barbiturates have additive effects with other CNS depressants.

Phenobarbital

Mephobarbital (Mebaral)

Pentobarbital (Nembutal)

*Benzodiazepines* like diazepam (Valium) are frequently used to terminate status epilepticus because the onset of effect is rapid. They can cause respiratory and cardiovascular depression when given too rapidly. The anticonvulsant action is short-lived, however, so should be followed by phenytoin to avoid the recurrence of seizures. Clonazepam (Klonopin) is used to treat absence, myoclonic, and atonic seizures and may be effective when other treatments fail. Frequent adverse effects include drowsiness, lethargy, ataxia, and behavioral changes, especially in children.

*Succinamides* are used to control absence seizures that are refractory to other drugs. Adverse reactions include gastrointestinal upset, blood disorders, neurological effects, and dermatologic manifestations.

Methsuximide (Celontin)

Phensuximide (Milontin)

Ethosuximide (Zarontin)

*Valproic acid* (Depakene, Depakote) is indicated to treat simple and complex absence seizures and adjunctively in patients with multiple seizure types, including absence seizures. Valproic acid should not be used in patients with hepatic disease or dysfunction. Other adverse reactions include gastrointestinal upset, sedative effects, hair loss, skin rashes and sensitivity, some behavioral problems, and metabolic changes.

*Acetazolamide* (Diamox) is sometimes effective in controlling absence seizures resistant to other agents. Tolerance develops rapidly, however.

*Phenacemide* (Phenurone) is used to treat complex partial seizures only when other agents have failed. Serious toxicity limits its usefulness.

*Lamotrigine* (Lamictal) is indicated as adjunctive therapy to treat partial seizures. It has nervous system side effects, runny nose, rash, double and blurred vision, and some digestive effects.

*Gabapentin* (Neurontin) is used as adjunctive therapy to treat partial seizures and may cause CNS depression.

*Felbamate* (Felbatol) is recommended only for use in patients who fail to respond to other treatments and whose epilepsy is so severe as to justify the risk of aplastic anemia and/or liver failure associated with its use.

Chapter 21

# The Musculoskeletal System

**Disciplines**

Sports medicine

Orthopedic surgery

Physiatry

Osteopathy

Physical medicine and rehabilitation

Reconstructive surgery

Physical therapy

Chiropractic

Podiatry

The musculoskeletal system describes the structure of the human body—the materials that hold it together. This chapter will deal with the structure particularly as it pertains to trauma. Any anatomical text will provide additional descriptions.

## THE AXIAL SKELETON

The body is constructed by the bones of the skeletal system, which can be broken down into the *axial* and the *appendicular* skeleton. Bones of the skeletal system are connected by joints.

The *axial* skeleton (See Figure 21.1) is the principal structure about which the rest of the body is arranged. The axial skeleton includes the *cranium* (protecting the brain) or skull, which is situated on the first cervical vertebra, or

**Figure 21.1**
**The Axial Skeleton**

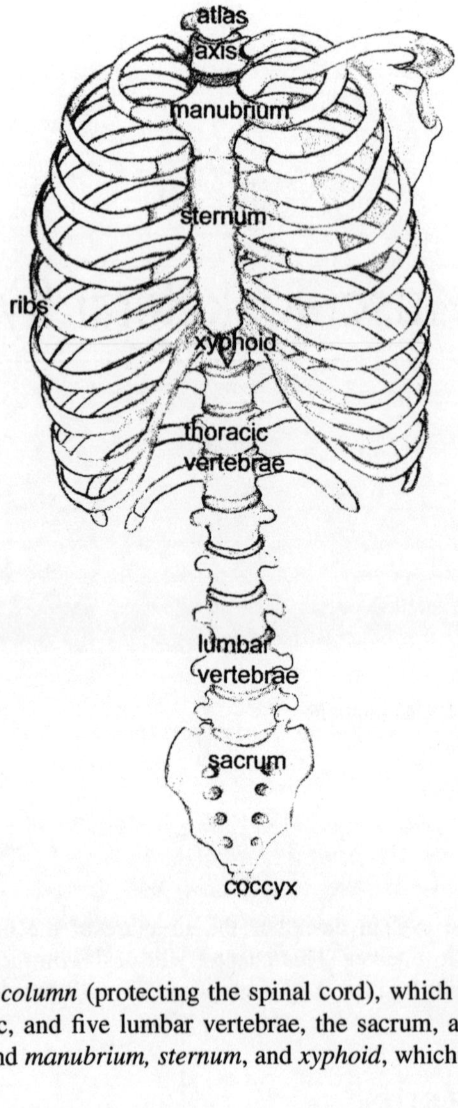


*atlas*; the *spinal column* (protecting the spinal cord), which contains seven cervical, 12 thoracic, and five lumbar vertebrae, the sacrum, and coccyx; and the 12 *ribs* (*costo*) and *manubrium, sternum*, and *xyphoid*, which protect the thoracic organs.

## THE SKULL

The skull (Figure 21.2) is the entire bony structure that sits above the first cervical vertebra, the atlas. The skull is assembled by the precise articulation of bones connected by sutures:

**Figure 21.2**
**The Skull**

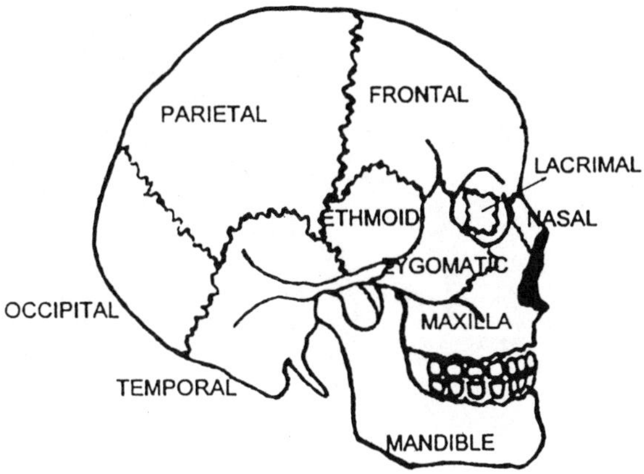


| | |
|---|---|
| frontal | parietal |
| nasal | occipital |
| maxilla | temporal |
| zygomatic | sphenoid |
| mandible | lacrimal |
| hyoid | vomer |

Each of these bones may be subdivided into smaller sections, processes, fossae, sinuses, and foramen. In the child, soft *fontanelles* may be felt where the skull bones have not yet *ossified* (hardened to bone).

## THE APPENDICULAR SKELETON

The *appendicular* skeleton consists of two parts: upper and lower. The upper part is the *pectoral* girdle from which arise the bones of the upper extremity (Figure 21.3)

A clavicle
B scapula
C humerus
D radius
E ulna

carpal bones (wrist):
F trapezium
G trapezoid

**Figure 21.3**
**Upper Appendicular Skeleton**

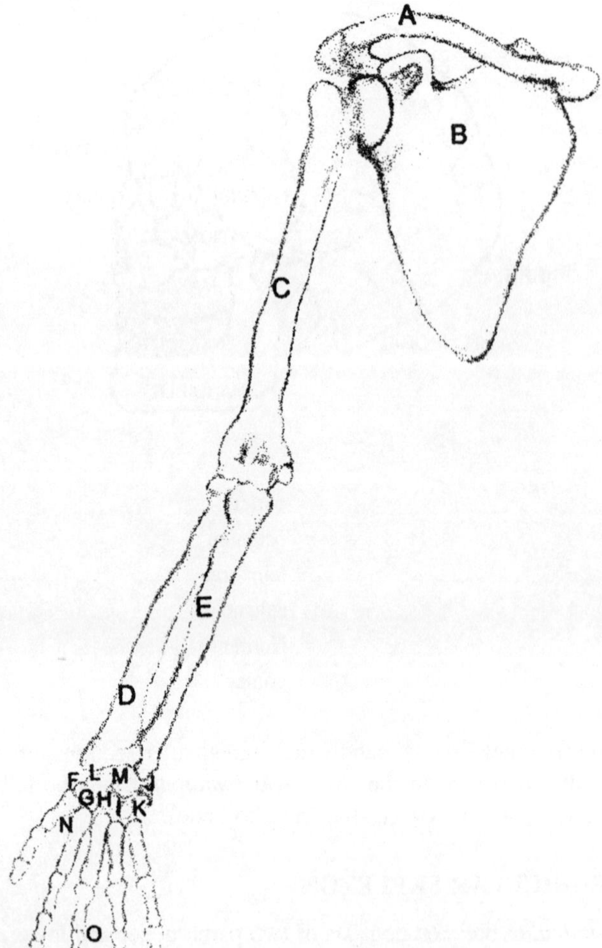


- H capitate
- I hamate
- J pisiform
- K triquetral
- L scaphoid
- M lunate

N five metacarpals
O fourteen phalanges (two on the thumb and three on each finger)

The lower part is the *pelvic* girdle (Figure 21.4), the bones through which the lower extremity is attached to the trunk:

**Figure 21.4**
**Pelvic Girdle**

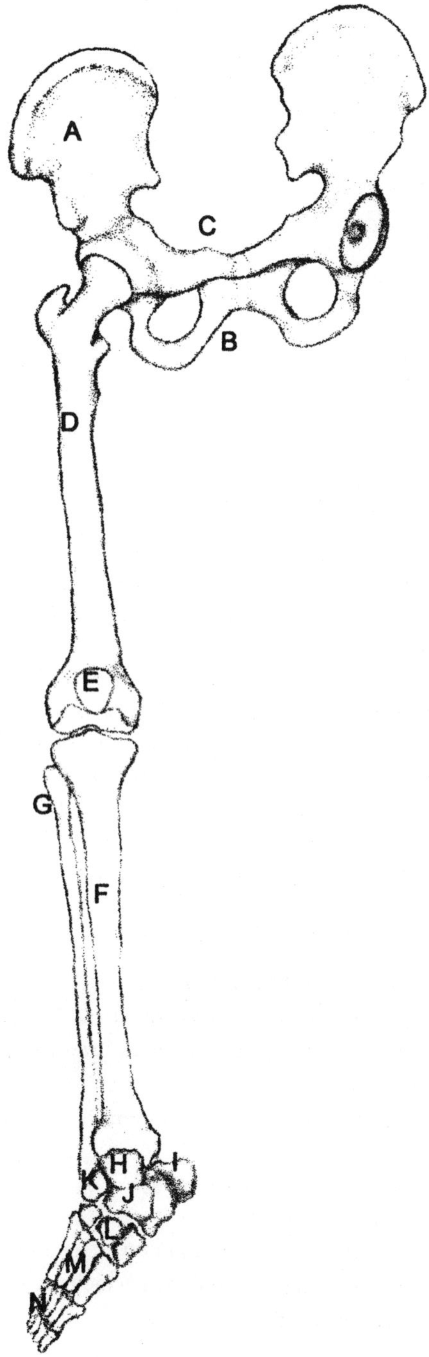

A ilium
B ischium
C pubis
D femur
E patella
F tibia
G fibula
  tarsal bones (ankle)
  H talus
  I calcaneus
  J cuboid
  K navicular
  L three cuneiforms
M five metatarsals
N fourteen phalanges (two for each hallux, or big toe; three for each other toe)

## JOINTS AND LIGAMENTOUS STRUCTURES

Joints are known as *arthroses*—articulations or the site of union between bones. They are classified according to the type of movement they allow and how they are connected. Some are connected by *cartilaginous* tissue (word element, *chondro*), *fibrous* tissue (cranial sutures), or *fibrocartilaginous* tissue (symphysis pubis). Their movement is limited. *Synovial* joints are freely movable and have a structure that contains a fluid-filled cavity (synovium). Synovial joints are further broken down into *ball and socket* joints like the shoulder and hip, *hinge* joints like the elbow, and *pivot* joints like the cranium on the first cervical vertebra. Some synovial joints like the knee and shoulder contain fluid-filled sacs called *bursae*, which decrease friction. There are also *condyloid* joints (at the wrist), *saddle* joints (thumb at carpal-metacarpal), *plane* joints, and others.

Any joint condition is described by the prefix *-arthro*.

*arthrochondritis*—inflammation of the cartilage of a joint
*arthrocentesis*—a procedure to puncture and aspirate joint fluid
*arthrodesis*—a surgical fixation of a joint (also called *artificial ankylosis*)
*arthrodynia*—pain in the joint
*arthrokatadysis*—the head of the femur protrudes through the floor of the acetabulum of the hip
*arthroneuralgia*—pain arising in or around a joint
*arthropathy*—used to describe any joint disease
*arthroscopy*—examination of the interior of a joint with an endoscope
*arthrosynovitis*—inflammation of the sunovial membrane of a joint
*costochondritis*—inflammation of a rib and its cartilage

*Ligaments* are strong, flexible bands of connective tissue that surround movable joints and hold the bones together. They are especially susceptible to tear from traumatic injuries. The *anterior cruciate ligament* of the knee is especially prone to injury from any knee trauma.

*Tendons* are fibrous tissue that connect bones to muscles. These also will tear from trauma. Muscles are described with the term *myo*.

*myositis*—muscle inflammation

*Fascial sheaths* provide additional connective tissue support around muscular structures. Fascia is often interrupted during trauma, including surgery.

*fasciitis*—inflammation of the fascia surrounding muscle

The body is made up of hundreds of muscles. Often these muscles are named for their location or the function they perform. For example, *flexor carpi ulnaris* is a muscle of the forearm that flexes the hand at the wrist (*carpus*). It is innervated by the ulnar nerve. The *extensor pollicis brevis* is the shorter muscle, which extends the thumb (pollex). The *adductor hallucis* muscle adducts the big toe.

## TRAUMATIC INJURY

A number of common terms are associated with trauma:

*abrasion*—a scrape, interrupting the skin's surface

*contusion*—a bruise

*hematoma*—bleeding in the tissues, usually clotted, and producing increased pressure

*lacerations*—cuts or torn wounds

*fractures*—breaks in the bone. They may be traumatic due to an accident or injury, or pathological, due to weakening of the bone by a cancerous lesion or age. These may be described as *simple* (these breaks do not protrude through the skin) or *compound* (the broken bone(s) project through ruptured skin).

Fractures may be further described according to their configuration:

*avulsion*—a small fragment of bone separated at the site of attachment of a ligament or tendon

*Colles'*—fracture along the lower end of the radius

*comminuted*—shattered

*complete*—all the way through the entire cross section of the bone

*composite*—the fracture lines branch without bone displacement

*compression*—crushed together

*depressed*—a skull fracture in which one fragment is pressed downward
*fissure*—a crack
*greenstick*—one side is broken, the other bent
*impacted*—one fragment is driven into another
*Jefferson*—fracture of the first cervical vertebra
*Le Fort*—bilateral horizontal fracture of the maxilla
*linear*—the break is parallel to the long axis of the bone
*Monteggia's*—fracture of the proximal ulna with dislocation of the head of the radius
*ping-pong*—same as depressed
*ring*—a skull fracture involving the occipital bone; the skull is jammed against the atlas.
*Smith's*—a reverse Colles' fracture
*spiral*—encircles the bone
*spontaneous*—pathologic
*sprain*—separation of a tendon from its insertion, taking with it a bone fragment
*transverse*—across the bone
*trophic*—due to a nutritional disturbance

Fractures are repaired by realigning and stabilizing the break. This repair may require surgery: *open reduction* (ORIF—open reduction, internal fixation—usually requires hardware insertion), or *closed reduction* (manipulating the bone back into place and immobilizing with a cast or splint).

Complications can follow fractures:

infection
gangrene
decreased range of motion
fat emboli, which may lodge in the lung (pulmonary embolism)
chronic pain
arthritis
further surgery
impinged nerves
permanent functional damage
discrepancy of limb length
compartment syndrome (compromises circulation as muscle groups swell without expanding)

**The Vertebral Column**

The spinal column is made up of cervical (the smallest), thoracic (intermediate), and lumbar (largest) vertebrae, sacrum, and coccyx. The vertebrae are stacked on one another to form the spine. Between each spinal vertebra, a nerve root emerges from the spinal cord and becomes a nerve designed to innervate a particular area of the body. Also interposed between each vertebral body from C1 to L5 are extremely strong fibrocartilaginous structures called *intervertebral discs*. These may be thought of as immensely tough cushions containing an outer covering of concentric layers of fibers, called *annulus fibrosus*. These fibers are stuffed with a central core composed of a springy, pulpy material called the *nucleus pulposus*. In healthy adults, these discs comprise about one-fourth the length of the vertebral column. They are largest in the lumbar region, where more shock absorption is required. With age, the composition of the intervertebral discs undergoes changes, with the core losing its liquid and becoming more fibrous-like.

When any disease process or trauma interrupts the cushioning between vertebral bodies, the vertebrae become more condensed, thereby compressing the space from which the nerve roots emerge. This squeezing may cause pain and dysfunction. Trauma may also tear the ligamentous structures surrounding the vertebrae, weakening their binding nature. It is as if a truss is loosened, causing the structure to become subject to further compromise.

Trauma may also induce the disc itself to distort in a number of possible ways. The disc may bulge, herniate, or rupture. This process can have disabling consequences, causing pain, impingement on the nerve root that emerges adjacent to the disc, and restriction. These may be treated in a number of conservative manners, including bed rest or restriction of activity, pain relievers, anti-inflammatory medication, and muscle relaxers. Chiropractic care may be sought, physical therapy modalities and exercises may be prescribed, and surgery may become necessary to fuse the vertebrae together.

*Spondylolisthesis* is forward displacement of one vertebra over its lower segment—either congenital or traumatically induced.

*Spondylolisis* is the breaking down of a vertebra.

### Spinal Cord Injury

The most severe form of traumatic injury to the vertebral column is a mishap (usually by an automobile accident) that causes one of the vertebral bodies to break, shatter, or dislodge itself to the point of impinging on the spinal cord itself. Damage to the spinal cord may also be caused by a sharp instrument, birth trauma, diving accidents, and pathological processes. The resulting compromise inhibits the spinal cord from transmitting impulses from the brain to the nerve areas for which they are intended. The result may be partial or complete paralysis, temporary or permanent. The vasculature is often interrupted as well. The extent of paralysis also depends on the level at which the impingement occurred. *Paraplegia* affects the lower limbs; *quadraplegia* affects all four limbs. Surgery may correct the displacement in some cases, and the vertebrae may be surgically realigned.

Victims of spinal cord injuries are not only physically disabled; they are affected in every other aspect of their lives as well. They must be cared for by others. Their normal body functions must be assisted through artificial means. They are susceptible to sores and infections. Their careers, their home life, their relationships, and their emotional state are all invariably disrupted to some extent.

Incomplete spinal cord syndromes may be encountered with traumatic cervical spine injuries. A hyperextension injury may produce what is known as the *central cord syndrome*, which involves a contusion to the central portion of the spinal cord. Symptoms include a painful, burning, *dysesthesia* in the arms, upper extremity weakness, and loss of sensation to pain and temperature along the back, shoulders and arms. *Anterior spinal artery syndrome* produces bilateral paralysis and loss of pain and temperature sensation below the injured level, yet vibrational and positional sense remains intact. *Brown-Séquard syndrome* is when half the cord is damaged. This produces one-sided paralysis, loss of vibrational and positional sense on the ipsilateral (same) side, and contralateral (other-sided) loss of pain and temperature. With the *posterial column syndrome*, which is uncomon, loss of vibration and proprioception occur below the damaged level.

## Whiplash Injury

*Whiplash* injuries are caused by excessive forces propelling the neck into hyperextension, hyperflexion, or both. The injury may damage the cervical vertebrae themselves, the ligamentous structures holding the cervical vertebrae in place, and surrounding soft tissue. There are numerous ligamentous structures in the cervical spine, which can become damaged in a whiplash injury:

anterior atlantooccipital membrane
posterior atlantooccipital membrane
articular capsules
lateral atlantooccipital ligaments
anterior longitudinal ligament
atlantoaxial ligaments
ligamentum nuchae
ligamenta flava
tectoral membrane
posterior longitudinal ligament
median atlantoaxial pivot joint
transverse ligament of the atlas
superior longitudinal fascicles

inferior longitudinal fascicles

cruciform ligament

apical ligament

alar ligaments

lateral atlantoaxial joints

accessory ligament

interspinous ligaments

Injuries to the cervical spine are classified as *flexion, flexion-rotation, hyperextension, extension-rotation*, and *compression* injuries. These classifications depend on which way the neck was bent when the injury occurred. After injury, the spine should always be immobilized to prevent further damage, although damage to the spinal cord cannot be cured. The means of immobilization depend on the type and extent of damage. These may involve bracing and traction through various tongs, boards, halos, collars, and jackets. Management may be conservative or surgical. Surgical intervention usually involves various methods of fusing the cervical vertebrae affected.

### Other Traumatic Injuries

These injuries include:

*sprain*—a joint injury wherein the ligamentous fibers are ruptured

*strain*—overstretching of a muscle, tendon, or ligamentous structure

*tear*—a common site of muscular tear is the shoulder cuff, where individual muscles may became traumatically torn

*Overuse syndromes*, also known as repetitive stress injuries, result from repetitive tasks using the same group of muscular structures—for example:

*carpal tunnel syndrome*—from compression of the median nerve as it passes through the transverse superficial carpal ligament at the wrist; produces symptoms ranging from swelling and pallor to numbness, tingling, and pain.

*bursitis, tenosynovitis*—inflammation of a tendon sheath or bursa. This may occur at the wrist, the elbow, the shoulder, the hip, the knee, or combinations of these joints. Treatment is aimed at alleviating symptoms, prescribing anti-inflammatory medication, and exercise.

*TMJ* (temperomandibular joint dysfunction)—a syndrome manifested by facial, jaw, and neck pain with mandibular restriction.

## DRUGS

### Pain Relievers

*NSAIDS* (nonsteroidal anti-inflammatory drugs) inhibit the synthesis of prostaglandins and thromboxanes. These mediate pain, fever, and inflammation. NSAIDS can also cause premature closure of the ductus arteriosus in the fetuses of pregnant women. That is why their unrestricted use is contraindicated, especially in the latter stages of pregnancy. These drugs are widely used for pain, fever, rheumatoid diseases, and other conditions but are not harmless. The main category of these drugs are known as *analgesics*:

Aspirin (Bufferin, Easprin, Ecotrin)

(There are many aspirin combinations too.) Aspirin inhibits platelet production, so has been used as a blood thinner. It has also been associated with the development of Reyes syndrome in children. Aspirin has an irritating effect on the gastrointestinal system so should not be used in those with a sensitive or hyperactive stomach. Overdoses interrupt the acid-base balance and can be extremely toxic.

Acetaminophen (Tylenol)

Acetaminophen combinations include many over-the-counter preparations for pain, sleeping aids, cold remedies, and so forth.

Ibuprofen (Advil, Motrin, IBU, Dristan Sinus, Nuprin, Pedia-Profen)
Naproxen (Naprosyn)
Naproxen sodium (Anaprox)
Sulindac (Clinoril)
Meclofenamate (Meclomen)
Indomethacin (Indocin)

### Anti-Inflammatory Agents

Glucocorticoids function to inhibit the physiological or pathological inflammatory response.

**Inhalers**
Beclomethasone (Beclovent [oral inhaler], Vanceril, Beconase [nasal inhaler], Vancenase)
Flunisolide (AeroBid, Aerobid-M, Nasalide Nasal Solution)
Tramcinolone acetonide (Amacort, Nasacort)

**Oral**

Prednisone (Metocorten)

Prednisolone (Delta-Cortef)

Methylprednisolone (Medrol)

**Parenteral Other Prophylactic**

Methylprednisolone sodium succinate (Solu-Medrol)

(prevents release of chemical mediators from mast cells)

Cromolyn sodium (Intal, Nasalcrom)

### Skeletal Muscle Relaxants

This group of drugs is often employed to decrease muscle spasms and spasticity associated with cerebral palsy, multiple sclerosis, stroke, and musculoskeletal conditions. Drugs that may be employed for treatment include the following:

*diazepam* (Valium)—a benzodiazepine that may aid in skeletal muscle relaxation by reducing spasticity with its sedative properties.

*Baclofen* (Lioresal)—effective in reducing spasms associated with spinal injury or multiple sclerosis. It acts on the spinal cord to reduce spasticity. It is not used as an antianxiety agent.

*Dantrolene* (Dantrium)—produces muscle relaxation outside the central nervous system. Used to treat malignant hyperthermia, a rare disorder triggered by inhalational anesthetics and neuromuscular blocking agents. Its adverse effects include general muscle weakness, sedation, and occasional hepatitis.

*Cyclobenzaprine* (Flexaril)—used for acute, painful muscle spasms. Adverse reactions include drowsiness, dry mouth, dizziness, and other rare reactions. Flexaril should not be used in patients with a history of urinary retention, glaucoma, and in those taking MAOIs or anticholinergic medications.

*Chlorzoxazone* (Paraflex)—a centrally acting agent for painful musculoskeletal conditions. Gastrointestinal symptoms followed by drowsiness and dizziness are symptoms of overdose.

*Methocarbamol* (Robaxin)—acts as a CNS depressant but is often prescribed to relieve acute musculoskeletal pain. Adverse reactions include lightheadedness, dizziness, drowsiness, nausea, headache, and fever.

*Metaxalone* (Skelaxin)—prescribed for acute muscle conditions and functions with a sedative effect as well.

*Carisoprodol* (Soma)—a centrally acting muscle action that relieves the pain of acute muscle spasm due to its sedative properties. Should not be used with bleeding disorders.

Appendix

# Medical Abbreviations

An informative medical reference such as a medical dictionary or encyclopedia, as well as individual references pertaining to the applicable specialty, are essential tools for working up a medical case. Often, however, only abbreviations are used in the medical records. This catalog of abbreviations will enable you to make sense of them. Some abbreviations have more than one meaning and will have to be put in context with the substance of the records.

| | |
|---|---|
| aa | each |
| AA | Alcoholics Anonymous |
| AAA | abdominal aortic aneurysm |
| AAE | active assisted exercises<br>acute allergic encephalitis |
| AAL | anterior axillary line |
| AAO | awake, alert, and oriented |
| $A_2$ | second aortic sound (heard on stethoscope) |
| ab | abortion<br>abnormal<br>antibody |
| AB | active bilaterally (on both sides)<br>ace bandage<br>asthmatic bronchitis |
| ABC | air and bone conduction |
| abd | abduction (movement away from)<br>abdomen |
| ABE | acute bacterial endocarditis |
| ABG | arterial blood gases (lab test) |
| abn | abnormal |
| ABP | arterial blood pressure |
| ABR | absolute bed rest |
| abs | absent |
| ABS | absent bowel sounds (physical exam finding)<br>acute brain syndrome |
| ac | before meals |
| AC | acromioclavicular (joint)<br>adrenal cortex<br>air conduction |

| | |
|---|---|
| | anterior chamber (eye) |
| | anticoagulant (blood thinner) |
| A/C | assist control (ventilator setting mode) |
| ACa | adenocarcinoma |
| ACA | anterior cerebral artery |
| | anterior coronary artery |
| ACC | accommodation (pupil) |
| ACE | angiotensin-1–converting enzyme |
| ACI | acute coronary insufficiency |
| ACIOL | anterior chamber intraocular lens (of eye) |
| ACL | anterior clavicular line (front of shoulder) |
| | anterior cruciate ligament (of knee) |
| ACLS | advanced cardiac life support |
| AcP | acid phosphatase |
| ACTH | adrenocorticotropic hormone |
| ACTS | acute cervical trauma syndrome |
| ACU | adolescent care unit |
| ACVD | acute cardiovascular damage |
| AD | right ear |
| | admitting diagnosis |
| | alternating days |
| A&D | admission and discharge |
| ADA | anterior descending artery |
| ADD | adduct (move toward center of body) |
| | adduction |
| ADH | adhesions |
| | antidiuretic hormone |
| ADJ | adjacent |
| ADL | activities of daily living |
| ad lib | as often as desired |
| ADM | admit, admission |
| ADM WT | admission weight |
| ADR | adverse drug reaction |
| ADV | arterial deep venous |
| AE | above the elbow |
| | active and equal |
| AER | auditory evoked response (hearing) |
| AF | adult female |
| | amniotic fluid |
| | aortic flow |
| | atrial fibrillation (heart) |
| | atrial flutter (heart) |
| AFB | acid-fast bacilli (bacterial designation) |
| AFL | artificial limb |
| AFTR | atrophy, fasciculation, tremor, rigidity |
| A/G | albumin-globulin ratio |
| AGA | appropriate for gestational age (referring to fetal weight) |
| AGE | acute gastroenteritis |
| | angle of greatest extension |
| AGF | angle of greatest flexion |
| agg | aggravated, aggravation |
| AGL | acute granulocytic leukemia |
| AGN | acute glomerulonephritis (kidney disease) |
| AGTT | abnormal glucose tolerance test |
| AH | abdominal hysterectomy |
| | arterial hypertension |
| AI | aortic insufficiency |
| | artificial insemination |
| AID | acute infectious disease |
| | artificial insemination by donor |
| AIDS | acquired immune deficiency syndrome |

| | |
|---|---|
| AIIS | anterior inferior iliac spine |
| AIT | acute intensive treatment |
| AJ | ankle jerk |
| AK | above the knee |
| AKA | above-the-knee amputation |
| AL | left ear |
| ALB | albumin |
| ALC | approximate lethal concentration |
| ALD | alcoholic liver disease |
| ALG | allergies |
| A line | arterial line |
| ALK | alkaline |
| alk phos | alkaline phosphatase |
| ALL | acute lymphocytic (or lymphoblastic) leukemia<br>allergies |
| ALMI | acute lateral myocardial infarction |
| ALS | acute lumbar strain<br>amytrophic lateral sclerosis<br>anterolateral sclerosis |
| ALT | alternate<br>alanine aminotransferase |
| ALVF | acute left ventricular failure |
| AM | adult male<br>before noon |
| AMA | against medical advice<br>American Medical Association |
| AMB | ambulate, ambulatory |
| AMI | acute myocardial infarction |
| AML | acute myelocytic (or myeloblastic) leukemia |
| amp | ampule |
| amt | amount |
| amy | amylase |
| ANA | anesthesia<br>antinuclear antibody |
| ANAL | analysis<br>analgesic |
| ANES | anesthesia |
| ang | angle |
| ANI | acute nerve irritation |
| ANRI | acute nerve root irritation |
| ANS | autonomic nervous system |
| ant | anterior |
| anti-HAV | hepatitis A antibody |
| anti-HBc | hepatitis B core antibody |
| anti-HBe | hepatitis Be antibody |
| anti-HBs | hepatitis B surface antibody |
| anx | anxiety |
| AO | angle of aorta |
| AOB | alcohol on breath |
| AOD | arteriosclerotic occlusive disease |
| AODM | adult-onset diabetes mellitus |
| AOM | acute otitis media (ear infection) |
| AP | anteroposterior (direction of x-ray)<br>abdominal-perineal (resection)<br>angina pectoris<br>after parturition |
| A&P | anterior and posterior<br>auscultation and palpation<br>auscultation and percussion |
| APB | atrial premature beat |
| APC | aspirin, phenacetin, caffeine |
| APGAR | appearance, pulse, grimace, agitation, respiration |
| APH | anterior pituitary hormone<br>aphasia (cannot speak) |
| AP&L | anteroposterior and lateral |

| | |
|---|---|
| APP | appears, appearance<br>appendix<br>approximate |
| APPT | appointment |
| AR | active resistance<br>admitting room<br>apical rate<br>artificial respiration<br>assisted respiration<br>at risk |
| ARC | AIDS-related complex |
| ARD | acute respiratory disease |
| ARDS | adult respiratory distress syndrome |
| ARE | active resistance exercise |
| ARF | acute respiratory failure<br>acute rheumatic fever |
| ARI | anxiety reaction, intense |
| ARM | anxiety reaction, mild |
| AROM | active range of motion<br>artificial rupture of membranes |
| ART | Achilles tendon reflex test<br>artery<br>articulation<br>artificial |
| AS | anal sphincter<br>arteriosclerosis<br>astigmatism<br>left ear (auris sinistra) |
| ASA | acetylsalicylic acid (aspirin) |
| ASA I, II . . . | American Society of Anesthesiology surgery risk assessment |
| ASAP | as soon as possible |
| ASC | arteriosclerosis<br>ascending |
| ASCAD | arteriosclerotic coronary artery disease |
| ASPC | American Society of Clinical Pathology |
| ASCVD | arteriosclerotic cardiovascular disease |
| ASD | atrial septal defect |
| ASHD | arteriosclerotic heart disease |
| ASIS | anterior superior iliac spine |
| ASO | antistreptolysin-O |
| ASPVD | arteriosclerotic peripheral vascular disease |
| AST | aspartate aminotransferase<br>astigmatism |
| AT | anterior tibial<br>atlas |
| ATC | adult therapeutic community |
| ATN | acute tubular necrosis |
| ATP | attending physician |
| ATR | Achilles tendon reflex<br>art therapy, registered<br>atrophy |
| ATS | anxiety tension state<br>arteriosclerosis |
| AU | both ears |
| AV | aortic valve<br>arteriovenous<br>atrioventricular<br>avulsion |
| avg | average |
| AVH | acute viral hepatitis |
| AVM | arteriovenous malformation |
| AV node | atrioventricular node |
| AW | able to work |
| A&W | alive and well |
| AWA | as well as |
| AX | axial<br>axillary |
| AZT | azidothymidin |
| BA | backache<br>barium<br>blood alcohol |

| | |
|---|---|
| | bone age<br>brachial artery<br>brisk and active<br>bronchial asthma |
| BAB | Babinski sign |
| BAC | blood alcohol concentration |
| bact | bacteria |
| BaE | barium enema |
| baso | basophil |
| BB | bed board<br>blood bank<br>both tones<br>breakthrough bleeding<br>breast biopsy |
| BBB | blood-brain barrier<br>bundle branch block |
| BB/FS | breast biopsy/frozen section |
| BBS | bilateral breath sounds |
| BBT | basal body temperature |
| BC | back care<br>birth control<br>bone conduction |
| BCC | basal cell carcinoma |
| BCP | birth control pills |
| BD | birthdate |
| BDR | background diabetic retinopathy |
| BE | barium enema<br>below the elbow<br>brisk and equal |
| Bender | Bender Gestalt |
| BF | black female<br>blood flow<br>bone fragment |
| BG | blood gases<br>bone graft |
| BGS | balance, gait, station |
| BGTT | borderline glucose tolerance test |
| BHP | benign hypertrophic prostate |
| BHS | beta-hemolytic streptococcus |
| bid | brought in dead<br>twice a day |
| bil | bilateral |
| bili | bilirubin |
| BiPap | biphasic positive airway pressure |
| BJ | biceps jerk<br>bone and joint |
| BJE | bone, joints, extremities |
| BJM | bone, joints, muscles |
| BK | back<br>below the knee |
| BKA | below-the-knee amputation |
| BL | blood loss |
| BLL | bilateral lower lung fields |
| BLU | bilateral lower extremities |
| BLQ | both lower quadrants |
| BM | basal metabolism<br>black male<br>body mass<br>bone marrow<br>bowel movement |
| BMcT | bilateral myringotomy with tubes |
| BMR | basal metabolic rate |
| BND | barely noticeable difference |
| BNO | bladder neck obstruction |
| BOE | bilateral otitis externa |
| BOM | bilateral otitis media |
| BOP | blood, ova, parasites |
| BOW | bag of water |
| BP | blood pressure<br>body part |
| BPC | blood pressure cuff |
| BPH | benign prostatic hypertrophy |
| BPM | breaths per minute |
| BPP | blood pressure and pulse |

BR bathroom
bed rest
BRB bright red blood
BRBPR bright red blood per rectum
BRP bathroom privileges
BRVO branch retinal vein occlusion
BS blood sugar
bowel sounds
breath sounds
BSA body surface area
bowel signs active
BSC bedside commode
BSD bedside drainage
BSN bowel sounds normal
BSO bilateral salpingo-oophorectomy
BSP Bromsulphalein
BT bowel tones
BTB breakthrough bleeding
BTL bilateral tubal ligation
BTR biceps tendon reflex
BTW back to work
BUE both upper extremities
BUN blood urea nitrogen
BUQ both upper quadrants
BUS Bartholin's, urethral, and Skene's
BV blood vessel
blood volume
BW birth weight
body weight
twice per week
BX biopsy

c with
C centigrade
C1–C7 cervical vertebrae 1–7
Ca calcium
CA cancer, carcinoma
cardiac arrest
caucasian adult
chronological age
C&A clinitest and acetone
CAB coronary artery bypass
CABG coronary artery bypass graft (pronounced ''cabbage'')
CAC certified alcoholism counselor
CAD coronary artery disease
CAH chronic active hepatitis
cal calorie
CAO chronic airway obstruction
cap capillary
caps capsule
cat cataract
CAT computerized axial tomography
cath catheter
CB chest-back
chronic bronchitis
CBC complete blood count
cc cubic centimeter
CC chief complaint
clean catch
clinical course
cold and clammy
color and circulation
common cold
costochondral
critical condition
current complaint
with meals
CCJ costochondral junction
CCMS clean catch midstream
CCOT cervical compression overloading test
CCU coronary care unit
CD cardiovascular disease
cause of death

| | |
|---|---|
| | childhood disease |
| | cigarettes per day |
| | communicable disease |
| | convulsive disorder |
| CDB | cough, deep breathe |
| CDE | common duct exploration |
| CDH | congenital disease of the hip |
| CDI | chemonucleolysis disc injection |
| CDS | cervico-dorsal syndrome |
| Cdyn | compliance dynamic |
| CEA | carcinoembryonic antigen |
| cf | compare, refer to |
| CFNS | chills, fever, night sweats |
| CH | characteristic |
| | chest |
| | chief |
| | chronic |
| CHD | congenital heart disease |
| CHF | congestive heart failure |
| chg | charge |
| CHG | change |
| CHI | closed head injury |
| CHO | carbohydrate |
| chol | cholesterol |
| CHP | child psychiatry |
| chr | chronic |
| | chronological |
| CI | cardiac index |
| | cardiac insufficiency |
| | cerebral infarction |
| CIA | common iliac artery |
| CIC | crisis intervention clinic |
| CICU | cardiac intensive care unit |
| CIE | counterimmunodiffusion |
| CIM | cortically induced movements |
| circ | circulation |
| | circumference |
| CIS | carcinoma in situ |
| | central inhibitory state |
| ck | check |
| CK | creatinine kinase |
| CKC | cold knife conization |
| CKMB | isoenzyme of creatinine phosphokinase |
| CL | chlorid |
| | clavicle |
| | clean |
| | closed |
| | cloudy |
| | contact lens |
| CLBB | complete left bundle branch block |
| CLD | chronic liver disease |
| | chronic lung disease |
| CLL | chronic lymphocytic leukemia |
| Cl Liq | clear liquid |
| cm | centimeter |
| CM | costal margin |
| cm $H_2O$ | centimeters of water |
| CMC | carpometacarpal |
| CMG | cystometrogram |
| CME | cervical mediastinal exploration |
| CMS | circulation, motion, sensation |
| CMV | continuous mandatory ventilation |
| | cytomegalovirus |
| CN | cranial nerve |
| CNS | central nervous system |
| CNV | cranial nerve 5 |
| CNX | cranial nerve 10 |
| c/o | care of |
| | complains of |
| CO | carbon monoxide |
| | cardiac output |
| | check out |
| $CO_2$ | carbon dioxide |
| CO60 | radioactive cobalt |
| COA | condition on admission |
| COAD | chronic obstructive airway disease |

| | |
|---|---|
| coag | coagulation |
| COAG | chronic open angle glaucoma |
| COC | coccyx/coccygeal |
| COD | cause of death<br>codeine<br>condition on discharge |
| COLD | chronic obstructive lung disease |
| comm | communication<br>communicative |
| comp | comprehend |
| cond | condition |
| cont | continue |
| COPD | chronic obstructive pulmonary disease |
| COPE | chronic obstructive pulmonary emphysema |
| CORD | chronic obstructive respiratory disease |
| COTA | certified occupational therapist assistant |
| CP | cerebral palsy<br>chest pain<br>constant pressure<br>cor pulmonale |
| CPAP | continuous positive airway pressure |
| cpd | compound |
| CPD | cephalopelvic disproportion |
| CPE | chronic pulmonary emphysema<br>complete physical examination |
| CPH | chronic pulmonary hypertension |
| CPK | creatinine phosphokinase |
| CPM | continuous passive motion |
| CPN | chronic pyelonephritis |
| CPPB | continuous positive pressure breathing |
| CPR | cardiopulmonary resuscitation |
| CPT | chest physiotherapy |
| CPU | child psychiatry unit |
| CPX | complete physical examination |
| CR | cardiorespiratory<br>clinical records<br>closed reduction |
| CRAO | central retinal arterial occlusion |
| CRBB | complete right bundle branch block |
| CR&C | closed reduction and cast |
| CRD | chronic renal disease<br>chronic respiratory disease |
| creat | creatinine |
| crep | crepitation |
| CRF | chronic renal failure |
| crit | critical<br>hematocrit |
| CRNA | certified registered nurse anesthetist |
| CROM | cervical range of motion |
| CRP | C-reactive protein |
| CRVO | central retinal vein occlusion |
| C&S | culture and sensitivity |
| CS | central supply<br>cervical spine<br>cesarean section |
| CSF | cerebrospinal fluid |
| CSM | cerebrospinal meningitis<br>color, sensation, motion |
| CSp | cervical spine |
| CSR | Cheyne-Stokes respiration<br>corrected sedimentation rate |
| CST | convulsive shock therapy |
| Cstat | compliance static |

| | |
|---|---|
| CT | carpal tunnel<br>cerebral thrombosis<br>cervical-thoracic<br>cervical traction<br>computerized tomography |
| CTA | clear to auscultation |
| CTB | confined to bed |
| CTL | cervical, thoracic, lumbar |
| CTS | carpal tunnel syndrome |
| CU | cause unknown<br>clinical unit<br>cubic |
| CUA | complete urinalysis |
| CUC | chronic ulcerative colitis |
| CUD | cause undetermined |
| CUG | cystourethrogram |
| cult | culture |
| CV | cardiac volume<br>cardiovascular<br>cerebrovascular<br>cervical vertebra<br>color vision<br>concentrated volume<br>costovertebral |
| CVA | cerebrovascular accident<br>costovertebral angle |
| CVAT | costovertebral angle tenderness |
| CVD | cardiovascular disease<br>cerebrovascular disease |
| CVP | central venous pressure |
| CVR | cardiovascular respiratory |
| CVS | cardiovascular status<br>cardiovascular system<br>cerebrovascular sclerosis<br>clean voided specimen |
| CW | chest wall<br>crutch walking |
| CX | cervix<br>consciousness |
| CXR | chest x-ray |
| cy | cyanosis |
| cysto | cystoscopy |
| D | divorced<br>dead |
| D5LR | dextrose 5 percent with lactated Ringer's |
| D5NS | dextrose 5 percent in normal saline |
| D5W | dextrose 5 percent in water |
| DA | degenerative arthritis |
| D/A | date of accident<br>date of admission |
| DAT | diet as tolerated |
| DB | date of birth<br>disability |
| DBP | diastolic blood pressure |
| DC | damp, cold<br>dilation, curettage<br>direct current<br>discharge<br>discontinue<br>Doctor of Chiropractic |
| D&C | dilatation & curettage |
| D/C | discharge<br>discontinue |
| DC&B | dilatation, curettage, and biopsy |
| DD | differential diagnosis<br>discharge diagnosis<br>dry dressing |
| DDD | degenerative disc disease |
| D/DW | dextrose distilled in water |
| D5%DW | dextrose 5% in distilled water |
| D/E | day/evening |
| D&E | dilatation and evacuation |
| DEC | deceased<br>decrease |
| decub | decubitus |
| def | defecation<br>deferred<br>deficiency |

| | |
|---|---|
| | deficient |
| | definite |
| | deformity |
| deg | degeneration(ive) |
| D/E/N | day/evening/night |
| derm | dermatology |
| des | describe |
| det | determine |
| dev | deviation |
| DF | dorsiflexion |
| DG | discharge goal |
| DH | delayed hypersensitivity |
| DHEA | dehydroepiandrosterone |
| DHEAS | dehydroepiandrosterone sulfate |
| DI | date of injury |
| | diabetes insipidus |
| diam | diameter |
| diath | diathermy |
| DIC | disseminated intravascular coagulation |
| Dig | digoxin |
| Dig Tox | digitalis toxicity |
| Dil | dilatation |
| dim | diminished |
| DIP | distal interphalangeal |
| DIPJ | distal interphalangeal joint |
| dir | direct |
| dis | disabled |
| | disease |
| DISI | dorsiflexion intercalated segment instability |
| disl | dislocate, dislocation |
| disp | disposition |
| dist | distal |
| | distance |
| | distended |
| | distilled |
| | distinguish |
| DJD | degenerative joint disease |
| DKA | diabetic ketoacidosis |
| | didn't keep appointment |
| DKB | deep knee bends |
| DL | date of loss |
| | deciliter(s) |
| | direct laryngoscopy |
| DL&B | direct laryngoscopy and bronchoscopy |
| DLCO | diffusing capacity of lung for carbon monoxide |
| DM | diabetes mellitus |
| | diastolic murmur |
| DME | defense medical examination |
| DNA | deoxyribonucleic acid |
| DNKA | did not keep appointment |
| DNR | do not resuscitate |
| | dorsal nerve root |
| DNS | did not show |
| D/NS | dextrose in normal saline |
| DO | Doctor of Osteopathy |
| DOA | date of accident |
| | date of admission |
| | dead on arrival |
| DOB | date of birth |
| DOC | died of other causes |
| | documented |
| DOD | date of death |
| DOE | date of examination |
| | dyspnea on exertion |
| DOI | date of injury |
| DOS | date of surgery |
| DOT | date of transfer |
| DP | deep pulse |
| | diastolic pressure |
| | distal phalanx |
| | dorsalis pedis |
| | dyspnea |
| DPC | delayed primary closure |
| DPD | diffuse pulmonary disease |
| DPP | dorsalis pedis pulse |

| | |
|---|---|
| DPT | diphtheria, pertussis, tetanus immunization |
| Dr | doctor<br>dressing |
| DR | diabetic retinopathy<br>dorsal root |
| D&S | dextrose in saline |
| DSD | discharge summary dictated<br>dry sterile dressing |
| DSG | dressing<br>dry sterile gauze |
| DSP | decreased sensory perception |
| D-Spine | dorsal spine |
| DT | date and time<br>date of treatment<br>delirium tremens<br>due to |
| DTP | distal tingling on percussion (Tinel's sign) |
| DTR | deep tendon reflexes |
| DTs | delirium tremens |
| DTV | due to void |
| DU | diagnosis undetermined<br>diagnosis unknown<br>duodenal ulcer |
| DUB | dysfunctional uterine bleeding |
| DVA | distance visual acuity |
| DVT | deep vein thrombosis |
| DW | dextrose in water<br>distilled water<br>doing well |
| Dx | diagnosis<br>difficulty<br>discharge<br>disease |
| Dxd | diagnosed<br>discontinued |
| DXR | deep x-ray |
| dys | dysfunction |
| dysp | dyspnea |
| ea | each |
| EA | early antigen |
| EAB | elective abortion |
| EAC | external auditory canal |
| EBL | estimated blood loss |
| EBNA | Epstein-Barr nuclear antigen |
| EBV | Epstein-Barr virus |
| EC | *Escherichia coli*<br>eyes closed |
| ECC | endocervical curettage |
| ECCE | extracapsular cataract extraction |
| ECG | electrocardiogram |
| ECHO | echocardiogram |
| ECT | electroconvulsive shock therapy |
| ECU | extensor carpi ulnaris |
| ED | edema<br>emergency department |
| EDC | estimated date of confinement ("due date") |
| EdS | Educational Services |
| EEG | electroencephalogram |
| EENT | eyes, ears, nose, throat |
| EF | ejection fraction |
| e.g. | for example |
| EG | external genitalia |
| EGD | esophagogastroduodenoscopy |
| EHL | extensor halluces longus |
| EIB | exercise induced bronchospasm |
| EJ | elbow jerk |
| EKG | electrocardiogram |
| el | elbow |
| elim | elimination |

| | |
|---|---|
| ELISA | enzyme-linked immunosorbent assay |
| EM | ejection murmur<br>endometrial |
| EMB | embolus |
| EMG | electromyogram<br>electromyography |
| EMS | electrical muscle stimulation<br>emergency medical service<br>eosinophilic myalgia syndrome |
| EMT | emergency medical technician |
| emuls | emulsion |
| endo | endoscopy<br>endotracheal |
| ENG | electronystagmogram |
| enl | enlarged |
| ENT | ear, nose, throat |
| EOM | equal ocular movements<br>external otitis media<br>extraocular movement<br>extraocular muscles |
| EOMI | extraocular movements intact |
| EOMM | extraocular movements, muscles |
| eos | eosinophils |
| EP | ectopic pregnancy<br>expiratory pressure |
| EPAP | expiratory positive airway pressure |
| EPI | epinephrine |
| epith | epithelium |
| ER | emergency room<br>equal and reactive<br>evoked response<br>external rotation |
| ERA | estrogen receptor assay |
| ERA/PRA | estradiol and progesterone receptor assays |
| ERCP | endoscopic retrograde cholangiopancreatography |
| ERE | external rotation in extension |
| ERF | external rotation in flexion |
| ERV | expiratory reserve volume |
| ES | electrical stimulation |
| ESR | erythrocyte sedimentation rate |
| ESRD | end-stage renal disease |
| ESRF | end-stage renal failure |
| EST | electroshock therapy |
| ESWL | extracorporeal shockwave lithotripsy |
| et | also<br>and |
| ET | endotracheal<br>etiology<br>eustachian tube |
| $ETCO_2$ | end tidal carbon dioxide |
| ETI | endotracheal intubation |
| ETime | expiration time |
| etiol | etiology |
| ETKM | every test known to man |
| ETOH | ethyl alcohol |
| ETT | exercise tolerance test |
| ETTube | endotracheal tube |
| EUA | examination under anesthesia |
| eval | evaluate |
| ex | exacerbate<br>examination<br>example<br>exercise |
| exc | excellent<br>except<br>exchange<br>excise, excision |
| exp | expand<br>expecting |

| | |
|---|---|
| | expired, expiration<br>explain<br>explore<br>expression |
| exp lap | exploratory laparotomy |
| ext | extend, extension, extensive<br>extensor<br>exterior<br>external<br>extract<br>extreme<br>extremity |
| ext rot | external rotation |
| f | breaths |
| F | Fahrenheit |
| FA | failed appointment<br>femoral artery<br>functional activities |
| FABERE | flexion, abduction, external rotation, extension |
| FAC | fellow of the American College (P = of Physicians; S = of Surgeons; OG = of Obstetrics and Gynecology) |
| FADIR | flexion, adduction, internal rotation |
| FADIRE | flexion, adduction, internal rotation, extension |
| FB | foreign body |
| FBD | functional bowel disorder |
| FBS | fasting blood sugar |
| FBU | fingers below umbilicus |
| FCA | fracture, complete, angulated |
| FCC | fracture, complete, comminuted<br>fracture, compound, comminuted |
| FCCC | fracture, complete, comminuted, compound |
| FCD | fracture, complete, deviated |
| FD | family doctor |
| Fe | iron<br>female |
| FEF | forced expiratory flow |
| fem | femoral |
| fem-pop | femoral-popliteal |
| FER | flexion, extension, rotation |
| FEV | forced expiratory volume |
| FF | forward flexion |
| FFC | fixed flexion contracture |
| FFD | free from disability |
| FFT | forward flexion, fingertips to toes |
| FFROM | full, free range of motion |
| FH | family history |
| FHT | fetal heart tones |
| F/I | fever/infection |
| fib | fibrillation<br>fibrous<br>fibula |
| FIF | forced inspiratory flow |
| $FIO_2$ | fraction of inspired oxygen |
| FJRM | full joint range of motion |
| fl | flank<br>flexion<br>fluid |
| FL | full fluid |
| flex | flexion |
| FMD | family medical doctor |
| FNA | fine needle aspiration |
| FNF | finger-nose-finger test |
| FOB | fiberoptic bronchoscopy |
| font | fontanelle |
| FPM | full passive movements |
| fr | fracture<br>frequency of respiration |
| FR | full range |
| FRBB | fracture of both bones |

| | |
|---|---|
| FRC | functional residual capacity |
| freq | frequency |
| FRJM | full range of joint movement |
| FROM | full range of motion |
| FS | frozen section |
| FSC | fracture, simple, comminuted |
| FSCC | fracture, simple, complete, comminuted |
| FSH | follicle-stimulating hormone |
| ft | foot, feet |
| FT | family therapy<br>full term |
| FTA | fluorescent treponema antibody |
| FTD | full-term delivery |
| FTI | free thyroxine index |
| FTKA | failed to keep appointment |
| FTSG | full thickness skin graft |
| FU | follow up |
| FUB | functional uterine bleeding |
| FUO | fever of undetermined origin |
| FV | femoral vein |
| FVC | forced vital capacity |
| FWB | full weight bearing |
| fx | fracture |
| FXBB | fracture of both bones |
| g | gram |
| G6PDH | glucose-6-phosphate dehydrogenase |
| GA | gastric analysis<br>general anesthesia<br>general appearance |
| GB | gall bladder |
| GBD | gall bladder disease |
| GC | general condition<br>gonococcus |
| GE | gastroenteritis |
| GEA | general endotracheal anesthesia |
| GER | gastroesophageal reflux |
| GERD | gastroesophageal reflux disease |
| GG | gamma globulin |
| GGTP | gamma-glutamyl transpeptidase |
| GH | general health |
| GI | gastrointestinal |
| GI series | gastrointestinal tract study |
| gl | glaucoma |
| gm | gram |
| GM | grand mal |
| GMA | gross motor activity |
| GP | general practitioner |
| GPU | general psychiatric unit |
| GR | gastric resection<br>grain<br>great<br>gross |
| grav | pregnancy |
| grav I | primigravida (first pregnancy) |
| grav II | secundigravida (second pregnancy) |
| GS | Gram's stain |
| GSW | gunshot wound |
| GT | gait training |
| GTT | glucose tolerance test |
| gtt | drops |
| GU | gastric ulcer<br>genitourinary |
| GXT | graded exercise test |
| gyn | gynecology |
| H | hour |

| | |
|---|---|
| $H_2O_2$ | hydrogen peroxide |
| HA | headache<br>hospital admission |
| HAA | hepatitis-associated antigen |
| HAS | hospital ambulatory surgery |
| HBD | has been drinking |
| HBeAg | hepatitis Be antigen |
| HBDH | hydroxybutyrate dehydrogenase |
| HBF | hepatic blood flow |
| HBP | high blood pressure (hypertension) |
| HbSAg | hepatitis B surface antigen |
| HCG | human chorionic gonadotrophin |
| HCL | hydrochloric acid |
| $HCO_3$ | hydrogen bicarbonate |
| HCT | hematocrit |
| HCTZ | hydrochlorothiazide |
| HCVD | hypertensive cardiovascular disease |
| hd | heart disease<br>hemodialysis |
| HDL | high-density lipoprotein (cholesterol) |
| HDS | herniated disc syndrome |
| He | helium |
| H&E | hematoxylin and eosin |
| HEENT | head, ears, eyes, nose, throat |
| HEP | heparin lock<br>home exercise program |
| HEV | home evaluation visit |
| HF | hay fever<br>heart failure |
| hgb | hemoglobin |
| HH | hard of hearing<br>hiatal hernia |
| H&H | hemoglobin and hematocrit |
| HHN | hand-held nebulizer |
| HIF | higher intellectual function |
| HJR | hepatojugular reflex |
| HL | hearing loss<br>heart and lungs |
| HLA | human leukocyte antigen |
| HLK | heart, liver, kidney |
| HLV | herpes-like virus |
| HM | heart murmur |
| HME | heat moisten |
| HMO | health maintenance organization |
| HMP | hot, moist packs |
| HNP | herniated nucleus pulposus |
| HNV | has not voided |
| HO | history of |
| HOB | head of bed |
| HP | hot packs |
| H&P | history and physical |
| HPE | history and physical examination |
| HPF | high-power field |
| HPI | history of present illness |
| HR | heart rate<br>hospital record |
| hr | hour |
| hs | at bedtime |
| HS | heart sounds |
| HSM | hepatosplenomegaly masses |
| HSV | herpes simplex virus |
| ht | height |
| HT | hospital treatment<br>hyperthyroidism |
| HTAA | 5–hydroxyindolacetic acid |
| htn | hypertension |
| HV | hepatic vein<br>herpes virus<br>home visit<br>hyperventilation |

| | |
|---|---|
| HVD | hypertensive vascular disease |
| HW | healing well |
| HWP | hot, wet pack |
| hys | hysterectomy |
| | hysterical |
| Hx | history |
| $^{131}I$ | iodine |
| IA | incurred accidentally |
| | intra-arterial |
| | intra-articular |
| | intra-atrial |
| IAC | internal acoustic canal |
| IBW | ideal body weight |
| ic | between meals |
| IC | inspiratory capacity |
| | intensive care |
| | intercostal |
| | intracerebral |
| | intracutaneous |
| | irritable colon |
| ICC | intensive coronary care |
| ICCU | intensive coronary care unit |
| ICDA | International Classification of Diseases, Adapted |
| ICF | intensive care facility |
| ICFX | intracapsular fracture |
| ICM | intercostal margin |
| ICN | intensive care nursing |
| ICP | intracranial pressure |
| ICS | intercostal space |
| ICT | intermittent cervical traction |
| ICU | intensive care unit |
| id | during the day |
| ID | identification |
| | idiopathic (unknown origin) |
| | ill defined |
| | ineffective dose |
| | infectious disease |
| | initial dose |
| | intradermal |
| IDA | iron-deficiency anemia |
| IDD | insulin-dependent diabetes |
| IDK | internal derangement of the knee |
| IDR | intradermal reaction |
| IDVC | indwelling venous catheter |
| i.e. | that is |
| IE | inner ear |
| I&E | inspiration and expiration |
| I/E ratio | inspiration/expiration ratio |
| IFA | indirect fluorescent antibody |
| IFR | inspiratory flow rate |
| IgA | immunoglobulin A |
| IgE | immunoglobulin E |
| IgG | immunoglobulin G |
| IgM | immunoglobulin M |
| IH | infectious hepatitis |
| | interval history |
| IHD | ischemic heart disease |
| IHO | idiopathic hypertrophic osteoarthropathy |
| IHR | intrinsic heart rate |
| IHSS | idiopathic hypertrophic subaortic stenosis |
| IL | ilio-lumbar |
| IM | infectious mononucleosis |
| | internal malleolus |
| | internal medicine |
| | intramuscular |
| IMBC | indirect maximum breathing capacity |
| IME | independent medical examination |
| IMI | intramuscular injection |
| imm | immediate |
| | immobolize |
| | immunize |

| | |
|---|---|
| imp | impression<br>improved |
| IMV | intermittent mandatory ventilation |
| in | inch |
| inc | incomplete<br>inconclusive<br>increase |
| ind | independent<br>index<br>indicated |
| inf | infant<br>infarction<br>infected<br>inferior<br>influenza |
| ing | inguinal |
| inj | inject, injected<br>injection<br>injury |
| INK | injury not known |
| ins | insulin<br>insurance |
| insp | inspiration |
| int | internal<br>intestinal |
| int. med. | internal medicine |
| int. rot. | internal rotation |
| IO | intestinal obstruction<br>intraocular |
| I&O | intake and output |
| IOFB | intraocular foreign body |
| IOL | intraocular lens |
| IOP | intraocular pressure |
| IOU | intensive therapy observation unit |
| IP | inpatient<br>inspiratory pressure<br>interphalangeal<br>intraperitoneal |
| IPAP | inspiratory positive airway pressure |
| IPF | idiopathic pulmonary fibrosis |
| IPL | intrapleural |
| IPPA | inspection, palpation, percussion, auscultation |
| IPPB | intermittent positive-pressure breathing |
| IPPO | intermittent positive-pressure inflation with oxygen |
| IPPR | intermittent positive-pressure respiration |
| IPPV | intermittent positive-pressure ventilation |
| IR | internal rotation |
| IRE | internal rotation in extension |
| IRF | internal rotation in flexion |
| IS | in situ<br>incentive spirometry<br>intercostal space<br>interspace<br>isolation |
| ISL | interscapular line |
| iso | isometric |
| IST | insulin shock therapy |
| IT | individual therapy<br>inhalation therapy<br>intensive therapy<br>interdermal test<br>intermittent traction<br>intertrochanteric<br>intratracheal tube |
| ITH | intrathecal |
| Itime | inspiration time |
| ITP | idiopathic thrombocytopenic purpura |
| ITT | internal tibal torsion |
| IU | immunizing unit<br>international unit<br>intrauterine |

| | |
|---|---|
| IUD | intrauterine death<br>intrauterine device |
| IUFB | intrauterine foreign body |
| IUGR | intrauterine growth retardation |
| IUP | intrauterine pregnancy |
| IUT | intrauterine transfusion |
| IV | in vitro<br>in vivo<br>intervertebral<br>intravascular<br>intravenous |
| IVC | intravenous cholangiogram |
| IVD | intervertebral disc |
| IVJC | intervertebral joint complex |
| IVP | intravenous pyelogram |
| IVPB | intravenous piggy-back |
| JAMA | *Journal of the American Medical Association* |
| JCAHO | Joint Commission on Accreditation of Health Care Organizations |
| jct | junction |
| jd | jaundice |
| JJ | jaw jerk |
| JND | just noticeable difference |
| JRA | juvenile rheumatoid arthritis |
| jt | joint |
| juv | juvenile |
| JV | jugular vein |
| JVD | jugular vein distension |
| JVP | jugular vein pulse |
| K | potassium |
| KA | ketoacidosis |
| KB | knee bearing |
| KCL | potassium chloride |
| KFT | kidney function test |
| kg | kilogram |
| KI | potassium iodide |
| KJ | knee jerk |
| KK | knee kick |
| KLS | kidney, liver, spleen |
| KOH | potassium hydroxide |
| KUB | kidneys, ureter, bladder |
| KVO | keep vein open |
| K-W | Keith-Wagener (eyes) |
| L | left<br>liter(s) |
| L1–L5 | lumbar vertebrae |
| LA | left arm<br>left atrium<br>local anesthesia<br>long action<br>long arm |
| L&A | light and accommodation<br>living and active |
| lab | laboratory |
| lac | laceration |
| LAC | long arm cast |
| LAD | left anterior descending<br>left axis deviation |
| LAE | left atrial enlargement<br>long above elbow (cast) |
| LAHB | left anterior hemiblock |
| LAM | laminectomy<br>laminogram |
| LANC | long arm navicular cast |
| LAP | laparotomy |
| LAPB | long arm plaster bandage |
| LAR | left arm recumbent |
| LAS | long arm splint |
| LASER | light amplification by stimulated emission of radiation |
| lat | lateral |
| LATS | long-acting thyroid-stimulating hormone |

| | |
|---|---|
| lb | pound |
| LB | large bowel<br>lateral bending<br>live birth<br>low back |
| L&B | left and below |
| LBB | low back bend |
| LBBB | left bundle branch block |
| LBE | long below elbow |
| LBH | length, breadth, height |
| LBP | lower back pain<br>low blood pressure (hypotension) |
| LBT | low back tenderness |
| LBW | low birth weight |
| LC | left cornea<br>lethal concentration<br>living children |
| LCB | left costal border |
| LCFA | long-chain fatty acids |
| LCM | left costal margin |
| LD | left deltoid<br>lethal dose<br>light difference perception<br>living donor |
| $LD_{50}$ | median lethal dose of radiation |
| LDD | light-dark discrimination |
| LDH | lactic dehydrogenase |
| LDL | low-density lipoprotein (cholesterol) |
| LE | laboratory examination<br>last examination<br>left eye<br>lower extremity<br>lupus erythematosus |
| LES | lower esophageal sphincter |
| LEVA | left eye visual acuity |
| LF | left foot<br>linear fracture<br>low frequency |
| LFA | left forearm |
| LFT | liver function test |
| lg | large |
| LG | laryngectomy<br>left gluteal |
| LH | left hand<br>luteinizing hormone |
| L&H | lungs and heart |
| LHG | left-hand grip |
| LHS | left-hand side |
| LIC | left iliac crest |
| LICM | left intercostal margin |
| LICS | left intercostal space |
| LIF | left iliac fossa<br>left index finger |
| LIG | ligament |
| LIH | left inguinal hernia |
| lim | limited |
| LIO | left inferior oblique |
| LIQ | left inner quadrant<br>liquid |
| LIR | left iliac region |
| LK | left kidney |
| LKS | liver, kidney, spleen |
| LL | left lateral<br>left leg<br>left lower<br>left lung<br>lethal level<br>lithium level<br>long leg<br>lower lobe |
| LLB | left lateral bending<br>long leg brace |
| LLC | long leg cast |
| LLCC | long leg cylinder cast |
| LLD | leg length discrepancy |
| LLE | left lower extremity |
| LLF | left lateral flexion<br>left little finger |

| | |
|---|---|
| LLL | left lower leg<br>left lower lid<br>left lower lobe |
| LLN | lower limit of normal |
| LLQ | left lower quadrant |
| LLR | left lateral rectus<br>left lumbar region |
| LLS | left leg spling |
| LLWC | long leg walking cast |
| LLX | left lower extremity |
| LMD | local medical doctor |
| LMF | left middle finger |
| L/min | liters per minute |
| LMP | last menstrual period |
| LN | lymph node |
| LNMP | last normal menstrual period |
| LOA | leave of absence |
| LOC | level of consciousness<br>loss of consciousness |
| LOM | left otitis media<br>limitation of motion |
| LOP | left occipitoposterior |
| LOQ | left outer quadrant |
| LOS | length of stay<br>loss of sight |
| LOT | left occipitotransverse |
| LP | light perception<br>low pressure<br>lumbar puncture |
| LPA | licensed physician's assistant |
| LPH | left posterior hemiblock |
| LPI | laser peripheral iridotomy |
| LPN | licensed practical nurse |
| LPO | light perception only |
| LQ | lower quadrant |
| LR | lactated Ringer's solution<br>left rotation<br>lethal range<br>light reaction |
| LRF | left ring finger |
| LRQ | lower right quadrant |
| LRS | lactated Ringer's solution |
| LRT | lower respiratory tract |
| LS | left side<br>liver, spleen<br>lumbar spine<br>lumbosacral |
| L/S | lecithin/sphingomyelin ratio (determining lung maturity in premature infants) |
| LSK | liver, spleen, kidneys |
| LSO | left superior oblique |
| LSP | licensed speech pathologist |
| LT | left<br>left thigh<br>left thumb<br>long term |
| LTC | laparoscopic tubal cauterization |
| LTD | limited |
| LTP | laser trabeculoplasty |
| LTS | laparoscopic tubal sterilization<br>long tract sign |
| LU | left upper |
| LUA | left upper arm |
| LUE | left upper extremity |
| LUL | left upper lid<br>left upper lobe |
| LUOQ | left upper outer quadrant |
| LUQ | left upper quadrant |
| LV | lung volume |
| LVE | left ventricular enlargement |
| LVEDP | left ventricular end diastolic pressure |
| LVH | left ventricular hypertrophy |
| LVN | licensed vocational nurse |
| LVR | lumbar ventral nerve root |
| LW | Lee-White (method) |

| | |
|---|---|
| L&W | living and well |
| LX | lower extremity |
| lymphs | lymphocytes |
| m | meter |
| MA | medical authorization<br>menstrual age<br>mental age<br>moderately advanced<br>muscle activity |
| MAC | macerated<br>maximum allowable concentration |
| MAJ | major<br>majority |
| MAL | malignant |
| MAO | monoamine oxidase |
| MAP | mean arterial pressure |
| MAS | manifest anxiety scale |
| mass | massage<br>massive |
| mat | maternal |
| max | maxilla<br>maximal/maximum |
| MB | muscle balance |
| MBC | maximum breathing capacity |
| MBH | maximum benefit from hospitalization |
| mc | millicurie |
| MC | metacarpal |
| MCC | mean corpuscular concentration |
| mcg | micrograms |
| MCH | mean corpuscular hemoglobin |
| MCHC | mean corpuscular hemoglobin concentration |
| MCL | midclavicular line |
| MCP | metatarsophalangeal joint |
| MCV | mean corpuscular volume |
| MD | doctor of medicine<br>midnight |
| MDC | minimum detectable concentration |
| MDI | metered dose inhaler |
| MDV | multiple dose vial |
| ME | medical examiner<br>middle ear |
| mech | mechanics, pulmonary |
| MED | medial, median<br>medicine<br>minimum effective dose |
| MEDLARS | Medical Literature Analysis and Retrieval System |
| meds | medications |
| MEF | maximal expiratory flow |
| MEFR | maximal expiratory flow rate |
| MEH | medical eye history |
| mel | melanoma<br>melena |
| mEq | milliequivalent |
| mEq/L | milliequivalent per liter |
| M&F | mother and father |
| MFD | midforceps delivery<br>minimum fatal dose |
| MFT | muscle function test |
| MFU | medical follow-up |
| MFW | multiple fragment wounds |
| mg | milligram |
| Mg | magnesium |
| MG | muscle group |
| $MgSO_4$ | magnesium sulfate |
| MH | marital history<br>medical history<br>mental health |
| MHB | maximum hospital benefit |
| MHR | maximum heart rate |

MHW mental health worker
MI mental illness
mitral insufficiency
myocardial infarction
MIC minimal inhibitory concentration
micro microscopic
MICU mobile intensive care unit
MID minimum ineffective dose
MIF maximum inspiratory flow rate
min minimal, minimum
minor
minute
MKV measles, killed vaccine
ml milliliter
ML maximum to left
middle lobe
midline
MLC minimum lethal concentration
MLD minimum lethal dose
mm millimeter
movement
murmur
muscles
MM malignant melanoma
medial malleolus
mucous membrane
mm/hr millimeters per hour
MMF maximal midexpiratory flow
MMFR maximal midexpiratory flow rate
mm Hg millimeters of mercury
MMK Marshall-Marchetti-Krantz
MMPI Minnesota Multiphasic Personality Inventory
MMST muscle strength
mn midnight
mod moderate
MOD medical officer of the day
MOM milk of magnesia
mono monocyte
mononucleosis
monospot mononucleosis spot test
MP menstrual period
metacarpophalangeal
moist pack
multiparous
MPC maximum permissible concentration
MPD maximum permissible dose
myofascial pain disorder
MPI multiphasic personality inventory
MR maximum to right
mental retardation
MRI magnetic resonance imaging
MRM modified radical mastectomy
MRSA methicillin-resistant *Stapholococcus aureus*
MS medical student
mental status
minor surgery
morphine sulfate
multiple sclerosis
muscle strength
musculoskeletal
MSTI multiple soft tissue injuries
MT manual traction
maximal therapy
medical technologist
muscle test
muscles and tendons
music therapy
MTD maximum tolerated dose
MTP metatarsophalangeal (joint)
MTR masses, tenderness, rebound
MTRG masses, tenderness, rebound, guarding

| | |
|---|---|
| multip | multiparous |
| MUO | myocardiopathy of unknown origin |
| mur | murmur |
| mus | muscle |
| MV | minute volume<br>mitral valve |
| MVA | motor vehicle accident |
| MVC | maximum vital capacity |
| MVP | mitral valve prolapse |
| mvt | movement |
| MVV | maximal volume ventilation |
| MWD | microwave diathermy |
| Mx | management |
| N | nitrogen |
| Na | sodium |
| NA | no abnormalities<br>not admitted<br>not available<br>nursing assistant |
| N/A | not applicable |
| NAA | no apparent abnormalities |
| NaCl | sodium chloride |
| NAD | no active disease<br>no acute distress<br>normal axis deviation<br>nothing abnormal detected |
| NAG | narrow angle glaucoma |
| NAI | no acute infection |
| nar | narcotic |
| NAR | no action required |
| NB | newborn |
| NBI | no bone injury |
| NBM | nothing by mouth |
| NBP | needle biopsy of the prostate |
| NBS | normal bowel sounds |
| NC | nasal canula<br>no change<br>no complaint<br>noncontributory |
| N&C | nerves and circulation |
| NCD | not considered disabling<br>not considered disqualifying |
| NCNS | no complications, no sequelae |
| NCO | no complaints offered |
| NCS | nerve conduction studies |
| NCV | nerve conduction velocity |
| ND | nondisabling<br>not dictated<br>not done |
| NE | nerve ending<br>neurologic examination |
| Neb | nebulizer treatment |
| NED | no evidence of disease |
| neg | negative |
| neuro | neurology, neurological |
| NG | nasogastric |
| NH | nursing home |
| NIDDM | non–insulin dependent diabetes mellitus |
| NIH | National Institutes of Health |
| NIP | negative inspiratory pressure<br>no infection present<br>no inflammation present |
| NK | not known |
| NKA | no known allergies |
| NKD | no known disease |
| NKDA | no known drug allergies |
| Nl | normal |
| NL | normal limits |
| NLM | National Library of Medicine |
| NLP | no light perception<br>normal light perception |

| | |
|---|---|
| NM | neuromuscular<br>not measured<br>not mentioned |
| N&M | nerves and muscles |
| NMA | neurogenic muscular atrophy |
| NMI | no middle initial |
| NMJ | neuromuscular junction |
| NMN | no middle name |
| NMP | normal menstrual period |
| NMTS | neuromuscular tension scale |
| nn | nerves |
| NN | neonatal<br>nurses' notes |
| NNR | not necessary to return |
| no | number |
| NO | nursing order |
| $NO_2$ | nitrous oxide |
| noc | night |
| NOK | next of kin |
| NOP | no ocular pain<br>not otherwise provided for |
| nor | normal |
| NOS | not on staff<br>not otherwise specified |
| NP | nasopharynx<br>nerve palsy<br>neuropathology<br>neuropsychiatric<br>new patient<br>not palpable<br>not performed<br>nurse practitioner<br>nursing procedures |
| NPC | no previous complaint<br>nonproductive cough |
| NPH | no previous history |
| NPO | nothing by mouth |
| NOPMN | nothing by mouth after midnight |
| NPN | nonprotein nitrogen |
| NPT | normal pressure and temperature |
| NR | nerve root<br>no report<br>no respirations<br>no results<br>normal range<br>normal reaction<br>normal report<br>not remarkable |
| NRB | nonrebreather |
| NRBC | nucleated red blood cell |
| NRI | nerve root involvement<br>nerve root irritation |
| NRM | normal range of motion |
| NRN | no return necessary |
| NROM | normal range of motion |
| ns | nerves |
| NS | neurosurgery<br>nonspecific<br>normal saline<br>no-show<br>not significant<br>not specified<br>not sufficient |
| ½NS | one-half normal saline |
| NSA | no significant abnormalities |
| NSAD | no sign of significant disease |
| NSAID | nonsteroidal anti-inflammatory drug |
| NSC | no significant change |
| NSCSPT | no significant change since previous tracing |
| NSD | no significant defect<br>no significant difference<br>normal spontaneous delivery |
| NSF | no significant findings |
| nsg | nursing |

| | |
|---|---|
| NSI | no sign of infection<br>no sign of inflammation |
| NSR | normal sinus rhythm |
| NSS | normal saline solution<br>normal size and shape |
| NSU | nonspecific urethritis |
| NT | nasotracheal<br>nerve treatment<br>no test<br>normal temperature<br>nontender<br>not tested |
| N&T | nose and throat |
| NTG | nitroglycerine |
| NTP | normal temperature and pressure |
| NTT | nasal tracheal tube |
| NUA | nursing activity |
| NV | neurovascular |
| N&V | nausea and vomiting |
| NVD | nausea, vomiting, diarrhea<br>neovascularization of disc |
| NWB | non–weight bearing |
| NYD | not yet diagnosed |
| o | oral |
| $O_2$ | oxygen |
| $O_2$cap | oxygen capacity |
| $O_2$sat | oxygen saturation |
| OA | osteoarthritis |
| OAG | open-angle glaucoma |
| OAP | osteoarthropathy |
| OB | obstetrics |
| OBD | organic brain disease |
| obj | object, objective |
| obl | oblique |
| OBP | ova, blood, parasites |
| obs | observe, observed |
| OBS | organic brain syndrome |
| OC | on call<br>oral contraceptive(s) |
| occ | occasional, occasionally<br>occiput<br>occupation |
| OCD | osteochondritis dissecans |
| OCG | oral cholecystogram |
| OCU | outpatient care unit |
| o.d. | right eye (oculus dexter) |
| OD | occupational disease<br>officer of the day<br>once daily<br>overdose |
| OE | on examination<br>orthopedic examination<br>otitis externa |
| O&E | observation and examination |
| OH | occupational history<br>other |
| OI | otitis internus |
| OM | occupational medicine<br>osteopathic manipulation<br>otitis media |
| OMM | osteopathic manipulative medicine |
| ON | optic nerve |
| onc | oncology |
| OOB | out of bed |
| OOB as tol | out of bed as tolerated |
| OOP | out on pass |
| op | operation |
| OP | outpatient |
| O&P | ova and parasites |
| OPA | outpatient procedure admission |
| OPC | outpatient clinic |
| opp | opposite |
| OPT | outpatient treatment |

| | |
|---|---|
| OPV | oral polio vaccine<br>outpatient visit |
| OR | open reduction<br>operating room |
| or | oriented |
| org | organic |
| ORIF | open reduction internal fixation |
| ORT | operating room technician |
| os | mouth |
| o.s. | left eye (oculus sinister) |
| OS | oral surgery |
| OT | objective test<br>occupational therapy |
| OTC | over the counter |
| OTT | oral tracheal tube |
| OU | both eyes<br>observation unit |
| OUQ | outer upper quadrant |
| OV | office visit |
| OWNL | otherwise within normal limits |
| oz | ounce |
| P | pulse |
| P1, P2 . . . | number of (live birth) pregnancies |
| P2 | second pulmonary sound |
| PA | physician's assistant<br>posteroanterior<br>pulmonary artery |
| P&A | percussion and auscultation |
| PAC | phenacetin, aspirin, codeine<br>premature atrial contraction<br>pulmonary artery catheter |
| PACU | postanesthesia care unit |
| PAD | pulmonary artery diastolic |
| PAF | paroxysmal atrial fibrillation |
| $PaO_2$ | partial arterial pressure of oxygen |
| PAP | passive-aggressive personality disorder<br>Papanicolaou (smear, stain, test) |
| PAR | postanesthesia recovery |
| Para I | primipara |
| Para II | has given birth to more than one child |
| PAS | pulmonary artery systolic |
| PAT | paroxysmal atrial tachycardia<br>patella<br>patient |
| path | pathology |
| pb | problem |
| PB | phenobarbital<br>pressure breathing |
| PBA | pressure breathing assistor |
| PBI | protein-bound iodine |
| pc | after meals |
| PC | phone call<br>posterior cervical<br>posterior chamber<br>present complaint |
| PCA | patient-controlled analgesia |
| PCHE | pseudocholinesterase |
| PCIOL | posterior chamber intraocular lens |
| PCKD | polycystic kidney disease |
| PCN | penicillin |
| $pCO_2$ | partial pressure of carbon dioxide |
| PCP | "angel dust"<br>pneumocystis carinii pneumonia |
| PCS | postconcussion syndrome |
| PCU | progressive care unit |
| PCV | packed cell volume |
| PD | partial denture<br>per day<br>poorly differentiated<br>progression of disease<br>pulmonary disease |

| | |
|---|---|
| PDA | patent ductus arteriosus |
| PDE | paroxysmal dyspnea on exertion |
| PDH | past dental history |
| PDR | *Physicians' Desk Reference* |
| PE | pedal edema<br>pelvic examination<br>physical examination<br>point of entry<br>present examination<br>probable error<br>pulmonary embolism |
| ped | pediatric |
| PEEP | positive end-expiratory pressure |
| PEF | peak expiratory flow |
| PEFR | peak expiratory flow rate |
| PEN | penicillin |
| PEP | psychiatric evaluation profile |
| per os | by mouth |
| PERLA | pupils equal, reactive to light and accommodation |
| PERRL | pupils equal, round, regular, reactive to light |
| PERRLA | pupils, equal, round, regular, reactive to light and accommodation |
| PET | positron emission tomography |
| PF | past findings<br>peak flow<br>pertinent findings<br>plantar flexion |
| PFR | peak flow rate |
| PFT | pulmonary function test |
| PGP | progressive general paralysis |
| PH | past history<br>personal history<br>physical history<br>public health |
| phal | phalanx |
| PHN | public health nurse |
| phos | phosphorus |
| pH | hydrogen ion concentration |
| PHX | past history |
| PI | personal injury<br>present illness |
| PICU | psychiatric intensive care unit<br>pulmonary intensive care unit |
| PID | pelvic inflammatory disease<br>post-inertia dyskinesia<br>prolapsed intervertebral disc |
| PIF | peak inspiratory flow |
| PIFR | peak inspiratory flow rate |
| PIIS | posterior inferior iliac spine |
| PIP | peak inspiratory pressure<br>probable intrauterine pregnancy<br>proximal interphalangeal |
| pkg | package |
| PKU | phenylketonuria |
| PKV | peak flow |
| PL | plan<br>plasma<br>plastic surgeon |
| PLT | pinprick light touch |
| PM | after noon<br>physical medicine<br>postmortem<br>preventive medicine |
| PMA | positive mental attitude<br>progressive muscular atrophy |
| PMD | primary medical doctor<br>private medical doctor |
| PMH | past medical history |
| PMI | past medical illness<br>point of maximum impact<br>point of maximum impulse |

PMN polymorphonuclear neutrophil
PMP prior menstrual period
PM&R physical medicine and rehabilitation
PMS postmenopausal syndrome
premenstrual syndrome
PMT premenstrual tension
PN pain
peripheral neuropathy
postnasal
PNB prostate needle biopsy
PND paroxysmal nocturnal dyspnea
postnasal drip
PNF proprioceptive neuromuscular fasciculation
PNI peripheral nerve injury
PNPB positive-negative pressure breathing
PNPR positive-negative pressure respiration
PNS parasympathetic nervous system
peripheral nervous system
PO by mouth
parieto-occipital
period of onset
postoperative
$pO_2$ partial pressure of oxygen
$PO_4$ phosphates
POAG progressive open-angle glaucoma
POC products of conception
POD postoperative day
POMR problem-oriented medical record
POP popliteal
port portable
pos position
positive
possible
post posterior
post MI posterior myocardial infarction
postop postoperative
pot potential
POX point of exit
PP pedal pulses
peripheral pulses
pinpoint pupils
pinprick
positive pressure
postpartum
postprandial
presenting problem
private physician
private practice
pulse pressure
PP&A palpation, percussion, and auscultation
PPB positive pressure breathing
PPBS psychophysiological bowel syndrome
PPD packs per day
PPH past pertinent history
postpartum hemorrhage
PPL postpartum laxative
PPTL postpartum tubal ligation
PPV positive-pressure ventilation
PR partial remission
peer review
per rectum
precautions
progress record
progressive resistance
pulse rate
PRA progressive resistance to arms
PRC packed red cells
PRD partial reaction of degeneration
PRE physical reconditioning exercise

| | |
|---|---|
| | progressive resistance exercise |
| preg | pregnancy |
| pre-op | preoperative |
| prep | prepare |
| pres | present |
| prev | previous |
| PRH | past relevant history |
| PRL | passive resistance to leg |
| PRN | as often as necessary |
| procto | proctoscopy |
| PROM | passive range of motion<br>premature rupture of membranes |
| pro time | prothrombin time |
| prox | proximal |
| PRP | psychotic reaction profile |
| PRRE | pupils round, regular, and equal |
| PRT | patient refused test |
| PS | paraspinous<br>physical status<br>present symptoms<br>pulmonary support |
| P&S | permanent and stationary |
| PSIS | posterior superior iliac spine |
| PSP | phenolsulfonphthalein<br>posterior spinous process |
| PSR | paranoid schizophrenic reaction |
| PSV | pressure-support ventilation |
| PSVT | paroxysmal supraventricular tachycardia |
| PSW | psychiatric social worker |
| pt | patient |
| PT | permanent and total<br>physical therapy<br>pneumothorax |
| PTA | physical therapy assistant (licensed)<br>prior to admission |
| PTCA | percutaneous transluminal coronary angioplasty |
| PTD | permanent total disability |
| PTH | parathyroid hormone<br>prior to hospitalization |
| PTR | patellar tendon reflelx<br>pelvic traction |
| PTSD | posttraumatic stress disorder |
| PTT | partial thromboplastin time |
| PUD | peptic ulcer disease<br>pulmonary disease |
| pulm | pulmonary |
| PV | paravertebral |
| PVC | premature ventricular contraction |
| PVD | peripheral vascular disease |
| PVOT | peripheral vascular occlusive disease |
| PVR | pulmonary vascular resistance |
| pvt | private |
| PVT | pressure, volume, temperature |
| PWB | partial weight bearing |
| PX | physical examination<br>pneumothorax<br>prescription<br>prognosis |
| PY | pack-years (_____ packs per day × _____ years = pack year history of smoking cigarettes) |
| PZI | protime zinc insulin |
| q | every |
| q2h | every 2 hours |
| q4h | every 4 hours |
| qam | every morning |

qd every day
qh every hour
qhs bedtime
qid four times per day
QMT quantative muscle testing
qn every night
QNS quantity not sufficient
qod every other day
qoh every other hour
qon every other night
qp at will
qpm every afternoon
every evening
QS quantity sufficient
qt quantity
quart
quiet
quad quadriceps
quad cane cane with four supports
qual qualitative
quant quantitative
qv as much as desired

R right
RA rheumatoid arthritis
right angle
right arm
RAD radiate
radicular
radium
rad pros radical prostatectomy
RAE right atrial enlargement
RAM rapid alternative movements
RAP right atrial pressure
RAR right arm recumbent
RAST radio allergosorbent test
RBBB right bundle-branch block
RBBx right breast biopsy
RBC red blood cell count
RC respirations ceased
RCM right costal margin
rcvd received
RD radial deviation
Raynaud's disease
reaction of degeneration
renal disease
respiratory disease
RDM readmission
RDS respiratory distress syndrome
RDW red cell distribution width
re regarding
RE resistive exercises
right eye
rec receive
recommend
recurrent
REC rear end collision
red reduce, reduction
ref refer
reg regular
rehab rehabilitation
RELE resistive exercises, lower extremities
rem remove, removal
REM rapid eye movements
reps repititions
resp respiration
ret retain, retention
retire
return
ret cath retention catheter
retic reticulocyte
retro retrograde (backward)
REUE resistive exercises, upper extremities
rev review
RF renal failure
RFA right forearm
RFB retained foreign body

| | |
|---|---|
| RFT | renal function test |
| RH | Rhesus blood factor<br>right hand |
| RHA | rheumatoid arthritis |
| RHD | rheumatic heart disease |
| RHS | right-hand side |
| RI | respiratory illness<br>respiratory infection |
| RIC | right iliac crest |
| RICM | right intercostal margin |
| RICU | respiratory intensive care unit |
| RID | ruptured intervertebral disc |
| RIF | right iliac fossa<br>right index finger |
| RIH | right inguinal hernia |
| RIO | right inferior oblique |
| RIR | right iliac region |
| RIVD | ruptured invertertebral disc |
| RL | right leg<br>right lobe<br>right lower<br>right lung<br>routine lab |
| RLA | react to light and accommodation |
| RLB | right lateral bending |
| RLC | residual lung capacity |
| RLE | right lower extremity |
| RLF | right lateral flexion |
| RLIPP | resistive intermittent positive pressure |
| RLL | right lower lateral<br>right lower leg<br>right lower limb<br>right lower lobe |
| RLQ | right lower quadrant |
| RLR | right lateral rectus |
| RLX | right lower extremity |
| rm | room |
| RM | radical mastectomy<br>respiratory movement |
| RMF | right middle finger |
| RML | right middle lobe |
| RMT | registered music therapist |
| RN | registered nurse |
| RND | radical neck dissection |
| RO | routine order |
| R/O | rule out |
| ROA | right occiput anterior (fetal presentation) |
| ROM | range of motion<br>right otitis media<br>Romberg test<br>rupture of membranes |
| ROMCPF | range of motion complete and pain free |
| ROP | right occiput posterior (fetal presenting part) |
| ROQ | right outer quadrant |
| ROS | review of systems |
| ROSS | review of subjective symptoms<br>review of subject systems |
| rot | rotation |
| RP | radial pulse<br>referring physician |
| RPG | retrograde pyelogram |
| RPh | registered pharmacist |
| RPR | rapid plasma reagin (test for syphilis antibodies) |
| rpt | repeat<br>report |
| RPT | registered physical therapist |
| RR | recovery room<br>regular rate<br>regular rhythm<br>respiratory rate |
| RRCT | regular rate, clear tones |
| RR&E | round, regular, and equal |
| RRF | right ring finger |

| | |
|---|---|
| RRM | right radical mastectomy |
| RRR | regular rate and rhythm<br>round, reactive, regular<br>routine recovery room |
| RRT | registered rehabilitation therapist |
| RS | respiratory system<br>review of symptoms<br>review of systems<br>right side |
| RSI | repetitive stress injury |
| RSO | right superior oblilque |
| RSR | regular sinus rhythm |
| RT | radiotherapy<br>reaction time<br>recreational therapy<br>registered therapist<br>respiratory therapy |
| RTA | renal tubular acidosis |
| RTC | return to clinic |
| RTO | return to office |
| RTT | registered radiation therapy technologist |
| RTW | return to work |
| RU | right upper |
| RUA | right upper arm |
| RUE | right upper extremity |
| RUL | right upper lateral<br>right upper limb<br>right upper lobe |
| RUOQ | right upper outer quadrant |
| RUQ | right upper quadrant |
| RV | rectovaginal |
| RVC | return visit to clinic |
| RVE | right ventricular enlargement |
| Rx | prescription<br>treatment |
| RXN | reaction |
| /s | without |

| | |
|---|---|
| S1 | first heart sound |
| S1–5 | sacral vertebrae |
| SA | sinoatrial |
| SAB | spontaneous abortion |
| sac | sacrum, sacral |
| SAC | short arm cast |
| sag | sagittal |
| SAS | short arm splint |
| sat | satisfactory |
| SB | scleral buckle<br>small bowel<br>sternal border<br>standby |
| SBA | standby assist |
| SBD | senile brain disease |
| SBE | short below elbow<br>subacute bacterial endocarditis |
| SBO | small bowel obstruction |
| SBR | strict bed rest |
| SC | sacrococcygeal<br>scapula<br>self-care<br>sternoclavicular<br>subcutaneous |
| S&C | sclera and cornea |
| SCAT | sheep cell agglutination test |
| SCD | service-connected disability |
| SCFE | slipped capital femoral epiphysis |
| SCI | spinal cord injury |
| scl | scleroderma<br>sclerosis |
| SCM | sternocleidomastoid |
| SC&M | sensation, circulation, and motion |
| SD | septal defect<br>spontaneous delivery<br>sterile dressing<br>subdural<br>sudden death |

| | |
|---|---|
| SDD | sterile dry dressing |
| SDM | systolic/diastolic/mean |
| SDS | same-day surgery<br>sudden death syndrome |
| SDSA | same-day surgery admit |
| sec | second |
| sed | sedimentation |
| segs | segmented neutrophils |
| sem | semen, seminal |
| SEM | scanning electron microscope<br>systolic ejection murmur |
| sens | sensation<br>sensory |
| sep | separate, separation<br>septal, septum |
| sepMI | septal myocardial infarction |
| seq | sequela |
| SF | spinal fluid |
| SFD | silver fork deformity |
| SFP | spinal fluid pressure |
| SGOT | serum glutamic-oxaloacetic transaminase (liver enzyme) |
| SGTP | serum glutamic-pyruvic transaminase (liver enzyme) |
| sh | shoulder |
| SH | self-help<br>serum hepatitis<br>social history<br>surgical history |
| SHO | secondary hypertrophic osteoarthropathy |
| SI | sacroiliac<br>self-inflicted<br>stress incontinence |
| SIMV | spontaneous intermittent mechanical ventilation |
| sinus tach | sinus tachycardia |
| SICU | surgical intensive care unit |
| sid | once per day |
| SIDS | sudden infant death syndrome |
| SIJ | sacroiliac joint |
| SIQ | self-inflicted wound |
| sit | situational |
| sk | skeletal |
| SKTR | skeletal traction |
| sl | slight |
| SL | slit lamp |
| SLB | short leg brace |
| SLC | short leg cast |
| SLE | slit lamp examination<br>systemic lupus erythematosus |
| SLR | straight leg raising |
| SLS | short leg splint |
| slt | slight |
| sm | small |
| SM | simple mastectomy<br>staff meeting<br>systolic murmur |
| SMA | sequential multiple analysis<br>superior mesenteric artery |
| SMD | senile macular degeneration |
| smk | smoking |
| SML | suspension microlaryngoscopy |
| SMO | slip made out |
| SMR | submucus resection |
| SNB | scalene node biopsy |
| SNF | skilled nursing facility |
| SNS | sympathetic nervous system |
| SNST | sciatic nerve stretch test |
| SNT | sinuses, nose, and throat |
| SO | salping-oophorectomy (take out tubes and ovaries) |

| | |
|---|---|
| | supraorbital (above the orbits) |
| | sutures out |
| SOAP | subjective, objective, assessment, plan |
| SOB | short of breath, shortness of breath |
| SOER | special orthopedic examination and report |
| sol | solution |
| SOM | serous otitis media |
| SOP | standard operating procedure |
| SOS | repeat once if necessary |
| | stimulation of senses |
| sp | spine, spinal |
| SP | status-post |
| | suprapubic |
| spas | spasticity |
| SPC | suprapubic catheter |
| SPD | sociopathic personality disorder |
| SPE | serum protein electrophoresis |
| sp gr | specific gravity |
| spl | splint |
| $SpO_2$ | pulse oximetry |
| spont | spontaneous |
| spr | sprain |
| sput | sputum |
| sq | squamous |
| SQ | status quo |
| | subcutaneous |
| SR | schizophrenic reaction |
| | sensitization response |
| | side rails |
| | sinus rhythm |
| | stretch reflex |
| | systems review |
| SROM | spontaneous rupture of membranes |
| srv | service |
| SS | sacrosciatic |
| | saline soak |
| | sitting and standing |
| | soapsuds |
| | substernal |
| S/S | signs and symptoms |
| SSC | size, shape, consistency |
| SSCP | substernal chest pain |
| SSE | soapsuds enema |
| SSI | sliding-scale insulin |
| SSpine | sacral spine |
| SSS | sick sinus syndrome |
| ST | shock therapy |
| | slight trace |
| | soft tissue |
| | speech therapy |
| | sphincter tone |
| | stomach |
| staph | staphylococcus |
| stat | immediately |
| STD | sexually transmitted disease |
| | skin test dose |
| STG | split thickness skin graft |
| STL | swelling, tenderness, limitation |
| STLOM | swelling, tenderness, limitation of motion |
| STM | soft tissue massage |
| STN | sphincter tone normal |
| STP | standard temperature and pulse |
| str | straight |
| | strain |
| | strength |
| strep | streptococcus |
| STS | serological test for syphilis |
| STSG | split thickness skin graft |
| STx | suction therapy |
| subQ | subcutaneous |
| SUD | sudden unexpected death |
| | sudden unexplained death |

| | |
|---|---|
| SUDI | sudden unexpected death of an infant |
| sup | superior<br>supination<br>supine |
| SV | stroke volume |
| SVC | slow vital capacity<br>superior vena cava |
| SVD | spontaneous vaginal delivery |
| SVI | stroke volume index |
| SVR | surface vascular resistance |
| sw | swelling, swollen |
| SW | stab wound |
| SWD | short-wave diathermy |
| SWP | sterile whirlpool |
| Sx | symptoms |
| sym | symmetrical<br>symptom |
| sys | system<br>systemic<br>systolic |
| Sz | schizophrenia<br>seizure |
| T | tablespoon |
| T1–12 | thoracic vertebrae |
| T3 | triiodothyronine |
| T4 | thyroxine |
| TA | traffic accident |
| T&A | tonsillectomy and adenoidectomy<br>tonsils and adenoids |
| tab | tablet |
| TAB | therapeutic abortion |
| tach | tachycardia |
| TAH | total abdominal hysterectomy |
| TAT | tetanus antitoxin<br>thematic apperception test |
| TB | total body<br>tuberculosis |
| TBA | to be admitted<br>to be arranged |
| TBF | total body fat |
| TBG | thyroxine binding globulin |
| TBLC | term birth, living child |
| TBV | total blood volume |
| TBW | total body weight |
| TC | throat culture<br>tissue culture<br>total cholesterol |
| T&C | turn and cough<br>type and crossmatch |
| TCDB | turn, cough, deep breathe |
| TCI | transient cerebral ischemia |
| TCN | tetracycline |
| TCU | transitional care unit |
| TD | total disability |
| TDWB | touch down weightbearing |
| TE | therapeutic exercises |
| TED hose | antiembolic stockings |
| tele | telemetry |
| temp | temperature |
| ten | tension |
| tend | tender |
| TENS | transcutaneous electrical nerve stimulator |
| TF | tube feeding |
| th | thoracic |
| TH | total hip (replacement) |
| THR | total hip replacement |
| TIA | transient ischemic attack |
| tib | tibia, tibial |
| TIBC | total iron-binding capacity |
| tid | three times a day |
| tin | three times a night |
| tiw | three times a week |
| TJ | triceps jerk |

| | |
|---|---|
| TK | total knee (replacement) |
| TKO | to keep open |
| TKR | total knee replacement |
| TL | tubal ligation |
| TLC | total lung capacity |
| TM | temperature by mouth<br>temperomandibular<br>tender midline<br>tympanic membrane |
| TMAS | Taylor Manifest Anxiety Scale |
| TMJ | temperomandibular joint |
| TML | tender midline<br>tongue in midline |
| TMT | tarso-metatarsal |
| TNC | too numerous to count |
| TND | test not done |
| tns | tension |
| TNS | transcutaneous nerve stimulation |
| TNTC | too numerous to count |
| TOA | time of admission<br>time of arrival |
| tol | tolerated |
| tomo | tomogram |
| TOPV | trivalent oral polio vaccine |
| TORCH | toxoplasmosis, rubella, cytomegalovirus, herpes simplex |
| tot | total |
| TOW | transfer off ward |
| TP | total protein<br>transverse process |
| TPD | temporary partial disability |
| TPN | total parenteral nutrition |
| TPR | temperature, pulse, respiration |
| TQ | tourniquet |
| tr | tincture<br>trace<br>traction<br>trauma<br>treatment<br>tremor |
| TR | temperature, rectal<br>therapeutic radiology<br>total resistance<br>total response |
| T&R | tenderness and rebound |
| trach | tracheostomy |
| trans | transportation |
| trich | trichomonas |
| TRNBP | transrectal needle biopsy of the prostate |
| TRO | to return to office |
| TRS | therapeutic recreational specialist |
| trt | treatment |
| TS | thoracic spine |
| TSD | Tay-Sachs disease |
| TSH | thyroid-stimulating hormone |
| tsp | teaspoon |
| TSP | thoracic spine |
| TT | tactile tension<br>total time<br>transfer training |
| TTD | temporary total disability |
| TTP | thrombotic thrombocytopenic purpura |
| TUR | transurethral resection |
| turb | turbinate |
| TURB | transurethral resection of bladder |
| TURBN | transurethral resection of bladder neck |
| TURP | transurethral resection of the prostate |
| TV | tidal volume<br>tinea versicolor<br>total volume<br>trichomonas vaginalis |

| | |
|---|---|
| TVC | timed vital capacity |
| TVH | total vaginal hysterectomy |
| TVR | thoracic ventral root |
| TWHW | toe walking, heel walking |
| tx | traction |
| Tx | treatment |
| TX | transplant |
| typ | typical |
| u | unit(s) |
| UA | umbilical artery<br>uric acid<br>urinalysis |
| UC | ulcerative colitis<br>unchanged<br>unconscious |
| UCD | usual childhood diseases |
| UCG | urinary chorionic gonadotropin |
| UCHD | usual childhood diseases |
| UCR | unconditioned reflex response |
| UCS | unconditioned stimulus<br>unconscious |
| UD | ulnar deviation<br>underdeveloped<br>urethral discharge<br>urethral drainage |
| UDO | undermined origin |
| UE | undermined etiology<br>upper extremity |
| UGA | under general anesthesia |
| UGI | upper gastrointestinal |
| UH# | unit history number |
| UIQ | upper inner quadrant |
| UK | unknown |
| UL | upper lobe |
| U&L | upper and lower |
| ULN | upper limits of normal |
| ULOQ | upper left outer quadrant |
| ULQ | upper left quadrant |
| umb | umbilical |
| UMN | upper motor neuron |
| UMNL | upper motor neuron lesion |
| U&MNP | ulnar and median nerve palsy |
| UN | ulnar nerve |
| unc | uncertain<br>unchanged<br>uncomplicated<br>unconscious<br>uncooperative |
| und | undetermined |
| ung | ointment |
| unk | unknown |
| UO | undetermined origin<br>ureteral orifice<br>urinary output |
| U/O | under observation for<br>urinary output |
| UOQ | upper outer quadrant |
| UP | uteropelvic (x-ray) |
| UPOR | usual place of residence |
| UQ | upper quadrant |
| UR | unconditioned response<br>upper respiratory<br>urinary retention<br>utilization review |
| URD | upper respiratory disease |
| URI | upper respiratory infection |
| urol | urology |
| UROQ | upper right outer quadrant |
| URQ | upper right quadrant |
| US | ultrasound |
| ut | uterus |
| UT | urinary tract |
| UTI | urinary tract infection |
| UTOC | upper thoracic outlet compression syndrome |
| UV | ultraviolet<br>umbilical vein<br>urinary volume |

U/WB unit of whole blood

V vision

VA vacuum aspiration
vertebral artery
Veterans Administration
visual acuity

V-A ventriculoatrial (shunt)

vac vaccination

vag vaginal

VAH Veterans Administration Hospital

VALE visual acuity, left eye

VAOD visual acuity, right eye

VAOS visual acuity, left eye

VAOU visual acuity, both eyes

var variation
variety

VARE visual acuity, right eye

vas vasectomy

VBP venous blood pressure

VC ventricular contraction
vital capacity
vocal cord

VCG vectorcardiogram

VD venereal disease
venous dilation
ventrodorsal (front to back)

VDA visual discriminary acuity

VDRL Veneral Disease Research Laboratory

VE vaginal examination

vent ventilation (mechanical)

vert vertebra
vertical
vertigo

VF ventricular fibrillation
visual field

VFI visual fields intact

VH vaginal hysterectomy

VI vaginal infection
viral infection

VIP vasoactive intestinal peptide

Vit vitamin

VM vasomotor

VMA vanillylmandelic acid

VMO vastus medialis oblique

VMR vasomotor rhinitis

VMS visual memory span

VMT vasomotor tone

VNA Visiting Nurse's Association

VNR ventral nerve root

VO verbal order

voc vocal
vocational

vol volatile
volume
voluntary

VP venipuncture
venous pressure

VPB ventricular premature beats

VPC ventricular premature contractions
volume-packed cells

VPS vibrations per second

V&PS vibration and peripheral sensation

VQ voice quality

VR ventilation rate
ventral root
ventricular rate
vocational rehabilitation

VRC ventral root, cervical

VRL ventral root, lumbar

VRT ventral root, thoracic

VS vesicular sounds
vital signs

VSBE very short below elbow (cast)

VSD ventral septal defect

VSN vital signs normal

VSS vital signs stable

| | |
|---|---|
| VSTT | ventral spinothalamic tract |
| VT | ventricular tachycardia<br>tidal volume |
| V-tach | ventricular tachycardia |
| Vtx | vertex |
| vv | veins |
| VV | vericose veins |
| w/ | with |
| WA | while awake |
| W/A | weakness atrophy |
| WAIS | Wechsler's Adult Intelligence Scale |
| WB | weight bearing<br>whole blood<br>whole body |
| WBC | well baby care<br>well baby clinic<br>white blood cell |
| WC | wheelchair<br>will call<br>work capacity<br>workers' compensation<br>wound check |
| wd | wound |
| WD | well developed |
| W&D | warm and dry |
| WDWN | well developed, well nourished |
| WE | wound of entry |
| WF | white female |
| WFO | will follow in office |
| WH | walking heel cast<br>well healed<br>well hydrated |
| WHP | whirlpool |
| wk | weak<br>week<br>work |
| WL | workload |
| WM | white male |
| WMAF | white middle-aged female |
| WMAM | white middle-aged male |
| WMF | white middle-aged female |
| WMM | white middle-aged male |
| WN | well nourished |
| WNL | within normal limits |
| w/o | without |
| WO | written order |
| WOE | wound of entry |
| WOX | wound of exit |
| WP | wet pack<br>whirlpool |
| WPB | whirlpool bath |
| WPW | Wolff-Parkinson-White (syndrome) |
| wr | wrist |
| WR | weak response |
| wt | weight |
| WTB | weight bearing |
| w/u | workup |
| XIP | x-ray in plaster |
| XOOP | x-ray out of plaster |
| XOP | x-ray out of plaster |
| XR | x-ray |
| XT | exotropia |
| xyl | xylocaine |
| Y/A | years of age |
| YAG | yttrium aluminum garnet (laser) |
| yd | yard |
| yo | years old |
| YOB | year of birth |
| yr | year |
| Z | zero |
| ZD | zero defects |
| Z-plasty | plastic surgery skin repair technique |
| zyg | zygoma |

# Index

## About the Author

RANDINE A. LEWIS is founder and principal of Medicolegal Solutions, a consulting firm in Houston, Texas, that advises attorneys and health care professionals on matters involving medical litigation. She has studied both medicine and law on the postgraduate level and worked in various law firms and health care settings.

ISBN 1-56720-088-5

90000>

EAN

9 781567 200881

HARDCOVER BAR CODE